Logic, Language, Formalism, Informalism

Daniel Richardson

Logic, Language, Formalism, Informalism

Daniel Richardson

School of Mathematical Sciences
University of Bath, UK

INTERNATIONAL THOMSON COMPUTER PRESS
I ⓣ P An International Thomson Publishing Company

London • Bonn • Boston • Madrid • Johannesburg • Melbourne • Mexico City • New York • Paris
Singapore • Tokyo • Toronto • Albany, NY • Belmont, CA • Cincinnati, OH • Detroit, MI

Logic, Language, Formalism, Informalism

Copyright © 1995 International Thomson Computer Press

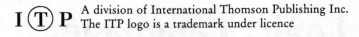

I ⓉP A division of International Thomson Publishing Inc.
The ITP logo is a trademark under licence

British Library Cataloguing-in-Publication Data
A catalogue record for this book is available from the British Library

Typeset in the UK by Hodgson Williams Associates, Tunbridge Wells and Cambridge
Printed in the UK by The Alden Press, Oxford

First printed 1995

ISBN 1-85032-127-2

International Thomson Computer Press   International Thomson Computer Press
Berkshire House   20 Park Plaza
High Holborn   14th Floor
London WC1V 7AA   Boston MA 02116
UK   USA

Imprints of International Thomson Publishing

Contents

To the Stueflotens, and to Judy Zaches, originally called Zellhoefer; and to the ghost of Enid Larson, once biology teacher at Carmell High School, passionate lover of chipmunks, ecological diversity, and critical intelligence.

And thanks to Bill Picksley for the cats.

Chapter 1

Introduction

Words are things. Do you agree with that? If not, what is it you see in front of you? Let's say that you see marks on paper and these marks are organised into words. As soon as you read a word, it is evaluated. This process happens so quickly in a literate adult it is almost impossible to observe. We can say that you first see the marks on the paper and then almost instantly organise them into words and then almost instantly evaluate them.

Sentences are things. If you have agreed that words are things I think you will agree that sentences are also things. Programs are things. A language is a thing.

Reasoning is a thing.

So we claim.

Of course these things, language and programs and reasoning, may have a complex internal structure. We can investigate this structure. Maybe we can understand language and reasoning as constructed by combinations of simpler things.

Not only is language a thing, the meaning of language is also a thing.

We will use "object" and "thing" as synonyms. So according to the way of talking which is being used in this book, an object could be a horse or a block of cement or an idea or a proof. Anything that can be named can be called an object, according to this way of using the word.

So language is an object, reasoning is an object and meaning is an object.

We can represent these interesting objects mathematically as sets or data structures (as described in chapter 2), and we can attempt to see how they work.

It is possible to look at language and reasoning, as if from the outside, as objects. Of course it is not quite reasonable to attempt to get outside all language and all reasoning in one big leap. But we can look at some of this objectively. Everyone does this anyway. But it is characteristic of logic, and of the logical study of computing, systematically to pursue this process of objectivisation.

If we look at mathematics and computing we see a range of different uses of language and proof. Some aspects of this are relatively easy to look at objectively and some are relatively hard.

We will call some languages and proofs formal and others informal. For example, we would say that a computer language is relatively formal, whereas the conversations which take place about the language are relatively informal. We will call an object formal if it is clearly defined and specified by some rules, which can be explicitly stated. A huge amount of intellectual effort goes into translation between formal and informal representations of ideas. It seems that being able to manage the translations in both directions is a sign of professionalism in both mathematics and computing.

Formalism is attractive in itself. People have always struggled to express what they know or intend or imagine, succinctly and formally.

Formalism is practically useful. Advances in mathematics and computing are accompanied by attempts to formalise the new experiences. On a more everyday level, the early part of writing a computer program is the process of making formal, and therefore explicit, ideas which are usually initially ambiguous.

The goal of education in computing and mathematics should be to encourage mathematical sophistication; this consists of critical awareness and the ability to translate back and forth between formal and informal representations of ideas.

This book is intended for undergraduate students of computing and mathematics (although it may be of interest to others) and is about the process of formalisation in computing, in language theory, and in mathematics. The book respects and follows the formalising urge and also constantly criticises the results of it. It is human nature to get things wrong, and when this trait is magnified and to some extent disguised by computer systems the consequences can be disastrous. Raising the level of critical awareness is the only way to alleviate this problem. We need a language and a tradition in which to express criticism. Formalisation of ideas is not just an end in itself but also serves to open the door to criticism.

Most readers of this book will have studied some discrete mathematics. The mathematical background is summarised in chapter 2: the ideas of sets and data structures, and the use of induction, well ordering and recursion.

Chapter 3 introduces formal languages, grammars and rewrite systems.

Chapter 4 gives definitions for the notions of logical equivalence and logical consequence for expressions built up using propositional operators $\land$, $\lor$, $\neg$, $\rightarrow$, $\leftrightarrow$.

The definitions given in chapters 3 and 4 provide us with useful ideas and a convenient notation, and are definitely of practical value. The point is made, however, that these formalisations are the result of trade offs in a process of intellectual design, and are in some ways flawed. They are subject to revision like all ideas. It is not true that such definitions as these *simply have to be accepted*. It is not somehow known beyond doubt that these ideas are correct.

Formalisations need to be constantly criticised by referring them back to reality. We should not just accept these things as games with language, and brush aside the questions of how good they are, or how appropriate they are.

This theme continues throughout the book.

Chapter 5 considers formal reasoning systems for the propositional calculus, especially semantic tableaux. The claim is made that formal reasoning systems really should attempt to reflect the actual process of thinking. Preposterous though it may seem, this modest desire for accord with experience was more or less abandoned by almost everyone in the field of formal logic at the beginning of the twentieth century development of this subject. (I believe the historical reason for this is that formal logic developed before computing so that on the one hand people expected too much from formal systems in the way of results and on the other hand their demands for closeness to experience were too modest.)

The problem of proving correctness of an algorithm is also discussed in chapter

5. As an important example of medium difficulty, soundness and completeness theorems are proved for the semantic tableau algorithm applied to the propositional calculus.

Chapter 6 introduces Prolog and the problem of formalising ordinary knowledge in this medium. Soundness and completeness properties are stated for Prolog. But it is made clear that Prolog does not always satisfy these desirable properties.

The computations of Prolog are explained via semantic tableaux. So chapter 6 follows directly from chapter 5. One of the central theses of this book is that the best way to look at logic programming is in the context of the semantic tableau method.

The Prolog used in chapter 6 does not have function symbols or lists, and the Herbrand universes are all finite. The situation changes radically as soon as lists (or any other function symbol) are introduced, since the minimal models become infinite. Chapter 7 is mostly about lists in Prolog. It should be clear after this chapter that almost anything which can be defined at all can be defined in terms of lists. Lists are to contemporary computing what sets were to early twentieth century mathematics.

In chapter 7 the semantic tableau algorithm for the propositional calculus is implemented in a very short sound and complete theorem prover in Prolog.

Chapter 8 introduces the predicate calculus and the problem of translating back and forth between informal ideas and formal expressions in first order languages, especially L_N, the language of first order arithmetic and L_{ZF} the first order language of Zermelo Fraenkel set theory.

Chapter 9 uses semantic tableaux to define a formal reasoning system for the predicate calculus. Soundness and completeness theorems are proved as before. This chapter gives us a non-deterministic algorithm, which is sound and complete, for first order reasoning. The problem of how to get computers to do such reasoning is only partly understood. This chapter ought to convince the reader that some progress is possible.

The axiomatic method is an ancient technique for getting a compact representation for a field of knowledge. The idea is to attempt to summarise everything we know in some area by a list of axioms. If this is done well, every known truth in this area can be naturally demonstrated as a logical consequence of the axioms. The axioms in that case explain everything else. In order to do this well, it is necessary to make good definitions, to use language very carefully and to understand the logical structure of the subject.

Chapter 10 discusses the axiomatic method in mathematics, and looks at axiomatic systems for partially ordered sets, group theory, number theory, set theory and category theory.

Thanks to the wonderful inventive work of Kurt Gödel, we know that there are essential limitations to the power of axiomatic systems, however useful they may be.

Chapter 11 sketches a proof of the Gödel incompleteness theorem for first order arithmetic. This shows that it will never be possible completely to formalise either mathematics or computing.

Chapter 12 describes one of the most interesting contemporary attempts at formalisation. What do we mean by a collection of interacting processes? How can we reason about such collections? There is as yet no consensus about how to represent the ideas which we all seem to have about such collections.

Chapter 12 is an introduction to the ideas of Hoare and Milner about interacting processes. The centre of it is a conversation between a group of people who are struggling with these ideas and criticising them.

It is a serious, even a barbaric, mistake to imagine that formal systems can replace informal understanding, or that formalism ought to separated from intuition, or protected from the contradictions and complexities of actuality. On the contrary, formal systems are always provisional and are only valuable scientifically if they are incessantly criticised by referring them back to their intended meanings.

"The greatest respect that we can pay to nature is not to trap it, but to acknowledge that it eludes us and that our own nature is also fluid, open and conditional." Gary Snyder, from *No Nature*, Pantheon, 1992.

1.1 Routes through the book

The core of this book is chapters 3, 4, 5, 6, 7, 8, and the first three sections of chapter 9.

If you know about context free grammars, you could just refer to the definition of the statement forms in section 3.3, and then begin immediately with chapter 4; and afterwards use chapter 3 as a reference.

The core of the core is the semantic tableau algorithm as described in sections 5.5, 5.6, and 5.7, and its later extension in the first section of chapter 9.

If you are in a hurry, you could skip the description of the Hilbert style system in section 5.2 and 5.3, and also all of chapter 7 after section 7.5.

If you are interested in using this book to get some ideas for research, my advice is to look for border areas where one subject diffuses into another, such as the boundary between the axiomatic method and logic programming, as described in chapter 10, or the boundary between computing and statistics as described in chapter 12. Good travelling.

A note on Problems

For clarity, the problems included have been ruled off from the surrounding text.

A number of the problems are decorated with stars. This is not meant to warn you away from trying them but just to indicate that they are thought to contain some unusual difficulties.

Answers to selected questions can be found in chapter 13.

Chapter 2

Preliminaries: a skeleton crew of ideas

In this book we wish to do mathematics about languages and about reasoning systems. Since the intention is to prove some theorems about such objects, we will need to make some assumptions, and to develop some techniques. The purpose of this chapter is to make a brief statement of the basic ideas and techniques which will be used, developed and explained in more detail later. (We will use some of these ideas also when we give examples of proofs for analysis.)

2.1 Design principles

There are two principles of intellectual design at work in the following.

First of all there is Occam's razor. One statement of this is: "Thou shalt not multiply entities unnecessarily." This means that our basic ideas should be as few and simple as possible. Thus, when possible we should try to reduce complex ideas to combinations of simple ones.

There is also another important principle, which is that our ideas should be close to experience and intuition. This will be called the naturalness principle.

Of course both principles are important. What we really want is simple elegant theories which are easy to understand and which seem correct in each detail. However this ideal case is quite uncommon. What usually happens is that a compromise is necessary. We sometimes have to accept some unnaturalness for the sake of structural simplicity, and we sometimes have to accept a bewildering complexity for the sake of closeness to experience.

2.2 Sets

A *set* is a collection of objects. The objects in a set can be physical things, such as chairs and tables, or they can be mathematical objects, such as numbers, or other sets. The objects in a set will be called its elements. We will write $x \in y$ to mean that x is an element of y. The set with elements $a_1, ..., a_n$ will be written $\{a_1, ..., a_n\}$.

In mathematics and computing, there are a number of words for ideas which are almost the same as sets. For example, people speak about collections, or classes or domains. There may be cases in which it is useful to make distinctions between these things. In this book, however, and in accordance with Occam's razor, we will suppose that all these words have just the same meaning.

So sets, collections, classes, and domains are all the same.

We assume that two sets are the same if they have the same elements. We do not assume any order on the elements of a set. So, $\{a,b,c\} = \{b,c,a\}$ for example. Also $\{a,b,a\}$ is exactly the same as $\{b,a\}$

We will say that a set X is a subset of another set Y if every element of X is also an element of Y. In particular, every set is a subset of itself. X is a subset of Y will be written $X \subseteq Y$.

So $\{2,1,3\}$ is a subset of $\{1,2,3,4\}$ and is also a subset of $\{1,2,3\}$.

We also need a notation for ordered sets. For finite, ordered sets we will use either square or round brackets. So (a,b,c) or $[a,b,c]$ will be used to denote the set with elements a and b and c, with a before b in the ordering, and b before c. An n-tuple is an ordered set $(x_1,...,x_n)$ with n elements.

We have that $(x_1,...,x_n) = (y_1,...,y_m)$ only if $n = m$ and $x_1 = y_1$ and $x_2 = y_2$ and... and $x_n = y_n$.

For example $(cat,cow,pig) \neq (cat,pig,cow)$, but $\{cat,cow,pig\} = \{cat,pig,cow\}$. Also $(1,1,1) \neq (1,1)$

So far we have mentioned sets and ordered sets. You may feel the desire at this point to wield Occam's razor. Is it possible to explain the concept of ordered set in terms of the concept of set? Or, alternatively, is it possible to explain "sets" in terms of "ordered sets"? Both of these possible lines of thought have been followed. But we will withhold judgement in this area and allow the two ideas of set and ordered set to coexist independently. It is of course up to you to decide whether or not you find it useful to explain one of these ideas in terms of the other.

We suppose that in some sense there *exist* sets with infinitely many elements. Some of these infinite sets have names, and are quite famous, for example the *natural numbers*.

We define the *natural numbers* **N**, to be the set of non-negative integers, $\mathbf{N} = \{0,1,2,3,....\}$.

If A and B are sets, we define $A \times B$, called the Cartesian product of A and B, to be the set of ordered pairs (x,y) with $x \in A$ and $y \in B$.

If A is any set we define A^n to be the set of all possible n-tuples $(x_1,...,x_n)$ with all of $x_1,...,x_n$ elements of A.

For example, if $A = \{a,b,c\}$, then

$$A^2 = A \times A$$

$$= \{(a,a),(a,b),(a,c),(b,a),(b,b),(b,c),(c,a),(c,b),(c,c)\}.$$

2.3 Functions

A function $f : A \rightarrow B$ is a process which, when given an object, x, in the set A produces another object, $f(x)$, in the set B. A is called the domain of the function, and B is called the codomain.

It is generally supposed in mathematics that if we know what a function is we also know its domain and the codomain. To say that we are given a function, according to the current mathematical convention, means that we are also somehow given its domain and the codomain.

If f is a function, the graph of f is the set $\{(x, f(x))$ such that x is an element of the domain of $f\}$.

Evidently there is something annoyingly vague about the idea of a function at this point. What is a process? It is quite important from the point of view of contemporary computing to keep this question open. This is because the idea needs more thought and discussion. In early twentieth century mathematics enthusiastic users of Occam's razor simply said that functions were exactly the same as their graphs. This has the virtue of being clear, and this is the source of the assumption that if you know the function you also know its domain and codomain. But it has the disadvantage of minimising the question of how one might obtain a value $f(x)$ in the codomain when given a value x in the domain. So we will not attempt to reduce the idea of a function to the idea of a set.

We will say that a function f is *injective* if $f(x) = f(y)$ never happens for two different values x and y in the domain of f. Injective functions are also called *one to one*.

We will say that a function f is *surjective* if for all y in the codomain of f there exists some x in the domain of f so that $f(x) = y$. Surjective functions are also said to be *onto*.

A function f is a *bijection* if it is both injective and surjective. Bijections are also called *one to one correspondences*.

If $f(x)$ is a function and S is a set, we will say that S is *closed* under application of f if $f(x)$ is defined and in S whenever x is in S. So, for example, the set of even natural numbers is closed under the operation of squaring.

We will use the same terminology for functions of several variables. So if $f(x, y)$ is a function of two variables we will say that a set S is closed under application of f if $f(x, y)$ is defined and in S whenever x and y are in S. For example, the set of odd natural numbers is closed under multiplication.

Problem 2.1 *Define $f(x) = x + 1$ for all real numbers x. What is the smallest set which contains 0 and is closed under application of f? Justify your answer.*

We define a *type* to be a set, together with a list of functions.

We can write a type as $(D, f_1, ..., f_n)$, where D is a set, which will also be called the domain of the type, and $f_1, ..., f_n$ are the functions which are associated with the domain by the type.

An example of a type would be $(\mathbf{Z}, +, *)$, where $\mathbf{Z}$ is the integers, and $+$ and $*$ are the usual addition and multiplication.

If we say that a variable has a certain type, say $(D, f_1, ..., f_n)$, this means that we know the domain of objects, D, over which the variable may range, and we also know the definitions of the associated functions on that domain.

2.4 Data structures

A *data structure* is a collection of objects, which we will call *nodes*, some of which are linked by *arrows*. Figure 2.1 shows a typical data structure.

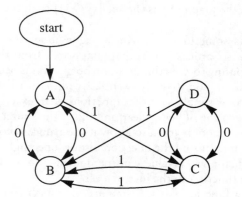

Figure 2.1 A typical data structure

In a data structure, there may be arrows which start and end at the same node. There may be no arrows between two nodes, or there may be many. There is no assumption here that data structures are finite.

Both the nodes and the arrows may be labelled with data, which may be numbers or text, or any set, or, in fact, any data structure. (We do not even forbid the possibility that a data structure, A, could have a node or arrow which was labelled with A.)

An arrow starts at one node, called its domain, or source, and ends at another node, called its codomain, or target. A *path* in a data structure is a sequence of nodes joined by arrows:

$$x_1 - -\alpha_1 - - > x_2 - -\alpha_2 - - > x_3 ... - -\alpha_{n-1} - - > x_n$$

A path can either have some number n of arrows in it, where n is a natural number, or it can be infinite. The number of arrows in a path is called its length. We can think of a path of finite length as a way of travelling from the source node at the beginning to the target node at the end. By convention, a single node, with no arrows, will be called a path, of length 0.

In general, there may be many different paths between any two nodes.

There may be a path, of length more than zero, which starts and ends at the same node. Such a path is called a *cycle*.

The *children* of a node, x, are all those nodes y so that some arrow goes from x to y.

The *frontier* of a data structure is the set of nodes with no children.

2.4.1 Lists

A *finite list* is a data structure of the form

$$x_1 - - > x_2 - - > ... - - > x_n$$

An *infinite list* is a data structure of the form

$$x_1 - - > x_2 - - > x_3 - - > ... x_n - - > x_{n+1} - - > ...$$

A list always has a first node, which is called its head. A finite list has just one node in its frontier; the frontier consists of the last node in the list. An infinite list goes on forever, and so has no nodes in its frontier.

We can make a few concessions to Occam at this point. Lists are particular kinds of ordered sets. Finite lists are exactly the same as finite ordered sets. Finite lists with n nodes are exactly the same as n-tuples. Sequences and lists are the same things.

2.4.2 Trees

Definition 2.1 *Rooted tree. A data structure consisting of a single node, and no arrows, is a rooted tree. If T is a rooted tree and x is on the frontier of T, we may add any finite or infinite list of new nodes $y_1, y_2, ...$ as children of x, and the new data structure T' is also a rooted tree, which is called an extension of T. The result of any finite or infinite number of extensions of a rooted tree is also a rooted tree.*

Rooted trees will just be called trees from now on.

In a rooted tree we suppose that the children of any node are added in a list. That is, the children of any node form an ordered set, not just a set. So we can talk about the first child, the second child, etc.

The *frontier* of a tree is the set of nodes which do not have children. The nodes on the frontier of a tree are also called *leaves*.

A tree is *infinite* if it has infinitely many nodes.

A *finite path* in a tree is a sequence $s_1, s_2, ..., s_k$ of nodes so that, for each $i < k$, the node s_{i+1} is a child of node s_i.

We said that trees were formed by sequences of extensions, and that when we made an extension, the nodes added were new. So there are no cycles in trees.

In computing it is conventional to draw trees with the root at the top of the picture, and all the children of any node directly below it, ordered left to right. If the extensions are understood as a form of growth, then the trees grow downwards according to this picture.

A *branch* of a tree is a maximal path, i.e. a path which starts at the root and continues to the frontier. If the tree is infinite, an infinite path starting at the root will also be called a branch.

In the tree shown in figure 2.2, the nodes are labelled with sets of animals.

The root of this tree is animals. The nodes on the frontier are labelled protozoa, porifera, invertebrates, and vertebrates. Three of the arrows are labelled with descriptive properties.

(Note that when drawing trees, we will usually not bother to put the arrowheads on the arrows. The convention is that all the arrows are directed downwards.)

One extension of this tree could add a list of children to the invertebrates, namely (worms, coelenterate, mollusca and arthropoda). After three extensions, we could have the tree shown in figure 2.3.

This example shows how trees can be used for classification. We will also use trees to indicate grammatical structure of expressions in a language, and logical structure of proofs. Trees can be used in many other ways also.

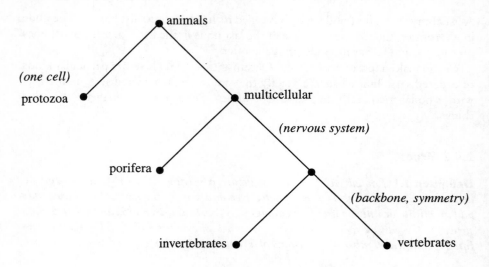

Figure 2.2   Animals

König's lemma *An infinite tree, in which no node has infinitely many children, must have an infinite branch.*

This famous lemma will be used later to prove termination of algorithms.

■

Problem 2.2 *A nineteenth century biologist claimed that it might happen that the population of descendants from some animal might never die out, although every individual path of descent might terminate. Show that if König's lemma is right, the famous biologist who said this must have been wrong.*

Problem 2.3 * *Obviously the tree of possibilities for a gambler is infinite, but if you continue gambling you eventually lose all of your money, and therefore there is no infinite path in this tree. Is this true? Does this show that König's lemma is false?*

Problem 2.4 * *Assume König's lemma is true. Consider the animal classification tree which was exhibited earlier. Imagine that a number of extensions have been made to the tree, so many that the frontier of the tree consists of all individual animals who have ever lived or will ever live. A branch of the tree corresponds to a descending sequence of sets of animals. Prove that if the tree has no infinite branch, then the whole tree is finite, provided that no node has infinitely many children.*

Problem 2.5 * *Do you think König's lemma requires proof? Try to argue that it does not require proof.*

Problem 2.6 * *Try to prove König's lemma. Hint: Assume tree T is infinite, i.e. has infinitely many nodes. Put a * by the nodes of T with the property that the subtree below that node is infinite. Now try to define an infinite path in T.*

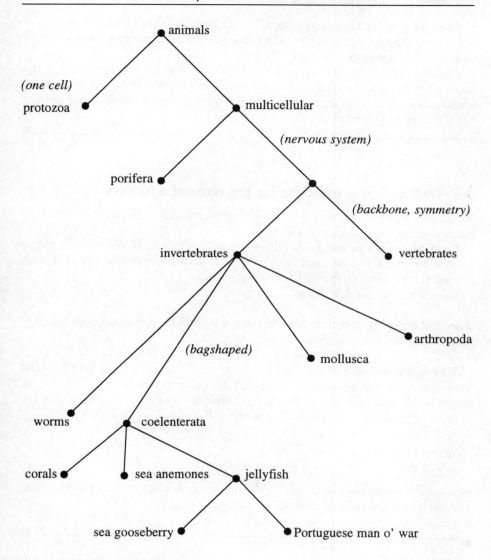

Figure 2.3 More animals

Problem 2.7* *Suppose we are given an infinite sequence of tiles: $t_0, t_1, t_2, t_3, \ldots$ Each tile is square, and each of the four edges is coloured in some way. We are required to put the tiles down on the plane in order so that they don't overlap, and each tile touches at least one other tile, with the edges aligned, and the colours of tiles match on touching edges. (We will not pay any attention to the colours on the corners.) Prove that it is possible to put all of the tiles down if and only if for each n it is possible to put down the first n tiles.*

Hint: Suppose we have played tiles $t_0, ..., t_k$. There are only finitely many ways of playing t_{k+1}. So we can represent all possible moves in this game by a tree in which each node has at most finitely many children.

Remark: Suppose we have succeeded in playing the first $k + 1$ of the tiles, $t_0, ..., t_k$, and we are confronted with t_{k+1}. We may not be able to just add t_{k+1} to the tiling we already have. It may be necessary to start over from the beginning and place the first $k + 1$ tiles in a different way.

2.5   Well ordering principle for the natural numbers

Recall that when we say that **S** is a *subset* of **N**, this does not imply that there is some element of **N** which is not in **S**.

Let **S** be any set of natural numbers, i.e. any subset of **N**. We will say that a natural number d is a *minimal element* of **S** if, firstly, d is an element of **S**, and, secondly, there is no element e of **S** so that $e < d$.

We will assume the following.

The well ordering principle for the natural numbers: *Any non-empty set, **S**, of natural numbers has a minimal element.*

Why is it reasonable to assume this? Suppose **S** is a non-empty set of natural numbers. Since it is non-empty, there must be a natural number k in **S**. It may be that k is minimal, and in that case the principle is satisfied. Otherwise, test the numbers from 0 up to k, in order, for membership of **S**. That is, we ask:

is 0 in **S**?

is 1 in **S**?

is 2 in **S**?

etc., until we get the answer "yes". This must happen before k steps. The first number d in **S** is a minimal element.

Problem 2.8 ** *Does the above text constitute a* proof *of the well ordering principle for the natural numbers?*

If you say it is a proof, try to say also what assumptions, if any, it uses.

Some possible responses to this question might begin:

a) It convinces me, it is a satisfactory proof, and it does not use any assumptions. b) It is a proof, and I think it might use some assumptions, but I don't know what they are. c) This is a proof. It is based on the following assumptions.... d) This is not a proof, but it convinces me that the well ordering principle is true. e) This is not a proof. The well ordering principle for the natural numbers is an assumption, and can't possibly be proved. f) The well ordering principle is obviously true, and the above thing is not a proof of it. g) This is not a proof of the well ordering principle for the natural numbers for the following reasons..... h) This is not a proof and I am not convinced that the well ordering principle for the natural numbers is true. g) In some circumstances some of the statements above could be false. For example.... Therefore this is a false proof. h) This is not a proof because I can't decide whether or not it is a proof. However the well ordering principle for the natural numbers is true for the following reasons....

■

In general if we have an ordering on a set (as we do have for the natural numbers) we will call it a *well ordering* if any descending sequence of elements in the set is necessarily finite.

2.6 Induction

Induction principle for the natural numbers: Let Δ be any subset of the natural numbers. Suppose 0 is in Δ and that whenever x is in Δ then $x + 1$ is also in Δ. Then every natural number is in Δ.

This is usually used to prove theorems about the natural numbers in the following alternative form.

Alternative form of the induction principle for the natural numbers: Any property holding for 0, and such that the successor of any number having the property also has the property, is true of every natural number.

■

Problem 2.9 * *The two induction statements given above are closely related. The first uses the idea of a set Δ and the second uses the idea of a property. They can be connected in the following way. Suppose that we are interested in some property, say P. We can define a set Δ as the set of natural numbers for which our property P holds. Use this to show that the first induction statement above implies the second one.*

Problem 2.10* *Show that the well ordering principle for the natural numbers implies the induction principle.*

■

There are many other induction principles in common use. For example, there is *complete induction*. The complete induction principle says that if a property holds for a natural number k whenever it holds for all natural numbers, if any, below k, then it holds for all natural numbers.

From the point of view of Occam's razor, it seems best to fix on one of the above principles as basic and to think of the others as secondary consequences.

We will take the well ordering principle for the natural numbers as our basic idea.

2.7 Definition and explanation by recursion

Ideas are often self-referential.

Definitions and explanations of ideas, which apply in a range of situations, are often done in the following manner.

Basis: We first explain the idea in the simplest possible situation.

Recursive step: We then explain the idea in a more complex situation in terms of the same idea in a simpler situation.

A definition or explanation which follows this pattern will be called *recursive*.

The recursive step is supposed to give a method to break complex situations into simpler ones. When this recursive step is applied repeatedly the ultimate result is supposed to be the reduction of the original situation to a number of instances of the simplest case.

Example 2.1 *Suppose we want to explain the exponential function x^y, where x and y are natural numbers. We could say:*

Basis*: The simplest situation occurs when $y = 0$. In this case, we decree*

$$x^0 = 1$$

Recursive step*: More complex cases occur for natural number exponents greater than zero. We can write such an exponent as $y + 1$. In this case we say*

$$x^{(y+1)} = x * (x^y)$$

This recursive definition reduces the problem of calculating $x^{(y+1)}$ to multiplication by x, and the simpler problem of calculating x^y.

Thus, to find 7^3, the recursive step would reduce this to $7 * 7^2$, and then again to $7 * 7 * 7^1$, and then again to $7 * 7 * 7 * 7^0$; and at this point we call on the basis, which gives $7^0 = 1$; and we see that $7^3 = 7 * 7 * 7$.

Example 2.2 *Another example is the Fibonacci sequence. The first Fibonacci number is 0. The second Fibonacci number is 1. For natural number n, the $(n + 2)^{th}$ Fibonacci number is obtained recursively by adding together the nth Fibonacci number and the $(n + 1)^{th}$ Fibonacci number. Thus the Fibonacci sequence begins:*

$0, 1, 1, 2, 3, 5, 8, 13, 21, 34, 55, 89...$

This sequence of numbers occurs in nature, and is quite difficult to describe without using recursion.

Example 2.3 *The ideas which we are discussing here can also be algorithms, and the situations can be problems.*

Problem*: To sort a list of numbers.*

A recursive solution:

Basis*: In the simplest situation, the list is empty or has only one number in it. This is already sorted, so there is nothing to do.*

Recursive step*: Given a list of length greater than 1, break it up into two non-empty lists of approximately equal size. Sort both these lists. Then shuffle the two sorted lists together into one big sorted list.*

This example shows how a complex procedure can be concisely described using recursion.

Of course, this recursive algorithm for sorting depends upon another simpler algorithm for shuffling together two sorted lists to obtain one big sorted list. But this shuffling procedure is relatively easy to describe. We want the final list to be either ascending or descending, and we have two sublists which are already properly ordered. At each stage we remove one of the heads of the two sublists and add it to the final list. We choose which head to remove according to the ordering we want.

■

Problem 2.11 ** *Consider the following alternative definition of rooted tree. A rooted tree consists of a set of nodes, one of which is called the root, and the rest of which are partitioned into a list of disjoint subsets, each of which is also a rooted tree. The nodes may be labelled with data. Do you think this is an acceptable definition? What do we require to make a recursive definition acceptable?*

■

Example 2.4 *One of the attractive features of recursion is that it allows compact description of infinite patterns. An example of this is Hoare's wonderful description of a clock.*

A clock is a process which first emits a "tick"; and thereafter behaves like a clock.

Example 2.5 *The Euclidean algorithm for finding the greatest common denominator of two natural numbers n and m was written down by Euclid. Not having the idea of recursion, he talks the reader through several loops of what we might call an iterative process. The explanation is fairly long, complicated, and incomplete. However if you persist in studying it, and try some examples, you eventually get the idea.*

In the computer language ML, we can express the same idea using recursion.

$fun\ gcd(m,n) =$
$\quad\quad\quad$ if $m = 0$ then n
$\quad\quad\quad\quad\quad$ else $gcd(n\ mod\ m, m)$;

Euclid codified a long tradition of mathematics. If you read Euclid's explanation, you may think it complicated and unclear. There was probably an original explanation, long before Euclid, which does not survive, and whose complexity and incompleteness we can only imagine.

There will be many other examples later.

Notice that the idea of well ordering is related to the idea of recursion. Roughly speaking, we can be sure that a recursive procedure terminates if the situations generated by trying to apply the explanation are descending in some well ordering.

2.8 Summary of chapter 2

All of mathematics and computing is constructed by logical combinations of the following basic ideas:

- A *set* is a collection of objects.
- A *function* is a process which, given an element of is domain as input, produces an element of its codomain as output.
- A *data structure* is a collection of nodes, some of which are joined by arrows. Both the nodes and the arrows may be labelled with data.

- Lists and trees are particular kinds of data structures.

The most important basic truth in mathematics is the well ordering principle for the natural numbers. The most important technique for defining functions is recursion.

Chapter 3

Formal grammars and languages

3.1 The problems of generation and recognition of languages

We are surrounded with proliferating languages, booming, beeping, drawling, chattering, some of them relatively natural, such as Urdu or English, and some of them relatively artificial, such as programming languages.

What is a language, and how does it work? In order to think about such questions, we imagine a *language system*. This system has two agents in it, a speaker and a listener. Some expressions, in some language, are being transmitted from the speaker to the listener. This text, for example, is being transmitted in some way from the writer to the reader. To start analysis of this situation, we refuse initially, to speculate about what is really going on in the minds of the speaker or the listener. (In fact we do not assume that they are human beings. The agents could be machines.) So all we look at are the expressions, which are being produced by the speaker. What can we say about these expressions? Each expression is a finite sequence of tokens of some kind, which we will call symbols. We will call these finite sequences strings. In the case of the text in front of you, the strings are sentences and the symbols are words. (It may be that from some other point of view, the symbols

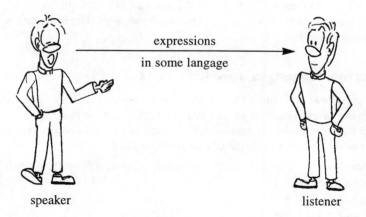

speaker   listener

Figure 3.1 Language system

could be broken up into parts in some way, but we treat the symbols as if they were atomic units.) We usually assume that the symbols are chosen from some finite set of possibilities, which is known in advance.

Definition 3.1 *Let Σ be a set of symbols. Define Σ^* to be the set of finite strings of symbols from Σ.*

Example 3.1 *Σ might be $\{a, b, c\}$, and a typical string in Σ^* could be bbaabbccba.*

Let λ be the empty string. So, for any string, X, we have $\lambda X = X$ and $X\lambda = X$.

We have decided so far that a language is going to have associated with it a finite set Σ of symbols, and that the language itself will be a subset of Σ^*.

When we know what language we are talking about, an expression in the language will be called grammatical. There may be many expressions in Σ^* which are not grammatical. Grammatical usually not is backwards written sentence a English in example For.

There are two basic problems in linguistics: the generation problem, and the recognition problem. These correspond to the activities of the speaker and the listener. How does the speaker generate grammatical expressions? How does the listener recognise them?

We wish eventually to be able to think about this problem in an abstract way. However it seems important also to keep ordinary reality in mind. [See Noam Chomsky's *Aspects of the Theory of Syntax*.]

How do children learn to use language? One idea is that they more or less repeat what they hear. However it seems that children very quickly start to say things which they never heard. It even seems that they say things that no one ever said before. So how can they have learned to do this? At this point the parsimonious refusal to look into the minds of the agents in our language system forces us to think about what is happening. It appears that a language may be something infinite. That is, the set of grammatical expressions may be infinite; or at least it is so large that it might as well be called infinite. The large amount of information involved in the use of language must be represented in some concise way.

The same remarks apply to any programming language. It is remarkable how quickly people can learn new languages. How can they possibly do this?

In this chapter we will look at the generation problem. The recognition problem will be considered later.

3.2 Formal languages, rewriting rules

One possible way to look at the situation is to consider that the behaviour of the speaker may be governed by some rules. The rules may be finite, even though the language itself is infinite. It may be that a complicated and beautiful language could be generated by a few simple rules, repeatedly applied.

Definition 3.2 *Let Σ be a finite set of symbols. Define a Σ rewriting rule to be an expression of the form*

   $A := B$

where A and B are in Σ^*.

A rewriting rule

A : = B

is understood to mean that A may be replaced by B in any string. A rewriting rule is also called a production.

An expression such as $A := B \mid C \mid D$ will mean that A can be rewritten as either B or C or D. This is an abbreviated way of giving three rewriting rules $A := B$, $A := C, A := D$.

Definition 3.3 *Define a rewrite system to be $(\Sigma, \mathcal{P})$, where Σ is a finite set of symbols and $\mathcal{P}$ is a finite list of Σ rewriting rules.*

We can think of a rewrite system as being like a game, with the rules giving the permitted moves in the game. A production tells us that wherever we see the left hand side we may, if we wish, replace it by the right hand side.

Example 3.2 $(\{0, 1\}, 01 := 00 \mid 11, 10 := 00 \mid 11\}$ *is a rewrite system.*

Definition 3.4 *Let $\mathcal{R} = (\Sigma, \mathcal{P})$ be a rewrite system, and let X and Y be strings in Σ^*. We will say that Y can be obtained from X in one step in $\mathcal{R}$, and write*

$$X \Rightarrow_{\mathcal{R}} Y$$

if X has the form CA_iD and Y has the form CB_iD, and

$$A_i := B_i$$

is a rule in our rule set $\mathcal{P}$. One or both of the surrounding strings C and D may be empty.

If the rewrite system is clear from the context we will leave off the subscript on $\Rightarrow$.

Definition 3.5 *We will say a string, X, is terminal in a rewrite system if none of the rules can be used to alter the string, i.e. if there is no string Y so that $X \Rightarrow Y$.*

This means that none of the left hand sides of the rules can be found contiguously as substrings of the string X.

Definition 3.6 *A derivation in a rewrite system is a sequence of strings*

$$X_0 \Rightarrow X_1 \Rightarrow ... \Rightarrow X_n$$

Definition 3.7 *We will say that $X \Rightarrow^* Y$ if there is a derivation which leads from X to Y.*

We allow derivations of length zero, so we will always have $X \Rightarrow^* X$.

Example 3.3 *Suppose we take our symbol set to be $\{v, a, b\}$, and our rewriting rules to be:*

$v := va$

$v := bv$

$v := a$

$v := b.$

A typical derivation in this system is: $v, va, vaa, bvaa, baaa$. We would write $v \Rightarrow^* baaa$, and the string baaa is terminal in this system.

Definition 3.8 *A phrase structure grammar is a rewrite system $(\Sigma, \mathcal{P})$, together with an initial word, I in Σ^*. The language generated by such a grammar is the set of strings W so that W is terminal and $I \Rightarrow^* W$.*

The idea of a phrase structure grammar seems to be the best contemporary solution to the generation problem. It also gives us quite a good, compact notation for describing languages.

We will say, in general, that a *formal* language is one which can be described by a phrase structure grammar. All programming languages are, in this sense, formal.

An important point to emphasise at this point is that whether or not a string is in a particular formal language has nothing at all to do with what the speaker or anyone else might mean by the string. This is a tactic which we have adopted in order to emphasise the formal aspect of languages. Eventually we want to consider languages with meaning attached to them. Our plan is first to try to pull language and meaning apart, and later to try to see how the pieces fit together.

3.3 Context free grammars and context free languages

The languages which we will actually use have an especially simple form: the left hand sides of the rules are all single symbols.

Definition 3.9 *Define a* context free grammar, *G, to be:*
1) *a finite set V of grammatical symbols*
2) *a finite set T of terminal symbols, with T disjoint from V*
3) *an initial symbol I in V*
4) *a finite set of rewriting rules* $A_1 := B_1, ..., A_n := B_n$, *where each left hand side,* A_i, *is a symbol in V, and each right hand side,* B_i, *is a string in* $(V \bigcup T)*$.

We will say that a string, X, is generated by a grammar G if it is possible to start with the initial string I of G and obtain the string X by applying the rewriting rules some finite number of times in any order. As before, a string X is terminal relative to a grammar G if there is no way to rewrite X using G.

The language $L(G)$ generated by the grammar G consists of all those strings which are generated by G and are also terminal. A context free language is one which can be generated in this way from a context free grammar.

Example 3.4 *Take the initial symbol to be x, and use rewriting rules*

$x := (x + x) \mid (x * x) \mid 0 \mid 1 \mid ... \mid 9$

There is just one grammatical symbol here, x, and the rest are terminal symbols. A typical derivation is: $x, (x + x), (x + (x * x)), (x + (1 * x)), (0 + (1 * x)), (0 + (1 * 1))$. *Note that in the course of the derivation different occurrences of x may be replaced by different expressions, and also that the rules can be applied in any order.*

Problem 3.1 *Here are the expressions in a language: La loo, La la loo, La la la loo, La la la la loo.... (The kth expression in this list consists of a La followed by $(k - 1)$ la's and a final loo, i.e. La la^{k-1} loo.) Find a context free grammar which generates this language.*

Example 3.5 *You have been kidnapped by aliens. One of them turns to you and says "Woogle Woogle Woogle Doo". The other one says "Woogle Shuffle Woogle Shuffle Woogle Woogle Doo". They turn to you expectantly and you say...? (You think to yourself Σ is at least Woogle, Shuffle, Doo, and $\mathcal{P}$ could be:*

A:= B Doo

B:= Woogle | Woogle Shuffle | B B

so we could have Σ as {A, B, Woogle, Shuffle, Doo}.)

You might say "Woogle Shuffle Woogle Doo". What you have said may be impolite but it is unlikely to be totally unrecognisable. By saying this you signal that you are listening, that you have enough brains so that you are potentially a force to be reckoned with, and that you wish to join the community of speakers. Evidently, any utterance may have several different levels of meaning.

Example 3.6 *We can write some simple facts of English grammar in our notation.*

sentence := **noun-phrase verb-phrase**

noun-phrase :=**determiner noun**

verb-phrase := **verb**

verb-phrase := **verb noun-phrase**

noun := horse

determiner := the

verb := likes

noun := man

etc. Note that all the left hand sides of the productions are grammatical symbols, and that all grammatical symbols correspond to important collections of expressions within the language. English grammar is concerned not only with what the sentences are, but also with noun-phrases, verbs and so on.

In general we will adopt the convention of writing grammatical symbols either in bold face or in italics, in order to distinguish them from the terminal symbols.

3.4 The language of statement forms

A *proposition name* will be a string of lower case letters and digits starting with a lower case letter. We can write a grammar for *proposition names* as follows.

---

proposition name := **lowercase** | **lowercase string**

string := **character string** | **character**

character := **lowercase** | **digit**

lowercase := *a* | *b* | *c* | *d* | ... | *z*

digit := 0 | 1 | 2 | ... | 9

In all the following we will use *proposition name* to stand for a string of this sort. Consider the grammar:

S := (¬S) | (S ∨ S) | (S ∧ S) | (S → S) | (S ↔ S)
S := *proposition name* (as described above)

---

with initial string S.

The expressions in this language will be called *statement forms*, and will play an important role in the rest of the course.

A complex statement in English may be expressed as a logical combination of simple statements. If this is done, and the simple statements are replaced by *proposition names*, and the logical combinations used are the propositional ones ∧, ∨, ¬, →, ↔, the result will be a statement form.

Example 3.7 *Take the statement "If the ladder slips, then the windows won't get cleaned and Paul will break his neck."*

($p \rightarrow ((\neg q) \wedge r))$ *is a statement form obtained from this, which shows its logical structure.*

3.5 The first order single sorted language of arithmetic

We define *variables* to be strings of letters and digits starting with an upper case letter.

Probably you can now invent a grammar for the *variables*.

The following will do.

---

variable := **uppercase** | **uppercase string**
string := **character string** | **character**
character := **uppercase** | **lowercase** | **digit**
uppercase := $A \mid B \mid C \mid D \mid ... \mid Z$
lowercase := $a \mid b \mid c \mid d \mid ... \mid z$
digit := 0 | 1 | 2 | ... | 9

L_N, the language of first order single sorted arithmetic, is defined by the following grammar.

---

wff := **(wff ∨ wff)** | **(wff ∧ wff)** | **(wff → wff)** | **(¬wff)** | **(wff ↔ wff)**
wff := **(∀ *variable*)wff** | **(∃ *variable*)wff**
wff := **AtomicFormula**
AtomicFormula := **(Term = Term)**
Term := **(Term + Term)** | **(Term * Term)** | **Term**′
Term := 0
Term := *variable* (as described above)

---

with initial string **wff**. The **wff** expressions will be called formulae of the language, the **AtomicFormula** expressions will be called atomic formulae of the language, and the **Term** expressions will be called terms of the language.

Example 3.8 *"X", "Xy", and "X77" are variables of L_N, but "x" is not a variable of L_N.*
  "$((X + Y) * X)$" is a term of L_N
  "$(\exists W)((W * (W * W)) = ((W * W) + 0''))$" is a formula of L_N.

We have defined L_N, using a certain context free grammar. This grammar is outside L_N. Part of the apparatus of this grammar is a small list of grammatical symbols. These are written in special ways typographically in order to distinguish them from strings in L_N. The grammatical symbols we have used are

- **uppercase**
- **lowercase**
- **digit**
- **string**
- *variable*
- **AtomicFormula**
- **Term**
- **wff**

3.6 The first order single sorted language of set theory

L_{ZF}, the language of Zermelo Fraenkel set theory, is defined by the following grammar.

---

wff := **(wff ∨ wff)** | **(wff ∧ wff)** | **(wff → wff)** | **(¬wff)** | **(wff ↔ wff)**
wff := **(∀ *variable*)wff** | **(∃ *variable*)wff**
wff := **AtomicFormula**
AtomicFormula := **(Term = Term)** | **(Term ∈ Term)**
Term := *variable* (as described above)

---

with initial string **wff**.

The expressions obtained in this grammar from rewriting the grammatical symbol **Term** will be called *terms* of L_{ZF}. Similarly, the expressions obtained in this grammar from grammatical symbols **AtomicFormula** will be called *atomic formulae* of L_{ZF} and the expressions obtained from grammatical symbol **wff** will be called *formulae* of L_{ZF}.

Note that each grammatical symbol corresponds to a natural collection of expressions in the language.

The variables are interpreted as ranging over sets. The consensus among contemporary mathematicians is that *almost all of current mathematics* can be expressed in L_{ZF}.

L_N and L_{ZF} are typical examples of *first order single sorted languages*, which will be defined in detail later. Note that in each case we have collections of expressions called variables, terms, atomic formulae, and formulae.

The formulae contain the atomic formulae and are closed under application of certain logical operators, $\wedge, \vee, \neg, \rightarrow, \leftrightarrow, \forall, \exists$. This means that, for example, if A and B are formulae then $(A \wedge B)$ is also a formula. Here we may think of $\wedge$ as an operator which, when applied to A and B gives $(A \wedge B)$.

There is only one type of object in the intended interpretation, and therefore only one type of variable is needed in these languages. For this reason, L_N and L_{ZF} are called single sorted languages.

An example of a multi-sorted language would be one in which there was one type of variable for real numbers and another type of variable for integers.

L_N and L_{ZF} are also called first order languages. This will be defined later.

We would say that one language has a higher order than another if the first language is able to say everything which can be said in the second language, i.e. if the second language can be directly translated into the first language, and also if the first language is able to talk about the second language as an object.

We are talking about these first order languages in a higher order multi-sorted informal language called English. Because this language uses many types, we need to declare or indicate the types of the variables as they occur. We might say, let A be a formula of L_N; or, let X be a natural number, or let S be a set of natural numbers. We can say: if A and B are formulae of L_N, then $(A \rightarrow B)$ is also a formula of L_N. A statement of this kind cannot be made directly inside L_N.

If you look back at the description of L_N, you will see immediately that the description itself is not in L_N. The description uses certain grammatical symbols, for example **wff** and **Term**. These grammatical symbols stand for types. For example, **wff** is a name for the set of formulae, which has associated with it certain functions, including the logical operators.

It is clear that multi-sorted languages can be useful. A number of difficult and important questions in computing and logic cluster around the question of how to deal with a multiplicity of types in language. In this book, however, we are dealing only with the simplest case of single sorted first order languages. We are hoping to get a clear understanding of this simplest case.

For the moment you should be happy if you understand the grammatical definition of L_N and L_{ZF}, and if you see that we ourselves are talking about these formal languages in another, relatively informal and much more complicated language.

3.7 Semantics and syntax

The syntax of a language is the collection of rules and conventions which determine whether or not an expression in the language is grammatical. In the context of a formal language, the syntax is exactly the information given by a phrase structure grammar.

The semantics of a language is the study of how meaning is attached to expressions in the language.

We are trying to understand semantics and syntax separately. However, from a human point of view it is difficult to look at syntax without some suggestion of meaning. As a small concession to this trait, we can say something now about the semantics of L_N and L_{ZF}.

Both L_N and L_{ZF} have variables of one type. These variables are intended to range over some domain. When we write a variable such as "X", we mean it to stand for some as yet unspecified element of the domain. So the first step in attaching meaning to a language such as L_N or L_{ZF} is to specify or describe the domain.

We previously defined the set of natural numbers, denoted **N** to be { 0, 1, 2, 3, ... }.

The variables of L_N are intended to range over the natural numbers. When we write "X" or "Y" or "Z" in L_N we mean them to stand for some unspecified natural number.

The variables of L_{ZF} are intended to range over objects and sets in "mathematical reality". In this case the intended domain is so large that it cannot be precisely specified, or constructed, but can only be informally described.

+ and * in L_N are intended to mean the usual addition and multiplication. X' is intended to mean $X + 1$.

In L_{ZF}, $\in$ is intended to mean set membership. So $(X \in Y)$ means that X is a member of Y.

L_N and L_{ZF} have the same set of logical operators, which are divided into two groups.

Propositional operators: $\land, \lor, \neg, \rightarrow, \leftrightarrow$

Quantifiers: $(\forall X), (\exists X)$.

We will study the behaviour of these operators in detail. The intended meaning of the operators is:

$\land$ is intended to mean "and"

$\lor$ is intended to mean "or"

$\neg$ is intended to mean "not"

$\rightarrow$ is intended to mean "implies "

$\leftrightarrow$ is intended to mean "if and only if"

$(\forall X)$ is intended to mean "for all X"

$(\exists X)$ is intended to mean "there exists X such that".

Example 3.9 *"X is the sum of two squares" expressed in L_N would be:*
$(\exists Y)(\exists Z)(X = ((Y * Y) + (Z * Z)))$.

Example 3.10 *"Set Z is the union of set X and set Y" can be translated into L_{ZF} by:*
$(\forall W)((W \in Z) \leftrightarrow ((W \in X) \lor (W \in Y)))$

Much of number theory can be translated into L_N, and much of contemporary mathematics can be translated into L_{ZF}. The reason for doing such a translation is that it helps us to see how relatively complex ideas are constructed out of combinations of relatively simple ones.

Much more will be said about semantics later.

Clearly the semantics of L_N and L_{ZF} is much more difficult than the syntax. The reader should not be dismayed if he or she is not yet able to use these languages.

However, at this stage we should be able to understand the syntax of L_N and

L_{ZF}. In each case we have a context free grammar. In each case three collections of expressions are defined: *terms, atomic formulae, and formulae.*

Given a string of symbols, we should be able to decide whether or not it is syntactically correct as a variable, term, atomic formula or formula of either L_N or L_{ZF}.

So, for example $(0 = 0)$ is not a term but it is both a formula and an atomic formula of L_N. We would say that $(X' = 0)$ is syntactically correct as a formula of L_N, even though you may believe that it is not semantically correct, i.e. true in the natural numbers. To say that something is syntactically correct just means that it is correctly put together. We would say also that

$$((X' = Y') \to (X = Y))$$

is syntactically correct as a formula of L_N. It is not a term, nor is it an atomic formula. We would say that $(p \to q)$ is a syntactic mistake in L_N, although it is syntactically correct as a statement form. You should check that the grammar of L_N does not allow derivation of $(p \to q)$ as a formula.

We would even say that strictly speaking

$$(X' = Y') \to (X = Y)$$

is a syntactic mistake in L_N, since it does not have the right number of brackets.

Problem 3.2 *Classify the following expressions as either variables, terms, atomic formulae, formulae or syntactic mistakes in L_N.*

$x32$

7

Sxz

$(\forall W3)(\exists Q)(Q = (W3 * W3))$

$A * (B * C)$

$(\forall X)(\forall Y)(\forall Z)((X * (Y * Z)) = ((X * Y) * Z))$

$(\neg x = Y)$

3.8 Pattern recognition, substitution and iteration

Definitions in mathematics are chosen, but some choices are much better than others. The purpose of a collection of definitions is to get into a situation in which very strong statements can be made very concisely and clearly. Making good definitions is a problem in design, like planning the structure of a computer program, or the layout of a cafe.

In the definition of phrase structure grammar given earlier, the intention is to describe language as generated from certain basic processes. These are pattern recognition, substitution, and iteration. Pattern recognition occurs when the left hand side of a rewrite rule is recognised, substitution occurs when the left hand side is replaced by the right hand side of a rule, and this pair of operations is iterated to produce derivations. I claim the phrase structure grammar definition is a good one. That means I am, so to speak, betting on the fundamental importance of pattern recognition, substitution and iteration.

The phrase structure grammar definition gives us a notation which is extremely powerful. A rich language, such as L_{ZF}, can be precisely specified in a few lines of text. The notation is of great practical use in computing, since it gives an unambiguous compact way to describe programming languages.

So, from a practical point of view, there is a lot of evidence that the phrase structure grammar definition is a good one, i.e. it is currently useful.

There is another part of the case for this definition, however. Associated with this definition is a belief that pattern recognition, substitution and iteration are basic human mental acts. The question is: do these things actually happen in human beings?

Noam Chomsky, in *Aspects of the Theory of Syntax*, argues that something like this does actually happen at some level inside human beings, and this is how they are able to use language.

Many computing professionals regard Noam Chomsky's assertions that something like a grammar must be built into the human mind as a pretentious embarrassment. After all, it may be said, it is *unnecessary* to make such grand claims.

My opinion, however, is that computer science and logic in particular are branches of applied mathematics which really should attempt to analyse certain types of human mental processes. From this point of view, Chomsky's argument strengthens the case for the importance of the phrase structure grammar idea.

Whether or not you agree with this, you should look carefully at the definition.

Accepting the definition gives us a purely syntactic way to describe many interesting languages. Take, for example, the statement forms defined above. We have defined them as a certain set of strings of symbols, without consideration of the meaning of the logical operators. The statement forms are therefore a combinatorial or mathematical structure, which can be studied with the same methods which are used for other structures.

Most definitions also have annoying limitations and side effects. In this case, for example, the insistence on initial separation of syntax and semantics is possibly a flaw. All such definitions should be seen as subject to possible future revision. If someone sees a better way to think about such things, they have to convince the community of people who are interested in such things to make a change.

3.9 Translation between formal and informal representations of ideas

Mathematical sophistication consists of critical awareness together with the ability to translate back and forth between formal and informal representations of ideas.

Much good mathematics consists in giving definitions, which are supposed to be in some sense "right". This means faithfully translating from an informal idea to a formal one. For example:

The ϵ and δ definition of continuity of $f(X)$ at a point x_1 (Weierstrass)
The definition of effective process (Turing)

The definition of rewrite system (Post)
The definition of Brownian motion

Any well constructed computer program.

The end product of formalism may not be useful in isolation. For example, the result of a translation into L_{ZF} may be more or less incomprehensible. It is the process of translation and partial translation which gives the end product its value.

If we are concerned about correctness, a computer program is not very useful without a record of the thinking behind it.

Mathematics and computing should be viewed as a collection of languages with translations between them. No one language (or mode of reasoning or attempt to establish correctness) is best for all purposes (or even sufficient for all purposes).

We live in the tower of Babel.

■

3.10 Problems

Problem 3.3 *Let G be the following grammar. The initial string is n, and the rewriting rules are:*

$n := n'$

$n := 0$

a) What is the alphabet of symbols used in G? What are the grammatical symbols? What are the terminal symbols?
b) What strings of Σ^* are terminal with respect to G?
c) Find three expressions in the language $L(G)$.

Problem 3.4 *Let G be the following grammar. The initial string is F, and the rewriting rules are:*

$F := (F + F)$

$F := (F * F)$

$F := 0$

$F := 1$

$F := x$

Let $p(x) = 3x^2 + 2x + 1$. Show that $p(x)$ can be represented by an expression in the language. Explicitly generate the expression from the rewriting rules. Show how to enlarge the grammar in order to represent polynomials in two variables. Show how to include division.

Problem 3.5 *Here are some expressions in a language: 1, 1.4, -34.9987, 999. Say what you think the terminal symbols of the language are, and define the language verbally. Give a grammar for the language.*

Problem 3.6 *Consider the following grammar G.*

Var := letter num

letter := $x \mid y \mid z$

num := num digit $\mid$ digit

digit := 0 | 1 | 2 | ... | 9

Initial string = Var

Decide whether or not X, Y, z32 are in the language L(G).

Problem 3.7 *Give a grammar which generates a language consisting of any string of letters followed by any string of digits.*

Problem 3.8 *Write a grammar for strings of one or more lower case letters, followed by zero or more digits.*

Problem 3.9 *Describe the language generated by:*

x := xax

x := b

with initial string x.

At this point we have precise definitions of the syntax of three interesting languages: statement forms, L_N and L_{ZF}. However we have not yet said anything very precise about the semantics. In some of the following problems, you are asked to attempt to make translations from informal expressions into these languages. You are of course entitled to refuse to do this on the grounds that the problem has not been specified. It is a fact that intelligent and conscientious people may disagree about the answers to these exercises. However, you are asked to put to one side the concept of the "right answer" for the time being, and to observe the ambiguities in our informal language. Hopefully this will help to convince you of the necessity of working toward clarification of the semantics of our formal languages.

Problem 3.10 *Show that $(p \lor q)$ is in the language of statement forms. Is $((p \land q) \to p)$ in the language?*

Say in the language that p and q are true if r is true. Say that either r is true or p is false if q implies p. Say that p and q and r can't all be false unless p implies q.

Problem 3.11 *Write expressions in L_{ZF} which mean a) Z is the intersection of Y and X; b) Z is the power set of X, i.e. the set of all subsets of X. Show derivations of these expressions in the grammar.*

Problem 3.12 *Look carefully at the differences and similarities between L_N and L_{ZF}.*

Interpret the variables of L_N as ranging over the natural numbers, + and ∗ as usual, and X' as $X + 1$. So $0'$ means 1, etc. Write expressions in L_N which say:

a) X is a prime number

b) X and Y are coprime

c) $X < Y$

d) ∗ *There are infinitely many numbers Y and Z so that $Z^3 - Y^2 = X$. (Hint: if there are only finitely many elements in a set of natural numbers, the set is bounded, and conversely.)*

Problem 3.13 ∗ *Write a context free grammar for a fragment of C which includes assignment and if and while constructions. Is C a formal language? Do you think it is a context free language?*

Problem 3.14 *Try to write a set of axioms for addition and multiplication in L_N.*

Problem 3.15 * *List and number all the symbols Σ in the alphabet for L_N. For s in Σ, let $g(s)$ be the number of s. Now let $S = s_1s_2...s_n$ be a string in Σ^*. Define $g(S)$ to be*

$$p_1^{g(s_1)} p_2^{g(s_2)} ... p_n^{g(s_n)}$$

where p_i means the ith prime. The number $g(S)$ is called the Gödel number of the string S. Find, but do not try to calculate, the Gödel number of $(\forall X)(\neg(X' = 0))$.

Find Gödel numbers for the answers to a), b), c), d) of Problem 3.12.

Problem 3.16 *List some true statements of L_N and some false ones. Give a statement of L_N which is grammatically correct and such that it is hard to decide whether it is true or false.*

Problem 3.17 * *(A sense of humour helps for this.) Define the following in L_{ZF}.*

a) $Z = \{X, Y\}$. That is, Z is the set with just two elements, X and Y.

b) $Z = \{\{X\}, \{X, Y\}\}$. Abbreviate this as $Z = (X, Y)$, and interpret it to mean that Z is the ordered pair with first element X and second element Y. (This is the usual way in which ordered sets are defined in terms of unordered sets.)

c) f is a function from domain X to codomain Y, assuming that functions are exactly the same as graphs of functions, i.e. sets of ordered pairs.

d) f is an injective function from domain X to codomain Y.

e) f is a bijection between X and Y.

In each case make abbreviations as you go along to try to keep things comprehensible, but try to estimate the sizes of the expressions for d) and e) if they were written out in full without abbreviations in L_{ZF}. It is this sort of thing which is meant when it is said that it is possible to translate all of mathematics into L_{ZF}. It is not being claimed that L_{ZF} is somehow better or more accurate than ordinary speech. The relationship between L_{ZF} and ordinary mathematics is something like, but more extreme than, the relationship between chemical formulae, and ordinary names, such as "sugar".

Problem 3.18 * *It can be argued that the statement forms as defined above have too many brackets. Identify cases in which you might like to leave brackets out, although the current definition requires them. Thus, produce a grammar for "relaxed statement forms", in which some of the brackets may be omitted, but the resulting expressions still seem to you to be unambiguous, in some sense.*

■

Example 3.11 *We can give a recursive definition of the statement forms.*

Basis: A proposition name *is a statement form.*

Recursive step: An expression of the form $(\neg A)$ is a statement form if A is a statement form. Expressions of the form $(A \land B), (A \lor B), (A \to B), (A \leftrightarrow B)$ are statement forms if A and B are statement forms.

Note that this definition suggests an algorithm for recognition of statement forms. (First (Basis) look at a given expression to see if it is a proposition name. *If it is, it is a statement form. Otherwise (recursive step) check to see if it is in one of the possible* *forms, either $(\neg A)$ where A is a statement form, or $(A \wedge B)$ or $(A \vee B)$ or $(A \rightarrow B)$ or $(A \leftrightarrow B)$ where A and B are statement forms.) In fact, we will be able to use this later to write a program to solve the recognition problem for statement forms.*

Problem 3.19 *Give a recursive definition of formulae of L_N, assuming that we already know what* terms *are.*

3.11 Well ordering principle for Σ^*

Let Σ be any alphabet of symbols. Suppose X is in Σ^*. Define $\mid X \mid$ to be the number of symbols in X. $\mid X \mid$ is called the *length of X*.

Example 3.12 $\mid \lambda \mid = 0$. *(λ is the empty string.) In the language of statement forms,* $\mid (p \rightarrow (q \vee r)) \mid = 9$. *The 9 symbols are 4 brackets, 2 logical operators, and 3 proposition names.*

The length function maps Σ^* onto **N**.

If S is a subset of Σ^*, and W is an element of Σ^*, we will say that W is *a minimal element of* S if, firstly, W is in S, and, secondly, there is no element V in S so that $\mid V \mid < \mid W \mid$.

Well ordering principle for Σ^*. *Any non-empty subset* S *of* Σ^* *has a minimal element.*

Problem 3.20* *Prove the well ordering principle for Σ^* from the well ordering principle for* **N**.

We will make extensive use of this well ordering principle later.

3.12 Summary of chapter 3

Formal languages are defined as the sets of strings of symbols generated by the rules written down in a phrase structure grammar.

A short phrase structure grammar can precisely define a rich and powerful language.

We have three important examples of formal languages:

- the statement forms
- L_N
- L_{ZF}.

These languages will be used and referred to in the following.

The most important fact about formal languages is that they are clearly defined combinatorial objects, which can be studied objectively. If a string of symbols is in some formal language, then there exists a derivation which demonstrates, beyond any doubt, that this is so.

Chapter 4

Propositional calculus semantics

4.1 An examination of the meanings of ∧, ∨, ¬, →, ↔

Logic considers the question: how does reasoning work? What is it that makes an argument valid?

Looking at this subject with mathematical eyes, we can see that in our mathematical languages there are a number of logical operators: ∧, ∨, ¬, →, ↔, ∃, ∀. The operators ∃ and ∀ are called quantifiers. The others are called propositional operators.

The propositional calculus is the study of the logical operators ¬, →, ∨, ∧, ↔. We will begin with this. To focus ideas, we consider the formal language of statement forms, defined earlier.

We will use upper case letters, such as A, B, C, as variables for statement forms. We make the following uniformity assumptions:

- The truth value of a statement form is determined by the truth values of the *proposition names* which occur in it.

- We will also assume that there are only two truth values, True and False, which we will write as T and F.

These seem fairly harmless assumptions. We will see, however, that imposing this sort of uniformity causes some trouble, especially with →.

This is an example of the difficulty of the art of making definitions. The need for uniformity in this case is allowed to modify the desire for intuitive correctness.

4.2 Truth tables

Our assumptions allow us to describe each of the propositional operators by a truth table.

To describe the logical operator ¬, we make a table to show how the truth value of $(\neg P)$ is related to the truth value of P.

P	$(\neg P)$
T	F
F	T

This just says that when P is true, $(\neg P)$ is false and vice versa. It seems quite acceptable. We can also easily make tables for $\vee$ and $\wedge$.

P	Q	$(P \vee Q)$
T	T	T
T	F	T
F	T	T
F	F	F

We note that $(P \vee Q)$ means P or Q or both. This truth table announces the fact that we intend to use $\vee$ to stand for the inclusive, rather than the exclusive "or". For example, if we say

"You are welcome if you are beautiful or talented (or both)."

this would have the form

((beautiful $\vee$ talented) $\rightarrow$ welcome))

P	Q	$(P \wedge Q)$
T	T	T
T	F	F
F	T	F
F	F	F

So far there does not seem to be any problem.

P	Q	$(P \leftrightarrow Q)$
T	T	T
T	F	F
F	T	F
F	F	T

This also seems intuitively correct. $(P \leftrightarrow Q)$ means that P is true if and only if Q is true. So $(P \leftrightarrow Q)$ is true just when P and Q have the same truth value.

Now we come to implication.

P	Q	$(P \rightarrow Q)$
T	T	a
T	F	b
F	T	c
F	F	d

We have to decide what a, b, c, d should be. We have stipulated that these should depend only on the truth values of P and Q, not on the meanings. Certainly b should be F, since if P is true and Q is false, $(P \rightarrow Q)$ can't be true.

According to our uniformity assumption, we can fill in the other values in this table, by looking at particular cases. For example, if it can ever happen that P, Q and $(P \to Q)$ can be simultaneously true, we will be forced to say that a is T.

Let P be $2^4 = 16$ and let Q be $2^4 + 1 = 17$. We would agree that $(P \to Q)$, and we also agree with P and Q. Thus a is T.

But what about statements $(P \to Q)$, where P is false. Consider

"If cows were blue, the sky would be the colour of a cow today."

I am forced to say this is true, even if I don't like the reasoning. (In fact, if I look out the window the sky is blue.) It seems from this that $(P \to Q)$ is going to be true if P is false and Q is true.

Consider:

"If this is Jane's shoe, then Alex is the murderer."

It seems that this statement can be true, although this is not Jane's shoe, and Alex is not the murderer. So we are compelled to accept:

P	Q	$(P \to Q)$
T	T	T
T	F	F
F	T	T
F	F	T

This table says that $(P \to Q)$ is to be considered true whenever P is false, as well as when both P and Q are true. In fact $(P \to Q)$ is synonymous with "Either P or not Q, or both".

We accept this, but with regrets. We have gained uniformity, but have lost part of the intuitive meaning of P implies Q, which suggests some logical connection between the meanings of P and Q.

We now have unambiguous definitions of $\neg, \vee, \wedge, \to, \leftrightarrow$ as operators on the truth values $\{$ T, F $\}$. We can write equations involving these operators. For example

$(T \to F) = F$

$(T \vee F) = T$

$(\neg F) = T.$

We can also combine the operators to get, for example,

$((T \leftrightarrow F) \to T) = T.$

In fact, by combining together the basic truth tables, it is now possible to construct truth tables for any statement form.

Consider, for example,

$((p \wedge q) \to ((\neg r) \wedge q))$

There are three proposition names in this statement form: p, q, r. Each can either be true or false, so there are $2^3 = 8$ possibilities. Our truth table for this statement form needs to show the final truth value for each of these possibilities, so it will need to have 8 rows.

Write the statement form, with extra spacing between the symbols, and put one column under each occurrence of a proposition name, and one column under each operator.

((p	∧	q)	→	((¬	r)	∧	q))

In this case there are 8 columns because there are four occurrences of proposition names and four operator occurrences.

Next we fill in all the possibilities for the proposition names. Note that if a variable occurs more than once in the statement form, as q does in our example, all the columns underneath it must be the same.

((p	∧	q)	→	((¬	r)	∧	q))
T		T			T		T
T		T			F		T
T		F			T		F
T		F			F		F
F		T			T		T
F		T			F		T
F		F			T		F
F		F			F		F

Now, using the values for the proposition names, and our basic truth tables, we can fill in the columns under the logical operators. We might, for example, first fill in the column under the first ∧.

((p	∧	q)	→	((¬	r)	∧	q))
T	T	T			T		T
T	T	T			F		T
T	F	F			T		F
T	F	F			F		F
F	F	T			T		T
F	F	T			F		T
F	F	F			T		F
F	F	F			F		F

In the next step we can fill in the column under the ¬, and in the next step we can fill in the column under the ∧ in ((¬r) ∧ q).

The last column to be filled in, under → in this case, is the final result column of the truth table.

Exercise: finish the example.

4.2.1 Interpretations

Associated with the set of statement forms is an infinite set of *proposition names*.

Intuitively, we imagine that an interpretation would associate some of the proposition names with an actual proposition in an actual situation in such a way that a truth value, either T or F, can be determined. To try to make matters simpler, we throw away all unnecessary information, and just keep the truth values. So an interpretation will just give us truth value for a subset of the proposition names. This leads to the following definition.

Definition 4.1 *An* interpretation, v, *is a function from a set of* proposition names *into the set* $\{\, T, F \,\}$ *of truth values.*

If v is an interpretation and X is a *proposition name* in the domain of v, let $v(X)$ be the truth value which v gives to X.

Definition 4.2 *If v is an interpretation, and S is a statement form, we will say that v defines a truth value for S if the domain of v includes all the proposition names which occur in S. In this case we will say that the interpretation covers S, and we will use the notation*

$$sat(S, v)$$

to denote the truth value which the interpretation v gives to S.

We are identifying the meaning of a statement form, S, with the mathematical object $sat(S, v)$, which is a function whose domain is the interpretations which cover S, and whose codomain is the set of truth values.

We could say that the truth value $sat(S, v)$ is determined by combining together the basic truth table definitions according to the structure of S. We can, if we wish, be more formal and give the following recursive definition:

Basis: If S is a *proposition name*, then $sat(S, v) = v(S)$.
Recursive step: $sat((A \land B), v) = (sat(A, v) \land sat(B, v))$
$sat((A \lor B), v) = (sat(A, v) \lor sat(B, v))$
$sat((\neg A), v) = (\neg sat(A, v))$
$sat((A \to B), v) = (sat(A, v) \to sat(B, v))$
$sat((A \leftrightarrow B), v) = (sat(A, v) \leftrightarrow sat(B, v))$

The recursive step above makes sense because we have previously defined how the propositional operators act on the truth values. We know $(T \lor F) = T$, etc.

4.2.2 Tautologies and contradictions

Definition 4.3 *A statement form S is a* tautology *if $sat(S, v) = T$ for all interpretations v which cover S.*

We will write

$$\models S$$

to mean that S is a tautology.

Definition 4.4 *A statement form S is a* contradiction *if $sat(S, v) = F$ for all interpretations v which cover S.*

Note that S is a contradiction if and only if $\models (\neg S)$.

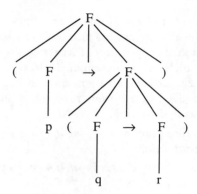

Figure 4.1   Parse tree for $(p \rightarrow (q \rightarrow r))$

4.2.3 Parse trees

It is possible to represent derivations in a context free grammar by trees. These are called parse trees. Put the initial string at the root. The initial string is just one grammatical symbol. Then if the first string in the derivation, s, has length n, the root will have n children, the ith one labelled with the ith symbol in s, for $i = 1, ..., n$. In general, each node of a parse tree is labelled with a symbol. If the symbol is replaced in the derivation by a string of length n, then the node will have n children, labelled according to the string.

The statement form $(p \rightarrow (q \rightarrow r))$ has the derivation: $F \Rightarrow (F \rightarrow F) \Rightarrow (F \rightarrow (F \rightarrow F)) \Rightarrow (p \rightarrow (F \rightarrow F)) \Rightarrow (p \rightarrow (q \rightarrow F)) \Rightarrow (p \rightarrow (q \rightarrow r))$. Notice that this derivation is not unique. There are several other ways to get from the beginning to the end. However all of these different derivations produce the *same parse tree*. The terminal string at the end of the derivation is obtained by reading the frontier of the tree, in order. See figure 4.1.

Suppose we have an interpretation σ. That means that we can attach truth values to the *proposition names* on the frontier of the tree. The expressions one level up from the frontier are then given truth values by the truth table definition. In general the truth table definition propagates up the tree from the bottom, eventually giving a truth value to the whole expression, represented by the initial F at the root of the parse tree.

In general, a derivation grows a parse tree, starting from the root, and using the rules in the grammar. On the other hand, meaning (in this case a truth value) begins at the frontier of the tree and propagates up the parse tree, eventually arriving at the root.

To go back to our original language system: a listener to an expression in a language observes the frontier of a parse tree. This listener then makes a hypothesis about what the whole parse tree must be. If we know the parse tree, and the definitions of the meanings of the operators of the language, we should be able to work out the meaning of the expression.

In our definitions of the language of statement forms, we used such an abundance of brackets in order to make each statement form correspond to a unique parse tree.

4.3 Translation between statement forms and ordinary explanation

Suppose we want to analyse the logical form of a complex statement in English. We can break it up as far as possible into simple statements combined together with logical operations $\neg, \vee, \wedge, \rightarrow, \leftrightarrow$. The statements can then be replaced by *proposition names*, and in this way we get a statement form.

It is not always clear how to do this.

Example 4.1 *Harry is the thief and the diamond is in the drawer, or the door is unlocked. This can be parsed as either $((ht \wedge dd) \vee (\neg ld))$, or $(ht \wedge (dd \vee (\neg ld)))$. Try to decide whether or not these two statement forms have the same meaning. If you become confused, look ahead to the definition of logical equivalence.*

Example 4.2 *Alice is guilty if George was at the party, unless January the thirteenth was a Wednesday. $(wednesday \vee (george - at - party \rightarrow alice - guilty))$. Even more compactly,*

$$((w \vee (g \rightarrow a))$$

English is quite ambiguous, and there are often many different ways to translate English into statement forms. For example, people disagree about what "A provided B" means. Some people understand this as $(B \rightarrow A)$ and other people understand it as $(A \leftrightarrow B)$. A similar situation occurs with "A unless B". Does this mean $(A \vee B)$? Or does it mean $(A \leftrightarrow (\neg B))$? Or what about $((\neg A) \rightarrow B)$?

The ambiguity of English helps to explain why people often become confused in mathematics lectures. It is very hard to follow an explanation if the speaker and listener have different understandings of the logical operators.

Everybody knows about the ambiguity of natural language. But the extent of it is surprising. We only become aware of it by having something unambiguous, such as the statement forms, to refer to. The reader is advised not only to try the translation exercises below, but also to discuss the results with others.

4.4 Logical consequence, logical equivalence, satisfiability

Definition 4.5 *Statement forms A and B are said to be* logically equivalent *if for all interpretations, σ, which cover both A and B, we have $sat(A, \sigma) = sat(B, \sigma)$.*

For example $(p \rightarrow q)$ is logically equivalent to $((\neg p) \vee q)$. Also, since we are only considering interpretations which cover both statement forms, *cat* is logically equivalent to $(cat \wedge (dog \vee (\neg dog)))$. This is because the extra proposition name, *dog*, does not influence the truth value of $(cat \wedge (dog \vee (\neg dog)))$.

Theorem *Let A and B be statement forms.*
A and B are logically equivalent if and only if $(A \leftrightarrow B)$ is a tautology.

Proof To begin with, suppose that A and B are logically equivalent. According to the definition, this means that $sat(A, \sigma) = sat(B, \sigma)$ for all interpretations σ. We wish to show that $(A \leftrightarrow B)$ is a tautology. Pick any interpretation σ. We have the truth table definition for $\leftrightarrow$, and we know that $sat((A \leftrightarrow B), \sigma)$ is $sat(A, \sigma) \leftrightarrow sat(B, \sigma)$. Since $sat(A, \sigma) = sat(B, \sigma)$ we have $(sat(A, \sigma) \leftrightarrow sat(B, \sigma)) = T$. But σ was arbitrary. So $\models (A \leftrightarrow B)$.

In order to do the proof in the other direction, suppose $\models (A \leftrightarrow B)$. Let σ be any interpretation. We know that $sat((A \leftrightarrow B), \sigma) = T$. So $sat(A, \sigma) = sat(B, \sigma)$. Thus A and B are logically equivalent.

Exercise: the DeMorgan laws. Show that $(\neg(P \vee Q))$ is logically equivalent to $((\neg P) \wedge (\neg Q))$. Also show that $(\neg(P \wedge Q))$ is logically equivalent to $((\neg P) \vee (\neg Q))$.

Definition 4.6 *A statement form B is a logical consequence of statement form A if for all interpretations σ which cover both A and B, $sat(B, \sigma) = T$ whenever $sat(A, \sigma) = T$.*

To say that B is a logical consequence of A means that any assignment of truth values which makes A true and covers B must also make B true.

Problem 4.1 *Prove that B is a logical consequence of A if and only if $(A \rightarrow B)$ is a tautology.*

We will write $A \models B$ to mean that B is a logical consequence of A.

We will say that a statement form B is a logical consequence of a set Γ of statement forms if $sat(B, \sigma) = T$ for any interpretation σ which covers Γ and B and is such that $sat(A, \sigma) = T$ for all A in Γ. If B is a logical consequence of Γ, we will write $\Gamma \models B$.

Definition 4.7 *A statement form S is* satisfiable *if there is an interpretation which makes S true. A set Γ of statement forms is* satisfiable *if there is an interpretation v which makes all of the statement forms in the set true.*

Problem 4.2 * *Prove that $\Gamma \models A$ if and only if $\Gamma \cup \{(\neg A)\}$ is not satisfiable.*

4.5 Validity of arguments

Statements in English or some other language may be combined together into arguments. Usually these have the form of a list of premises, and a conclusion. It is asserted that the conclusion follows logically from the premises.

In order to attempt to reveal the logical structure of an argument we can try, as before, to break the complex statements in the argument into simpler statements combined together with logical operators, and finally replacing the simplest statements by *proposition names* uniformly. From this process we will get a list

$A_1, ..., A_n$ of statement forms corresponding to the premises, and a statement form B corresponding to the conclusion.

Define an *argument form* to be an expression

$$A_1, ..., A_n$$

$$\overline{}$$

$$B$$

where $A_1, ..., A_n$ are statement forms, called the premises, and B is a statement form called the conclusion.

Example 4.3 Modus ponens

$$A, (A \to B)$$

$$\overline{}$$

$$B$$

is an argument form with premises A and $(A \to B)$ *and conclusion B. This is a famous argument form, called modus ponens.*

Example 4.4 *Another famous argument form is* proof by contradiction. *This may be written:*

$$((\neg T) \to S), (\neg S)$$

$$\overline{}$$

$$T$$

A typical pattern for the use of this form is as follows:

Theorem Thm

Proof by contradiction. *Assume Thm is false. Using this assumption we deduce a conclusion S. But we know that S is false. We have a contradiction, so our assumption that "Thm is false" must be incorrect. Thus Thm must be true.*

Example 4.5 *Here is an example of proof by contradiction.*

Induction principle *Let Δ be any subset of the natural numbers. If 0 is in Δ, and $x + 1$ is in Δ whenever x is in Δ then $\Delta = \mathbf{N}$.*

Proof by contradiction. Assume that the induction principle is false. Then there is a set Δ of natural numbers so that 0 is in Δ, and also $x + 1$ is in Δ whenever x is in Δ, but not every natural number is in Δ.

Let $S = \mathbf{N} - \Delta$. S is not empty, since not every natural number is in Δ. So, by the well ordering principle for $\mathbf{N}$, S has a minimal element; call this minimal element k. This number k is not 0, since 0 is in Δ. Let $j = k - 1$. This j is a natural number and $j < k$, and k was a minimal element of S, so j is not in S. Thus j is in Δ. But j in Δ implies $j + 1$ in Δ. So k is in Δ. Contradiction. Therefore the induction principle must be true.

Remark: The above proof of the induction principle uses more than just proof by contradiction. It also uses the well ordering principle for $\mathbf{N}$ and the fact that if k is a non-zero natural number, then $k - 1$ is also a natural number.

Definition 4.8 *We will say that an argument form*

$$A_1, ..., A_n$$

$$B$$

is valid if $((A_1 \wedge A_2 \wedge ... \wedge A_n) \rightarrow B)$ is a tautology.

Problem 4.3 *Prove that argument form*

$$A_1, ..., A_n$$

$$B$$

is valid if and only if $\{A_1, ..., A_n\} \models B$.

Example 4.6 *"If aardvarks have green teeth then Zorn's lemma implies that it is illegal to eat spaghetti. Also if aardvarks don't have green teeth its illegal to eat spaghetti. But it is legal to eat spaghetti. So Zorn's lemma is false." The form of this argument is*

$$(agt \rightarrow (zl \rightarrow (\neg ls))), ((\neg agt) \rightarrow (\neg ls)), ls$$

$$(\neg zl)$$

Note that the validity of the argument form does not depend on how the statements are interpreted. To decide whether or not this argument is valid we do not have to make up our minds about Zorn's lemma, or even understand what it is. In this sense it seems that a lot of mathematics can be followed, or even criticised, without knowing anything specific.

Example 4.7 *Another famous argument form is resolution:*

$$(A \vee C), (B \vee (\neg C))$$

$$(A \vee B)$$

4.6 Substitutions

Definition 4.9 *A substitution is a function from a set of proposition names to a set of statement forms. A finite substitution may be written as*

$$\alpha = \{(X_1, S_1), ...(X_n, S_n)\}$$

where $X_1, ..., X_n$ are proposition names and $S_1, ..., S_n$ are statement forms. Such a substitution α is applied to a statement form S by simultaneously replacing each occurrence of proposition name X_i by corresponding statement form S_i, for $i = 1, ..., n$.

The result of applying substitution α to statement form S will be written S_α.

For example, if S is $((p \wedge q) \rightarrow r)$, and $\alpha = \{(p, (p \vee q)), (r, (r \vee p))\}$, then $S_\alpha = (((p \vee q) \wedge q) \rightarrow (r \vee p))$. Note that in this case the substitution α has two components, and S_α is obtained by applying them together. If we had first substituted $(r \vee p)$ for r, and then substituted $(p \vee q)$ for p, we would have obtained a different result.

Substitution theorem *For all statement forms $S, A_1, ..., A_n, B_1, ..., B_n$, if A_i is logically equivalent to B_i for all i, and*

$$\alpha = \{(X_1, A_1), ..., (X_n, A_n)\}$$

and

$$\beta = \{(X_1, B_1), ..., (X_n, B_n)\}$$

are any substitutions, then S_α and S_β are logically equivalent.

Proof by contradiction. Suppose that this theorem were false. Then there would be a statement form S, and two substitutions α and β, as above so that S_α and S_β were not logically equivalent. We have $\alpha = \{(X_1, A_1), ..., (X_n, A_n)\}$ and $\beta = \{(X_1, B_1), ..., (X_n, B_n)\}$, and each A_i is logically equivalent to the corresponding B_i. Since the results of the two substitutions are not logically equivalent, there must an interpretation, v, so that

$$sat(S_\alpha, v) \neq sat(S_\beta, v)$$

For the rest of the argument, assume α, β, and v are fixed, i.e. constant. Define a set of statement forms

$$\Delta = \{statement form\ W : sat(W_\alpha, v) \neq sat(W_\beta, v)\}$$

We know Δ is non-empty, since S is in Δ. We now use the well ordering principle for Σ^*, where Σ is the set of symbols needed to define statement forms. The well ordering principle says that a set such as Δ must have a minimal element, say W. W is a statement form, so W is either a *proposition name*, or has one of the forms $(A \wedge B), (A \vee B), (\neg A), (A \rightarrow B), (A \leftrightarrow B)$. We consider each of these alternatives, and show that each implies a contradiction. The appearance of contradiction will be signified by $\otimes$.

Case 1. W is a *proposition name*. The substitutions α and β replace the same variables, $X_1, ..., X_n$. If W is not one of these, then $W_\alpha = W_\beta = W$. On the other hand, if $W = X_i$, then $W_\alpha = A_i$ and $W_\beta = B_i$, so in either case W_α is logically equivalent to W_β. $\otimes$.

Case 2. W has the form $(A \wedge B)$. Both A and B are shorter than W, and W was the minimal counterexample to the theorem. So the theorem must be true for A and also for B. Thus A_α is logically equivalent to A_β and B_α is logically equivalent to B_β. This implies

$$sat(A_\alpha, v) = sat(A_\beta, v)$$
$$sat(B_\alpha, v) = sat(B_\beta, v)$$

It follows from this that $sat(W_\alpha, v) = sat(W_\beta, v)$, which was assumed to be false. $\otimes$.

Do the other cases yourself, i.e. the cases for $\vee, \neg, \rightarrow, \leftrightarrow$.

All cases end in contradiction. So our original assumption that the substitution theorem was false must be wrong. Therefore the substitution theorem is true.

$\square$

■

Problem 4.4 * *In the archives of the former Soviet Union Siberian Cybernetics Institute, a manuscript was found with the following:*

Theorem. If A and B are logically equivalent, and α is any substitution, then A_α is logically equivalent to B_α.

Unfortunately the proof of this is missing. There is a handwritten note which says: I do not have time to write this proof. However it is obvious.

Do you think this statement is true or false. Present some evidence; if possible find either a proof or a counterexample.

■

Definition 4.10 *Two statement forms A and B are* unified *by a substitution α if $A_\alpha = B_\alpha$.*

4.7 Conjunctive normal form, disjunctive normal form

Statement forms have a lot of brackets, in order to make their parse trees unique. However, now we have decided on the semantics of statement forms, we see that $(p \vee (q \vee r))$ is logically equivalent to $((p \vee q) \vee r)$. In this sense, $\vee$ is associative. In a similar way, $\wedge$ is associative. From now on, we will feel free to leave brackets off, provided that the meaning of the resulting statement, i.e. the truth table, is unambiguous.

We will call $(p \vee q)$ the disjunction of p and q. Similarly we will call $(a \vee b \vee c)$ the disjunction of a and b and c. If $A_1, ... A_n$ are statement forms, we will write the disjunction of $A_1, ..., A_n$ as

$$\bigvee_{i=1}^{n} A_i$$

Similarly, we will call $p \wedge q \wedge r$ the conjunction of p, q and r. If $A_1, ..., A_n$ are statement forms, the conjunction of all of them will be written as

$$\bigwedge_{i=1}^{n} A_i$$

Definition 4.11 *A statement form is a* literal *if it is either a proposition name or the negation of a proposition name.*

So, for example, p is a literal, as is $(\neg p)$.

Definition 4.12 *A statement form is in* conjunctive normal form *(CNF) if it is in the form*

$$\bigwedge_i \bigvee_j A_{i,j}$$

where each $A_{i,j}$ is a literal.

Definition 4.13 *A statement form is in* disjunctive normal form *(DNF) if it is in the form*

$$\bigvee_i \bigwedge_j A_{i,j}$$

where each $A_{i,j}$ is a literal.

So conjunctive normal forms are conjunctions of disjunctions of literals, and disjunctive normal forms are disjunctions of conjunctions of literals. A simple conjunction of literals is both in CNF and in DNF, as is a simple disjunction of literals.

■

Problem 4.5 *Show that the negation of a statement form in conjunctive normal form is logically equivalent to a statement form in disjunctive normal form. Hint: use the DeMorgan laws.*

■

Conjunctive and disjunctive normal form theorem. *For any statement form X we can find a statement form $CNF(X)$ which is in conjunctive normal form and is logically equivalent to X. For any statement form X we can find a statement form $DNF(X)$ which is in disjunctive normal form and is logically equivalent to X.*

Remark. Two algorithms will be given below. Either one will find either of the normal forms for any given statement form X. You should learn to use these algorithms. The issue of proof of correctness for the algorithms will be discussed in the problems. Correctness would mean: 1) the given algorithm always terminates for any given statement form X, 2) at termination, the given algorithm produces as output a statement form in the desired normal form, and 3) the output statement form is logically equivalent to the input X.

Algorithm 1

We define a rewrite system which operates on statement forms, preserves logical equivalence, and eventually terminates with either conjunctive normal form or disjunctive normal form. Suppose we are given statement form X.

Apply the following in order.

1) get rid of all $\leftrightarrow$ operators, using

$$(A \leftrightarrow B) := ((A \rightarrow B) \wedge (B \rightarrow A))$$

2) get rid of all $\rightarrow$ operators, using

$$(A \rightarrow B) := ((\neg A) \vee B)$$

After 1) and 2) we have a statement form, logically equivalent to the original, but using only $\wedge, \vee, \neg$.

3) move all the $\neg$ operators to the inside as far as possible using the DeMorgan laws

$$(\neg(A \vee B)) := ((\neg A) \wedge (\neg B))$$
$$(\neg(A \wedge B)) := ((\neg A) \vee (\neg B))$$

In the process of doing this, we also get rid of double negations

$$(\neg(\neg A)) := A$$

We now have just $\vee$ and $\wedge$ applied to proposition names and negations of proposition names, i.e. to literals. We use the distributive law to move the $\vee$ operators inside the $\wedge$ operators, if we want conjunctive normal form, and vice versa if we want disjunctive normal form.

If we want conjunctive normal form, we use

$$(A \vee (B \wedge C)) := ((A \vee B) \wedge (A \vee C))$$
$$((B \wedge C) \vee A) := ((B \vee A) \wedge (C \vee A))$$

On the other hand if we want disjunctive normal form, we use the rewrite rules:

$$(A \wedge (B \vee C)) := ((A \wedge B) \vee (A \wedge C))$$
$$((B \vee C) \wedge A) := ((B \wedge A) \vee (C \wedge A))$$

Example $(p \leftrightarrow q)$

We get $((p \rightarrow q) \wedge (q \rightarrow p))$ at the first step. We then replace the implication. This gives $(((\neg p) \vee q) \wedge ((\neg q) \vee p))$. This is a conjunctive normal form. In order to get it in the other form, we need to use the distributive laws to move the conjunction inside the disjunctions.

Try this as an exercise.

A possible disjunctive normal form for the above would be

$$((p \wedge q) \vee ((\neg p) \wedge (\neg q)))$$

You may have got something else which is logically equivalent. Neither CNF nor DNF are unique. Strictly speaking, anything is correct as long as it is logically equivalent to the original and in the correct form.

Note that when the distributive laws are applied, the expressions tend to grow alarmingly in size. It can happen that the initial expression is small and the final expression is fairly small, but there is no obvious way to get from one to the other using the rewrite rules without passing through very large and complicated looking expressions.

Problem 4.6 *Show that the transformations of Algorithm 1 preserve logical equivalence. Use the substitution theorem.*

Problem 4.7 *Find conjunctive normal form for*

$$((winter \wedge (\neg shelter)) \rightarrow (coldfeet \wedge coldhands))$$

Because of the difficulty of applying the distributive law, another method for finding CNF and DNF is given below.

Algorithm 2 for the CNF and DNF theorem

We will prove a slightly stronger statement than the theorem. Define a truth function of n variables to be a function from n-tuples of truth values to truth values. If $h(x_1, ..., x_n)$ is such a function, $h(x_1, ..., x_n) : \{T, F\}^n \rightarrow \{T, F\}$. Suppose we are given a function, h, of this type in some way. We might be given a statement form with n *proposition name*s, for example. All we will assume is that we are somehow able to work out the truth value of $h(x_1, ..., x_n)$ for each n-tuple of truth values $x_1, ..., x_n$.

For each of the normal forms, we will show that we are able to find a statement form in the right normal form which has the same truth table as the given function $h(x_1, ..., x_n)$.

We begin by making a truth table for $h(x_1, ..., x_n)$. This will have 2^n rows and $n + 1$ columns, one column for each variable, and one column for the result.

Disjunctive normal form case.

Mark all the rows which have T in the result column. Call these the true rows.

These rows are the conditions which make $h(x_1, ..., x_n)$ true. Each row assigns truth values to the variables, one value, either true or false, to each variable. The condition expressed by a row is therefore a conjunction of n conditions on individual variables. So each row is equivalent to a conjunction of literals. For example, to say x_1 is true, x_2 is false, and x_3 is true is expressed by

$(x_1 \wedge (\neg x_2) \wedge x_3)$

So $h(x_1, ..., x_n)$ can be expressed as the disjunction of the conjunctive row conditions which come from rows which have T in the results column.

Example

P	Q	$h(P, Q)$
T	T	T
T	F	F
F	T	F
F	F	T

The true rows are (T, T) and (F, F). $h(P, Q)$ is true if and only if either the first true row occurs or the second true row occurs, or both. So we get

$((P \wedge Q) \vee ((\neg P) \wedge (\neg Q)))$

Conjunctive normal form case

Let the false rows be those which have F in the results column in the truth table for $h(x_1, ..., x_n)$. Suppose these false rows are $r_1, ..., r_k$. We have

$h(x_1, ..., x_n)$ is true if and only if

none of the false rows happens, i.e. r_1 does not happen and r_2 does not happen and ... and r_k does not happen.

So we can express $h(x_1, ..., x_n)$ as a conjunction of statements of the type

row r_i does not happen.

We want to express this as a disjunction. Suppose r_i is $(v_1, ..., v_n)$, an n-tuple of truth values. To say "r_i does not happen" means $(x_1, ..., x_n)$ is different from $(v_1, ..., v_n)$, that is

$(x_1$ is not $v_1)$ or $(x_2$ is not $v_2)$ or ... or $(x_n$ is not $v_n)$.

So we can express "row r_i does not happen" as

$a_1 \vee a_2 \vee ... \vee a_n$

where a_i is $(\neg x_i)$ if $v_i = $ T and a_i is x_i if $v_i = $ F.

We end up expressing "row r_i does not happen" as a disjunction of literals.

Example Referring to the previous truth table we get (T,F) and (F,T) as the false rows. To say that the first false row does not happen means $(P, Q) \neq $ (T, F), i.e. $((\neg P) \vee Q)$. The non-occurrence of the second false row is expressed by $(P \vee (\neg Q))$. So we get conjunctive normal form

$(((\neg P) \vee Q) \wedge (P \vee (\neg Q)))$

4.8 Clausal form

Suppose we have a statement form S and we write it in conjunctive normal form. This gives us a conjunction of disjunctions. Break the conjunction up into a list of disjunctions. Each of these disjunctions has the form

$$U_1 \vee U_2 \vee ... \vee U_n \vee (\neg V_1) \vee (\neg V_2) \vee ... \vee (\neg V_m)$$

where the U_i's and V_j's are *proposition names*. We will call the U_i terms the positive proposition names and the V_j terms the negative proposition names. This disjunction is logically equivalent to

$$(V_1 \wedge V_2 \wedge ... \wedge V_m) \to (U_1 \vee U_2 \vee ... \vee U_n)$$

Such an expression, i.e. a conjunction of *proposition names* implying a disjunction of proposition names is called a *clause*. Note that clauses do not use negation.

We have expressed any statement form as a list of clauses. This list of clauses is called a *clausal form* of the original statement.

It may happen that there are no proposition names in one of the two categories. Therefore the clauses are not always statement forms, even after brackets are added. For example, we would call

$$V_1 \wedge V_2 \wedge ... \wedge V_m \to$$

a clause, even though there is nothing to the right of the implication.

Clausal form is often a natural way to represent logical relationships. Consider for example the following text.

> "If the lights don't work then the battery is flat. If the lights were left on and the battery is flat then the battery is run down. If the battery fluid is not visible and the battery is flat then the battery fluid is low. However if the battery is flat and the lights were not left on we have a generator fault."

We can first translate this into a list of statement forms

$(\neg lw) \to bf$

$(llo \wedge bf) \to brd$

$((\neg bfv) \wedge bf) \to bfl$

$(bf \wedge (\neg llo)) \to genf$

Thus is not yet clausal form, because of the use of negation. We can put it into clausal form as follows.

$lw \vee bf$

$(llo \wedge bf) \to brd$

$bf \to (bfl \vee bfv)$

$bf \to (llo \vee genf)$

■

Problem 4.8 *Put $(dog \to (cat \to bird))$ into clausal form.*

A *headed Horn clause* is one in which there is just one positive proposition name. So headed Horn clauses can be written

$(V_1 \wedge V_2 \wedge ... \wedge V_m) \rightarrow A$

where $V_1, ..., V_m$ and A are all *proposition names*.

Later, we will write a clause of this type as:

A if $V_1, ..., V_m$.

It is *not* true that every statement form is logically equivalent to a conjunction of headed Horn clauses.

A clause conveys information in the following way: we give a list of conditions, such that if they are all true then at least one of a list of alternatives must hold. In the case of headed Horn clauses, only one alternative is allowed. Clearly, headed Horn clauses are easier to deal with than clauses in general.

In the construction of knowledge based systems, one of the strategies is to represent information using lists of headed Horn clauses.

4.9 Problems

Problem 4.9 *Expose the logical form of the following statements. Write them as proposition names combined together with propositional operators:* $\wedge, \vee, \neg, \rightarrow, \leftrightarrow$, *i.e. as statement forms.*

a) If Alex was at the party and this is Fred's shoe, then Jane is guilty.

b) If we had some ham, we could have ham and eggs, provided that we had some eggs.

c) We could have ham and eggs, provided that we had some ham.

d) If Jones is not elected leader of the party, then either Smith or Robinson will leave the cabinet, and we shall lose the election.

e) Assuming that this is not Fred's shoe, then Jane is only guilty if Alex wasn't at the party.

f) Zorn's lemma is true only if the well ordering principle is true.

Problem 4.10 *Write out the truth tables for the following:*

$\neg((p \rightarrow q) \rightarrow (\neg(q \rightarrow p)))$

Problem 4.11 *Write out the truth tables for the following:*

$(((p \wedge q) \leftrightarrow r) \rightarrow (p \vee q))$

Problem 4.12 *Find a statement form only using* $\vee, \wedge, \neg$ *which has the same truth table as* $(p \rightarrow q)$.

Problem 4.13 *Express* $\vee$, *and* $\wedge$ *in terms of* $\rightarrow$ *and* $\neg$.

Problem 4.14 *Show that* $(((\neg p) \wedge (\neg q)) \rightarrow (\neg r))$ *is logically equivalent to* $(r \rightarrow (q \vee p))$.

Problem 4.15 *Show that* $(((\neg p) \rightarrow q) \rightarrow (p \rightarrow (\neg q)))$ *is not a tautology. Find a substitution* $\alpha = \{(p, A), (q, B), (r, C)\}$ *which turns this statement form into a contradiction.*

Problem 4.16 *Find a substitution which unifies $(p \to (q \to r))$ and $((u \to v) \to w)$.*

Problem 4.17 *Show that for any statement forms A, B, C,*

$$((A \wedge B) \to B)$$

is a tautology.

Advice: make sure you know how to find CNF, DNF and clausal form.

Problem 4.18 *Put the following statements into conjunctive normal form, and also disjunctive normal form. Check that the truth tables are the same.*

a) $(((p \to q) \to r) \to s)$
b) $(p \leftrightarrow q)$

Problem 4.19 *Find clausal form for $(((p \wedge q) \to r) \vee (\neg s))$*

Problem 4.20 *Construct the argument form, and decide whether or not the argument is valid:*

Either Robin was a spy or he wasn't. If he was a spy, then they have all our secrets. If he wasn't a spy, then we hanged him unnecessarily. If we hanged him unnecessarily, Harry will defect. If Harry defects then they have all our secrets, unless we kill him. Therefore, either we kill him or they have all our secrets.

Problem 4.21 *Give an interpretation, σ, which makes $(p \to (q \to r))$ true, but makes q false.*

Problem 4.22 *If an interpretation σ makes $sat((A \to B), \sigma) = True$, what can you say about $sat(A, \sigma)$ and $sat(B, \sigma)$?*

Problem 4.23 *Write as a conjunction of clauses. The Q manuscript is not prior to the F manuscript unless both are derived from the Ur-Hamlet, or unless the letter is inaccurately dated.*

Problem 4.24 *Construct a parse tree for the statement forms of the previous problem. Pick an interpretation at random and label the proposition names on the frontier of the tree with this interpretation. Then propagate the truth values up the tree.*

Problem 4.25 *The problem of deciding whether or not a statement form is a tautology can be settled by constructing a truth table. Suppose you are given an hour to do this with paper and pencil. Estimate how large a statement form you can deal with.*

Problem 4.26 *Add ? to the truth values and extend the truth tables accordingly.*

Problem 4.27 *Assume the truth values are probabilities. Is it reasonable to continue to maintain the uniformity assumption? That is, does the truth value of a compound statement only depend on the truth values of its parts?*

Problem 4.28 *Express the following as an argument form and either prove that it is valid, or show that it is not valid.*

"If the axiom of choice is true, then Zorn's lemma implies the well ordering principle. But if the axiom of choice is false the well ordering principle is also false. We know that Zorn's lemma implies the axiom of choice. So therefore the axiom of choice and the well ordering principle are equivalent."

Problem 4.29 *Decide whether or not the following argument form is valid*

$(p \vee q), (r \vee (\neg q))$

$(p \vee r)$

Justify your conclusion.

■

4.10 Summary of chapter 4

We make two basic assumptions, that the truth value of a statement form depends only on the truth values of its constituent proposition names, and that there are only two truth values T and F. Using these assumptions, we get truth table definitions for all the propositional operators $\neg$, $\wedge$, $\vee$, $\rightarrow$, $\leftrightarrow$. We can then construct truth tables for all statement forms.

We define:

- interpretation
- tautology
- logical equivalence
- logical consequence
- validity of argument forms
- CNF, DNF
- clausal form.

We also have algorithms to find CNF, DNF and clausal form.

Chapter 5

Formal propositional reasoning

5.1 The idea of a formal reasoning system

We previously defined a formal language system to consist of two agents, a speaker and a listener. Expressions are in some manner generated by the speaker and, in some manner, processed by the listener. We have attempted to understand something about the structure of language without making assumptions about the intentions of the speaker and the listener. In this chapter we will begin to look at reasoning in the same way.

It appears that formal language theory is fundamental to contemporary computing, since so much of this computing has to do with translations of some type. Computer scientists are working to embed as much as possible of the richness of human understanding in computer systems. Human understanding is structured and generated by reasoning in a manner analogous to the structuring and generation of language by grammar. Therefore it seems likely that formal reasoning will become increasingly important in computing.

We will say that a *formal reasoning system* consists of two agents, one called a theorem prover and the other called a proof checker. Associated with the system

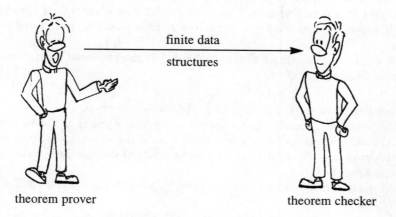

theorem prover   theorem checker

Figure 5.1   Reasoning system

is a formal language, L. The theorem prover produces finite data structures which purport to be proofs of statements in L. These data structures are typically lists or trees labelled with expressions in L, and some explanatory remarks in another language. Associated with a formal reasoning system is a definition of what constitutes a correct proof. This definition must be sufficiently precise so that the proof checker can decide whether any given finite data structure is or is not a proof of a given expression in L. The proof checker applies some checking algorithm and either accepts the proof or rejects it.

The essential property of a formal system is that proof checking can be effectively defined.

Part of the behaviour of the theorem prover may be random. The theorem prover may make lucky guesses, or may even be unreliable.

Generally speaking, however, there are two recognised types of strategy for the theorem prover.

- A bottom up strategy begins with a set of assumptions or axioms in the language L; these are supposed to be obviously true for the situation being considered. The theorem prover also has access to a collection of rules of inference, which are supposed to preserve truth. The conclusion of a rule of inference is suppose to follow, obviously, from the truth of its premises. So the theorem prover in this type of system begins with the axioms or assumptions and generates theorems by applying the rules of inference. This type of theorem generation is also called forward chaining.

- A top down, or goal directed strategy begins with a potential theorem, which is considered as a goal. The theorem prover begins by supposing that the potential theorem is *false* and deducing consequences from this until a situation has been obtained which can be recognised as impossible, or contradictory. Since in logic we assume that reality is not contradictory, and since the contradiction was obtained from the assumption that the potential theorem was false, it must be, in this case, that the potential theorem is true. This type of theorem generation is also called backwards chaining.

The advantage of a forward chaining system is that it manages to prove something, even if it is not what we wanted to prove. The advantage of a backwards chaining system is that when it succeeds it often produces short and natural looking proofs.

If F is a formal system of either type, and A is an expression in the associated formal language, we will write

$$\vdash_F A$$

to mean that there exists a proof of A in the formal system F.

$\vdash_F A$ means that, according to the formal system F, there is a data structure which passes the test for being a proof of A. If the theorem prover can somehow find this proof and give it to the proof checker, the proof checker will have to agree that it is a proof of A.

$\vdash_F A$ is a statement about the relationship between A and the rules defining the system F.

If F is a *good* formal reasoning system, there should be some notion of validity associated with it and there should be some clear relationship between

$\vdash_F A$

and the truth of A.

In the case of the statement forms, our notion of validity was $\models A$.

Advice to the reader: We have two notations which look alike:

$\models A$

and

$\vdash_F A$

It is quite important at this stage to distinguish between these. If A is a statement form we have defined $\models A$ to mean that A is a tautology. On the other hand, $\vdash_F A$ means that there is a proof of A in formal system F.

The central problem of the propositional calculus is recognition and proof of tautologies.

We will consider two different formal systems which attempt to solve this problem.

1) A bottom up Hilbert style system H. The proofs in this case are in the form of lists.

2) A top down, or goal directed system, called semantic tableaux, B. (B is for Beth, who invented semantic tableaux.) The proofs in this case are trees.

H is a system which, like all forward chaining systems, uses direct proof and B uses indirect proof. The next section briefly discusses these styles of proof.

5.2 Direct and indirect proof in mathematics

The *converse* of an implication $(A \rightarrow B)$ is the implication $(B \rightarrow A)$.

The *contrapositive* of an implication $(A \rightarrow B)$ is $((\neg B) \rightarrow (\neg A))$.

You should be able to show now that an implication is logically equivalent to its contrapositive but not necessarily to its converse.

There are several standard patterns to proofs of statements of the form $(A \rightarrow B)$ in mathematics. We can classify these proofs depending on which pattern they follow.

1) A *direct proof* of $(A \rightarrow B)$ has the following form. First assume that A is true. Then from this assumption draw one conclusion after another. Finally conclude that B is true. Therefore $(A \rightarrow B)$ must always be true.

2) A proof of the *contrapositive* of $(A \rightarrow B)$ has the following form. We first assume that B is false. We then draw one conclusion after another. Finally we come to the conclusion that A is false. We have a direct proof of $((\neg B) \rightarrow (\neg A))$. Therefore, we say $(A \rightarrow B)$. This uses the argument form

$$((\neg B) \rightarrow (\neg A))$$
$$\overline{}$$
$$(A \rightarrow B)$$

3) A *proof by contradiction* of $(A \rightarrow B)$ has the following form. We assume that A is true, and that B is false. We then draw one conclusion after another, until we arrive at some statement C which we know is false. *Contradiction*, we say. (We will write this as $\otimes$.) So it cannot happen that A is true and B is false. This means that

whenever A is true, B must also be true. Therefore $(A \rightarrow B)$. (A slightly different form of this was mentioned earlier in chapter 4.)

It is an interesting fact that it is often much easier to write down proofs using one of these patterns rather than the others. A proof of the contrapositive of $(A \rightarrow B)$ may be easier than a direct proof when $(\neg B)$ is in some sense simpler or easier to work with than A. Proof by contradiction is used very often in mathematics. The advantage of it is that the proof can use the information both that A is true, and that B is false. The argument form used is

$$((A \wedge (\neg B)) \rightarrow C), (\neg C)$$

$$\overline{\qquad\qquad\qquad\qquad\qquad}$$

$$(A \rightarrow B)$$

Example 5.1 *Let n be an integer. Let $odd(x)$ mean that integer x is odd. Suppose we want to prove*

$$odd(n) \rightarrow odd(n^2)$$

We can do this directly. Assume $odd(n)$. Then for some integer k, we have $n = 2k + 1$. Therefore $n^2 = (2k + 1)^2 = 2(2k^2 + 2k) + 1$. Thus $odd(n^2)$. We could also prove this by proving the contrapositive, or by contradiction, but in this case there is no advantage in doing so.

Example 5.2 *Suppose n and m are integers, and we want to prove*

$$odd(m * n) \rightarrow odd(m)$$

Suppose also that we have already established that all integers are either odd or even, and no integer can be both. A proof of the contrapositive would look as follows. Assume $(\neg odd(m))$. Then $even(m)$. Thus $m = 2k$, for some integer k. Thus $m * n = 2j$, for some integer j. Thus $even(m * n)$. Thus $(\neg odd(m * n))$. We have

$$(\neg odd(m) \rightarrow \neg odd(m * n))$$

and therefore $odd(m * n) \rightarrow odd(m)$.

This seems to be somewhat easier than a direct proof.

We could also write this as a proof by contradiction.

Assume $odd(m * n)$, $(\neg odd(m))$. As above we get $even(m)$ and then $even(m * n)$. But we know $odd(m * n)$ and $even(m * n)$ is impossible. $\bigotimes$. Therefore $(\neg odd(m) \rightarrow \neg odd(m * n))$.

It is often easier to see a contradiction in assuming A true and B false, rather than to see a direct proof of B from A.

So, in order to try to prove $(A \rightarrow B)$, a good technique is to try to imagine a world in which A is true but B is false. If you can show that in such a world impossible things must happen, then you have a proof.

Example 5.3 *For natural numbers X, define X is prime by*

$$(\forall Y)(\forall Z)(X = (Y * Z) \rightarrow (Y = 0' \vee Z = 0'))$$

Theorem *Every natural number is either a prime number or can be written as a product of prime numbers.*

Proof by contradiction. *Suppose the theorem were false. Let S be the set of natural numbers which are not prime and cannot be written as a product of prime factors. Since we suppose the theorem false, S is not empty. By the well ordering principle for*

N, *S has a minimal element, say d. The number d is not prime. So $d = e * f$ for some natural numbers e and f, neither of which are* 1. *So $e < d$ and $f < d$. Since d was minimal in S, both e and f can be written as a product of primes. Thus d also can be written as a product of primes.* $\bigotimes$.

Example 5.4 *Review the proof of the substitution theorem in the previous chapter.*

Do you think it is true that indirect proofs can always be changed into direct ones? If you say "yes", test your claim on the above example. If you say "no", how can you explain this?

An idea related to the above questions is the principle of the excluded middle. This says that a well defined proposition is either true or false. Proof by contradiction leans heavily on this principle. We say: since the proposition in question cannot be false, it must be true. The validity of indirect proof is derived from the assumption that there are only two truth values.

There exist mathematicians who do not accept the principle of the excluded middle, notably Brouwer. Brouwer rejected this principle in the middle of his distinguished career, repudiated his earlier theorems which used it, and founded a branch of mathematics, called Intuitionism, which only refers to constructible objects and only uses direct forms of proof. So, if you find you have reservations about proof by contradiction, you are in some good company.

5.3 A Hilbert style system, H

We will first briefly describe a reasoning system, H, based on direct proof.

H only deals with statement forms with operators $\rightarrow$ and $\neg$. This sublanguage will be called $sf(\rightarrow, \neg)$.

H has a set of axioms, written in $sf(\rightarrow, \neg)$, and a rule of inference. A proof in H is a finite list of statements of $sf(\rightarrow, \neg)$, so that each one is either an axiom of H, or follows by the rule of inference from earlier statements in the list. A proof is said to be a proof of its last statement. If we have a proof of X, we will say that X is a theorem of H and write $\vdash_H X$.

The rule of inference is called modus ponens. It says that from A and $(A \rightarrow B)$ we can deduce B. In other words,

$A, (A \rightarrow B)$

B

H has an infinite set of axioms, which occur in three forms. Let A, B, C be any statement forms in $sf(\rightarrow, \neg)$. Then the following are axioms of H.

a1) $(A \rightarrow (B \rightarrow A))$
a2) $((A \rightarrow (B \rightarrow C)) \rightarrow ((A \rightarrow B) \rightarrow (A \rightarrow C)))$
a3) $(((\neg A) \rightarrow (\neg B)) \rightarrow (B \rightarrow A))$

Note that the axioms of H are closed under substitution, i.e. if X is an axiom and α is a substitution then X_α is also an axiom. In fact, we could have defined the *axioms* as follows using substitution:

$(p \rightarrow (q \rightarrow p))$ is an axiom.

$((p \rightarrow (q \rightarrow r)) \rightarrow ((p \rightarrow q) \rightarrow (p \rightarrow r)))$ is an axiom

$(((\neg p) \rightarrow (\neg q)) \rightarrow (q \rightarrow p))$ is an axiom.

If X is an axiom and α is a substitution, then X_α is an axiom.

The theorems in this system are the smallest collection of statement forms which contain the axioms and are closed under application of the rule of inference, modus ponens. This means that if A is a theorem and $(A \rightarrow B)$ is a theorem, then B must also be a theorem in the system H.

To show that a statement form is a theorem, we are required to exhibit a proof. For example, $\vdash_H (p \rightarrow (p \rightarrow p))$. This theorem is also an axiom, of type a1). The one line sequence

$(p \rightarrow (p \rightarrow p))$

is also a proof. Similarly, every axiom in H is also a theorem, with a one line proof.

It is useful to number lines in a proof in H, and to annotate them with explanations.

Example 5.5 *An example of a proof in H.*

1) $(p \rightarrow (p \rightarrow p))$ *a1) axiom*

2) $((p \rightarrow (p \rightarrow p)) \rightarrow ((p \rightarrow p) \rightarrow (p \rightarrow p)))$ *a2) axiom*

3) $((p \rightarrow p) \rightarrow (p \rightarrow p))$ *MP from 1,2.*

So, $((p \rightarrow p) \rightarrow (p \rightarrow p))$ is a theorem of H.

■

Problem 5.1 *Modify the above formal proof, to show*

$\vdash_H ((p \rightarrow q) \rightarrow (p \rightarrow p))$

Evidently we can construct more theorems, just by writing down axioms and known theorems and observing patterns in which we can apply modus ponens. So if all we want is a large number of theorems, H is quite useful. The more usual situation, of course, is that we want to see if we can prove a particular statement. So we have in mind some statement B. If B is not an axiom, we have to find a statement A so that A and $(A \rightarrow B)$ are both theorems. There is no obvious way to do this. For this reason, H, although agreeable conceptually, is somewhat hard to use. It is like a vehicle with no steering.

Problem 5.2 * *Try to prove $(p \rightarrow p)$ in H. (It is possible.)*

H is acceptable as a source of puzzles. In this context its crablike, autonomous, oblique quality is an asset.

Problem 5.3 *** **Extremely hard.** *Try to prove*

$((\neg(\neg p)) \rightarrow p)$

in H.

5.4 Proof from assumptions in H

Let Γ be a set of statement forms. A list of statement forms

A_1

A_1

A_3

.

.

.

A_n

is a *proof in the Hilbert system H from assumptions* Γ if, for each $i \leq n$, either A_i is an axiom, or A_i is in Γ, or A_i is obtained from two previous statement forms in the list by modus ponens.

Such a proof is said to be a proof of the last statement form, A_n, in the list. We will write

$\Gamma \vdash_H A$

to mean that there is a proof of statement form A in H from assumptions Γ.

Of course $\Gamma \vdash_H A$ just tells us that there is some way of proving A from assumptions Γ and the axioms using modus ponens, but even if we know that a proof exists we may have a hard time finding a proof.

Example 5.6 *Let* $\Gamma = \{(q \rightarrow (p \rightarrow r)), p\}$. *Then* $\Gamma \vdash_H (p \rightarrow r)$. *Here is a proof.*

1) p , assumption

2) $(q \rightarrow (p \rightarrow r))$, assumption

3) $(p \rightarrow (q \rightarrow p))$, axiom

4) $(q \rightarrow p)$, MP 1,3

5) $((q \rightarrow (p \rightarrow r)) \rightarrow ((q \rightarrow p) \rightarrow (q \rightarrow r)))$, axiom

6) $((q \rightarrow p) \rightarrow (q \rightarrow r))$, MP 2,5

7) $(q \rightarrow r)$, MP 4,6

Problem 5.4 *With Γ as above, show that* $\Gamma \models (q \rightarrow r)$.

A great deal of work has been done on Hilbert style systems. (It is easier, and more enjoyable, to prove theorems about the system than it is to prove theorems within the system.) One of the most famous theorems about Hilbert style systems is the following.

Deduction theorem *Let Γ be any set of statement forms, and let A and B be any statement forms. Then*

$\Gamma \cup \{A\} \vdash_H B \Leftrightarrow \Gamma \vdash_H (A \rightarrow B)$

Proof *Try the problem below first*

■

Problem 5.5 *The theorem is an if and only if statement. One of the implications is much easier than the other. Decide which is the easy direction. Prove this half of the theorem.*

■

Now consider the implication in the other direction. Assume that from assumptions Γ and A we have a proof of B. Suppose this is

B_1
B_2
B_3
.
.
.
B_k

with $B_k = B$. Call this the old proof. We want to use this old proof to help us construct a proof of $(A \rightarrow B)$ from assumptions Γ. We will call the proof we are constructing the new proof. Begin by writing a skeleton for the new proof. Construct the skeleton by replacing each statement B_i in the old proof by $(A \rightarrow B_i)$.

$(A \rightarrow B_1)$
$(A \rightarrow B_2)$
$(A \rightarrow B_3)$
.
.
.
$(A \rightarrow B_k)$

This skeleton is almost certainly not a proof as it stands. But at least it has the right last line. The idea now is to fill in the gaps by adding lines between the lines of the skeleton in such a way as to make this a proof. The way we fill in the gap above a line $(A \rightarrow B_i)$ depends on how the line B_i was justified in the old proof.

There are four possibilities.

- B_i is an axiom. In this case we fill the gap with

  B_i, axiom
  $(B_i \rightarrow (A \rightarrow B_i))$, axiom
  $(A \rightarrow B_i)$, MP
- B_i is in Γ. Do this yourself.
- B_i is A. Fill in with a proof of $(A \rightarrow A)$.
- B_i was obtained in the old proof by modus ponens from two earlier lines B_j and $(B_j \rightarrow B_i)$. In the new proof there are two earlier lines

  $(A \rightarrow B_j)$

  and

$(A \rightarrow (B_j \rightarrow B_i))$.

We need to use these two lines to get a proof of

$(A \rightarrow B_i)$.

Exercise: Figure out how to do this, using one of the axioms.

$\square$

Problem 5.6 * *We said earlier that in a formal reasoning system, the notion of proof is so precisely defined that a proof checker, given a thing which purports to be a proof, can decide whether or not it is. In the case of the Hilbert style system H, suppose you are given a list of statement forms $(X_1, X_2, ..., X_n)$, without further explanation. Give an algorithm to decide whether or not this is a proof in H.*

5.5 Semantic tableau system

This is an indirect method of trying to prove a statement form X. We attempt to construct a counterexample to X. The general idea is to suppose X false, and deduce consequences from this supposition. If we eventually arrive at a contradictory situation, we know that X could not be false. So we have proved X.

We may have to deduce a large number of consequences of the falsity of X, and keep track of branching alternatives, before we decide falsity of X is impossible. To keep account of what we are doing, we will put the statements in a table, called a semantic tableau, with a true column and a false column.

We first give some examples and an informal description of the method.

5.5.1 Example 1

Consider $(A \rightarrow (B \rightarrow A))$. We want to decide whether or not this is a tautology. We say: what would happen if it were false? We make a semantic tableau, and put the statement to be tested at the top of the false column.

TRUE	FALSE
	1) $(A \rightarrow (B \rightarrow A))$

We think to ourselves: statement 1) has the form $(X \rightarrow Y)$. If this is false, it must happen that X is true and Y is false. So add these two statements, with a reference back to statement 1) as an explanation.

TRUE	FALSE
	1) $(A \rightarrow (B \rightarrow A)$
2) A, from 1)	3) $(B \rightarrow A)$, from 1)

Continuing with this, we see that statement 3) can be given the same treatment.

TRUE	FALSE
	1) $(A \to (B \to A))$
2) A, from 1)	3) $(B \to A)$ from 1)
4) B, from 3)	5) A, from 3), $\otimes$ 2

Statements 2) and 5) are now contradictory. This is indicated by $\otimes$. Therefore no counterexample to the original statement is possible. So the original statement form was a tautology. The tableau is a *proof* of the statement form in the semantic tableau system. We write this

$$\vdash (A \to (B \to A))$$

Sometimes it is necessary to split a semantic tableau into branches, in order to account for the fact that there are several alternative ways in which a situation can occur.

5.5.2 Example 2

Consider $(((p \to q) \land (\neg q)) \to (\neg p))$

TRUE	FALSE
	1) $(((p \to q) \land (\neg q)) \to (\neg p))$
2) $((p \to q) \land (\neg q))$, from 1)	3) $(\neg p)$, from 1)
4) p, from 3)	
5) $(\neg q)$, from 2)	
6) $(p \to q)$, from 2)	7) q, from 5)

Our problem now is that we have an implication $(p \to q)$ in the true column. There are two ways that such an implication can be true. Either p can be false, or q can be true. We split the tableau therefore into two branches, labelling them in some manner, say α and β. Both branches have true and false columns. All the statements up to 7) belong to both branches. The splitting gives:

TRUE	TRUE	FALSE	FALSE
α	β	α	β
		8) p, from 6) $\otimes$ 4)	
	8) q, from 6), $\otimes$ 7)		

There were two branches α and β and both ended in contradictions. So there is no possible counterexample.

$$\vdash (((p \to q) \land (\neg q)) \to (\neg p))$$

Definition 5.1 *We will say that a branch of a semantic tableau is* closed *if the same statement form appears on both the true and the false side of the branch. A branch is* open *if it is not closed. A tableau is said to be* closed *if every branch is closed.*

So far we have the following idea: to test whether or not a statement form X is a tautology, put X in the false column of an initial semantic tableau. Then apply the process described above, to try to construct a counterexample to X. If we eventually get a closed tableau, this constitutes a proof that X is a tautology. This is explained in more detail below.

5.5.3 *Example 3*

Suppose we want to test $((p \rightarrow q) \rightarrow (q \rightarrow (\neg p)))$.

TRUE	FALSE
	1) $((p \rightarrow q) \rightarrow (q \rightarrow (\neg p)))$
2) $(p \rightarrow q)$, from 1)	3) $(q \rightarrow (\neg p))$, from 1)
4) q, from 3)	5) $(\neg p)$, from 3)
6) p , from 5)	

At this point the only statement we have not considered is 2). We split the tableau into two subtableaux.

TRUE i)	TRUE ii)	FALSE i)	FALSE ii)
	7) q, from 2)	7) p, from 2), $\otimes$ 6	

There are two branches in this tableau, i) and ii), caused by the splitting of statement 2). Branch i) is closed. But branch ii) remains open. Also the procedure has terminated at this point. Every statement is either a proposition name or has been considered. All the statements from 1) to 6) are on both branches.

Branch ii) says q and p are both true. This defines an interpretation which makes the original statement form false, i.e. a counterexample.

In general the claim is that *the semantic tableau method always terminates after finitely many steps, and either produces a proof or a counterexample.*

We have seen that as the semantic tableau construction proceeds, the tableau may branch. Some statements may then be on more than one branch. It is usually a good idea to do non-branching operations before branching ones, so that the branchings occur as low as possible.

Statements are numbered consecutively on each branch. We can see whether or not a statement, with number n, has yet been considered on a given branch α. To do this, travel down the branch α and observe whether or not there is a reference back to n. Statements only have to be considered once on each branch.

■

Problem 5.7 *Prove $((\neg(\neg p)) \rightarrow p)$ using semantic tableaux.*

5.6 Representing semantic tableaux by trees

Consider the tableau shown in example 3 above. The tableau has two branches, which are called i) and ii). Each branch has a true side and a false side. The first six statements in the tableau are on both branches i) and ii). We would say, for example, that $(q \to (\neg p))$ is on the false side of branch i) and also on the false side of branch ii). But q appears on the true side of branch ii) as statement 7). Branch i) of this tableau is closed, but branch ii) is open. If we travel up branch ii) from the frontier, we get a list of statements which are asserted, on the true side, and another list which are denied, on the false side.

Our tableaux have a tree-like structure, and therefore it seems a good idea to represent them explicitly as trees. Example 3), written as a tree, would give figure 5.2.

Most people find the tree notation superior to the table notation.

From now on we will use trees. In these trees the nodes are labelled with assertions or denials of statement forms, corresponding to the true and false columns of a semantic tableau. The nodes will be labelled with consecutive natural numbers on each branch. We will put the statement form to the left of a node if it is meant to be in the true side, and on the right if it is meant to be on the false side. We can also put the justifications, i.e. the reference back to an earlier statement form at each node.

5.6.1 Example 4

Suppose we believe that the following is a tautology.

$$(((p \to q) \land (q \to r)) \to ((p \lor s) \to (r \lor s)))$$

We can give a proof of it in tree form as in figure 5.3.

It seems to me that the tree is a good picture of why the original statement is a tautology. In order to understand these trees, of course, it is essential to remember the convention that statements written to the left of a node are asserted, and statements written to the right of a node are denied. The left hand side of a branch is the true column and the right hand side is the false column.

5.6.2 Example 5

Suppose we want to test

$$(((p \to q) \land ((\neg p) \to q)) \to q)$$

Try to do this example, representing the tableau by a tree. You should get three branches, all of which eventually become closed.

At this point let us assume that we know how to operate the tree form of the semantic tableau algorithm.

We are systematically looking for a counterexample to a statement form X. We put X on the false side of the initial node. We then repeatedly apply the semantic

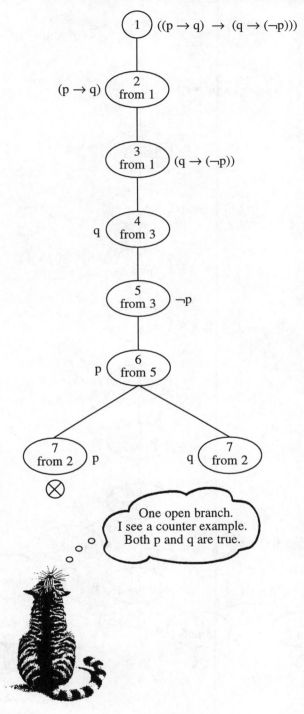

Figure 5.2 Test of $((p \to q) \to (q \to (\neg p)))$

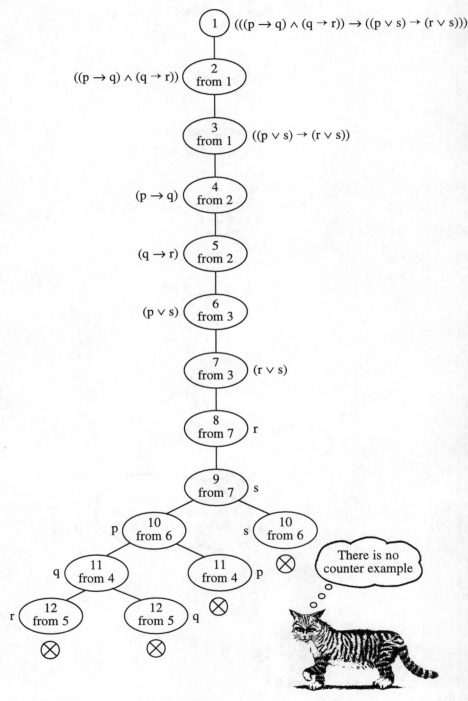

Figure 5.3   Proof of $(((p \rightarrow q) \wedge (q \rightarrow r)) \rightarrow ((p \vee s) \rightarrow (r \vee s)))$

tableau process, which appears to unfold the meaning of the falsity of X, and which gives us a tree of labelled nodes. The nodes are labelled with several different kinds of data. Each node has a number and these numbers are consecutive on each branch. Each node, other than the root, also has a reference back to an earlier node, which explains its origin. So far this is just a fairly arbitrary bookkeeping system. However, each node also has either an assertion or a denial of a statement form as part of its data. If we think of the data at a node as a record, it has four fields: a number, a reference number, a true field, a false field. Conventionally, we write the true field to the left of the node and the false field to the right of the node. (Evidently, if we wanted to deal with more than two truth values, the nodes would just have more fields; however the conventional picture would have to be altered.)

We may perfectly well know how to do the semantic tableau process. However the problem of saying in a clear way how we do what we do is still in front of us.

We know where to start. Our semantic tableaux are trees of a certain kind. We have a clear definition of a branch of a semantic tableau, and a clear definition of a closed branch and of an open branch. Also, a semantic tableau is closed if all of its branches are closed.

Here is one more necessary piece of our explanation:

Definition 5.2 *We will say that a statement is* alive *on branch α if the statement number is n, and if there is no reference back to n anywhere on α.*

So the alive part of a branch is the part that has not yet been done. A *proposition name* by itself on a branch is always alive, since there is nothing which can be done to it, i.e. it cannot be broken down any farther.

We need also to be clear about the operations of adding a statement form to either the true side or the false side of a branch α of a semantic tableau.

Suppose α is a branch of a semantic tableau and we are considering a statement S on α which has statement number n. Suppose as a result of this, we wish to add a new statement Y to either the true side or the false side of α. We will assume that this is always done in the following way. Go down to the frontier of α. Suppose the node at the frontier has number k. Extend α by one new node, with number $k + 1$. Put Y in one of the truth value fields of the new node. Inside the new node write a reference back to S -- from n -- which explains the origin of Y and also shows that S is no longer alive on this branch. Similarly, if we wish to split α into two branches, we would extend α by two new nodes, both children of the original frontier node, both numbered $k + 1$, and both with a reference back to S.

5.7 Semantic tableau algorithm

Input: statement form X.

1) Create an initial tableau with one node with X on the false side.

2) Apply the semantic tableau process, described in the subsection below, repeatedly until it terminates.

3) Examine the terminal tableau to see if it has any open branches. If all branches are closed in the terminal tableau, we will call this terminal tableau a proof of X.

In this case we will write $\vdash X$, and say that X is a theorem of the semantic tableau system.

On the other hand, suppose the terminal tableau has at least one open branch. It is claimed that any one of the open branches defines a counterexample to X. If α is an open branch, let σ be an interpretation such that, for each *proposition name* P,

$\sigma(P) = \text{T}$ if P is on the true side of α

$\sigma(P) = \text{F}$ if P is on the false side of α

It is claimed that $X(\sigma) = F$, i.e. σ is a counterexample to X.

(Note: The claims which are made here for the results of the semantic tableau algorithm will later be proved.)

5.7.1 Semantic tableau process

In this subsection, we will define the semantic tableau process, which is one step of the central loop in the semantic tableau algorithm.

The semantic tableau process has

Input: A semantic tableau T_x

Output: A new semantic tableau $T_{x'}$, or termination.

The semantic tableau process is non-deterministic. This means that many different output tableaux may correctly result from a given input tableau.

The given semantic tableau T_x may have several branches. Each branch has a true and a false side, containing statement forms.

The action of the process depends essentially on the definition of aliveness which was given earlier.

The alive part of a branch is the part which has not yet been considered on that branch.

Note that aliveness is a property of a statement form on a branch, not just of a statement form in isolation. A particular statement form may be on several branches, and it may be alive on some of them and non-alive on others.

Suppose now that input T_x is given.

(The non-determinacy occurs here.) Pick an open branch α of T_x, and a statement form S on α so that S is alive on α, and S is not a proposition name.

If no such α and S exists the process terminates.

Otherwise, there are several cases, depending on the form of S, and on which side of α it was found.

- If S is $(\neg Y)$ on the true side of α, add Y to the false side of α.
- Similarly, if S is $(\neg Y)$ in the false side of α, add Y to the true side of α.
- If S is $(Y \rightarrow Z)$ on the false side of branch α, put Y on the true side and Z on the false side of α.
- If S is $(Y \rightarrow Z)$ on the true side of a branch α, split the branch α into two subbranches. Put Y in the false side of one of the subbranches and Z on the true side of the other subbranch.

  (The tableau splits because there are two distinct ways in which the implication can be true.)

- If S is $(Y \wedge Z)$ on the true side of a branch α, add both Y and Z to the true side of α.
- If S is $(Y \wedge Z)$ on the false side of a branch α, split the tableau into two branches and put Y on the false side of one branch and Z on the false side of the other.
- (There are also rules for $\vee$ and $\leftrightarrow$. It is best to try out the above rules until you understand them well enough so that you can specify the other rules yourself.)

5.7.2 A summary of the semantic tableau rules in tree form

We are considering five propositional operators, and each one can occur either on the true side or on the false side of a branch of a tableau. The semantic tableau process can be summarised by the ten rules shown in figure 5.4.

Advice: try these problems now.

■

Problem 5.8 *Let A, B, and C be any statement forms. Use semantic tableaux to give formal proofs of:*

a) $(A \rightarrow (B \rightarrow A))$
b) $((A \rightarrow (B \rightarrow C)) \rightarrow ((A \rightarrow B) \rightarrow (A \rightarrow C)))$
c) $((A \rightarrow B) \rightarrow ((\neg B) \rightarrow (\neg A)))$
d) $(((A \rightarrow B) \rightarrow A) \rightarrow A)$

I hope you will agree that although the indirectness of the semantic tableaux system is annoying (and puzzling) it is *much* easier to use than the Hilbert system. Another point is that a semantic tableau proof seems to explain why the thing proved is true, but this is not the case for the Hilbert system. My opinion is that although we may think that we think in Hilbert style, the way we actually think is more like semantic tableaux. We will use semantic tableaux from now on.

Problem 5.9 *State the semantic tableau rules for $\vee$ and $\leftrightarrow$.*

Problem 5.10 *Give a semantic tableau tree in which some occurrence of a statement form is on two branches and is alive on one branch and not alive on another.*

■

It is important to realise that the semantic tableau algorithm only terminates when each statement form has been considered once *on each branch*. Suppose, for example, that there are two disjunctions $(A_1 \vee A_2 \vee ... \vee A_n)$ and $(B_1 \vee B_2 \vee ... \vee B_m)$ at the top of a semantic tableau on the true side. We may decide to work on the first of these, and so, after a while we will get a tree with n branches, the ith branch having statement form A_i on the true side. The other disjunction $(B_1 \vee ... \vee B_m)$ is on the true side of every one of these branches. Suppose we look first at the left most branch, with A_1 on the true side. We may then split $(B_1 \vee ... \vee B_m)$ into m subbranches. The original disjunction $(B_1 \vee ... \vee B_m)$ is no longer alive on these subbranches. However it is still alive on the $n - 1$ branches ending with $A_2, ..., A_n$

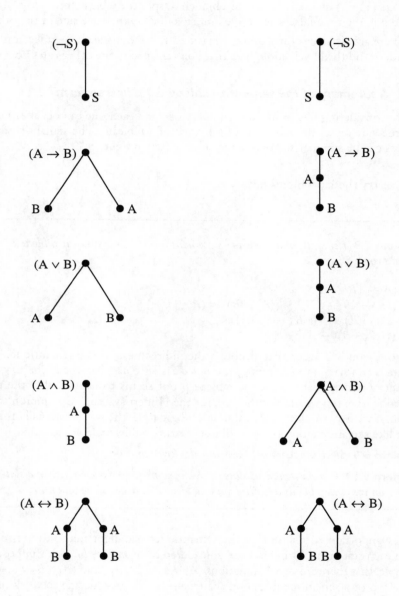

Figure 5.4 Propositional semantic tableau rules

on the true side. So the two disjunctions together will eventually split into $n * m$ branches. Clearly, the large number of branches can cause severe difficulties with the use of the semantic tableau algorithm.

5.8 Deeper waters: correctness

We now have a pair of ideas: a semantic idea

$$\models A$$

about the truth of A; and a syntactic idea

$$\vdash A$$

about the provability of A in the semantic tableau system.

We want to see the connection between these distinct ideas. We take $\models A$ as a given reality, and hope that $\vdash A$ will turn out to be closely related to it.

The semantic tableau algorithm has the following classic form

1) Initialise. (Form initial tableau)
2) Loop: Iterate some process until termination occurs. (In this case it is the semantic tableau process.)
3) Draw conclusions from terminal state. (In this case, we either get a proof or a counterexample from the terminal state.).

We are faced with the following problems. Does the process really terminate in all cases? How can we prove this? Is the algorithm correct? That is, does it do everything that it ought to do, and not do anything which it ought not to do? How can this be stated more clearly? How can it be proved?

It should be emphasized that these problems occur in just this form every time an algorithm is stated in mathematics, or a computer program is written. Also, there is a well known tendency for people who have written algorithms or programs, especially groups of people with financial or personal interests, to believe that they are correct. So the above technical looking questions are of practical importance.

The basic strategy for proving correctness is the following. We define some property which is true of the initial state, and which will imply correctness if it is true of the terminal state. We then try to show that the property is preserved by each iteration of the loop. The property means that "things are OK so far". Such a property is called a *loop invariant*. It is not a straightforward task to define such a loop invariant

Often, in fact, proving correctness of algorithms is difficult. Finding an appropriate loop invariant property often takes a real leap of the imagination, and stating it clearly requires care and technical skill. Once this is done, however, it usually happens that the proof that the property is preserved over the loops tends to be straightforward, although long.

In our case, after some experience using the semantic tableau algorithm, we feel that each step of the process neither adds nor subtracts from the information present. Our difficulty is to state this property sufficiently clearly so that we can prove something about it.

5.9 Soundness and completeness theorems

We previously defined Γ to be *satisfiable* if there is an interpretation σ so that for all statement forms A in Γ, $sat(A, \sigma) = T$. The next definition extends this idea to semantic tableaux.

Definition 5.3 *A semantic tableau, T_x, is satisfied by interpretation σ if there is a branch α of T_x so that, for all statement forms A, if A is on the true side of α then $sat(A, \sigma) = T$; and if A is on the false side of α, then $sat(A, \sigma) = F$.*

We will say that a semantic tableau, T_x, is satisfiable, if there is an interpretation σ which satisfies it.

A branch of a semantic tableau contains a list of statement forms which are asserted to be true, and another list which is asserted to be false. The previous definition says, in effect, that an interpretation satisfies the tableau if it agrees with the assertions and denials on one of the branches. The branches are alternative possibilities for satisfaction of the tableau.

Definition 5.4 *If σ is an interpretation, σ satisfies live(T) will mean that there is a branch α of T so that for all statement forms A on α which are alive on α, if A is on the true side of α then $sat(A, \sigma) = T$, and if A is on the false side of α then $sat(A, \sigma) = F$.*

Exercise: show that if σ satisfies a tableau T, then σ satisfies *live*(T). Show that if $T_{x'}$ is an extension of T_x and σ satisfies $T_{x'}$ then σ satisfies T_x.

Here is our loop invariance lemma.

Lemma *Let T_x be a semantic tableau. Suppose semantic tableau $T_{x'}$ is obtained from T_x by one step of the semantic tableau process. Let σ be any interpretation. Then*

a) *σ satisfies T_x iff σ satisfies $T_{x'}$*
b) *σ satisfies live(T_x) iff σ satisfies live$(T_{x'})$.*

Proof $T_{x'}$ is obtained from T_x as follows.

Pick statement form S, not a proposition name, on an open branch α of T_x, and apply the semantic tableau rules to get $T_{x'}$.

There are several cases now, depending on the form of S, and where it was found on α.

Case 1. S has the form $(\neg A)$ and it was found on the true side of α. According to the definition of the process, $T_{x'}$ is formed by adding A to the false side of α. Look at the two parts of the lemma. Note that only the α branch of T_x has been altered.

a) Suppose σ satisfies T_x. Then, according to the definition, σ satisfies some open branch of T_x. If this branch is not α, then σ also satisfies $T_{x'}$, since branches other than α are the same in T_x and $T_{x'}$. So suppose σ satisfies branch α in T_x. This must mean that $sat(S, \sigma) = T$. So, by the truth table definition of $(\neg A)$, it must happen that $sat(A, \sigma) = F$. But $T_{x'}$ is obtained just by adding A to the false side of α. So σ satisfies $T_{x'}$.

$T_{x'}$ includes T_x, so the implication in the other direction we get almost for free. If σ satisfies $T_{x'}$ then σ satisfies T_x.

b) Suppose σ satisfies *live*(T_x). As before, we may as well assume that α is the branch satisfied. What change has been made to the live part of branch α? $T_{x'}$ is obtained by removing S from the live part of α, and adding A to the false side of α. Suppose the live part of T_x has $\{A_1, ..., A_n, (\neg A)\}$ on the true side and $\{D_1, ..., D_m\}$ on the false side. Then the live part of $T_{x'}$ has $\{A_1, ..., A_n\}$ on the true side and $\{D_1, ..., D_m, A\}$ in the false side. So,

σ satisfies the live part of α in T_x

$\Leftrightarrow$

σ makes $\{A_1, ..., A_n, (\neg A)\}$ true and $\{D_1, ..., D_m\}$ false

$\Leftrightarrow$

σ makes $\{A_1, ..., A_n, \}$ true and $\{D_1, ..., D_m, A\}$ false

$\Leftrightarrow$

σ satisfies the live part of $T_{x'}$.

Case 2. S has the form $(\neg A)$ and it was found on the false side of open branch α on T_x. Do this yourself. That is, write out the argument in detail.

Case 3. S has the form $(A \to B)$ and it was found on the false side of open branch α in T_x. $T_{x'}$ is obtained by removing S from the live part of α, adding A to the true side and B to the false side of α.

Do parts a) and b) as above.

Case 4. S has the form $(A \to B)$ and it was found on the true side of open branch α in T_x. In this case we get a split of α. $T_{x'}$ is obtained by removing S from the live part of α, and then splitting α into α_1 and α_2, and adding A to the false side of α_1 and adding B to the true side of α_2.

a) Suppose σ satisfies α in T_x. We must then have $sat(S, \sigma) = $ T. According to the truth table definition, it follows that either $sat(A, \sigma) = $ F or $sat(B, \sigma) = $ T. Thus σ must either satisfy α_1 or α_2. On the other hand, if σ satisfies either α_1 or α_2 in $T_{x'}$, it must satisfy α in T_x. Thus σ satisfies T_x if and only if σ satisfies $T_{x'}$.

b) Do this yourself.

All the other cases are the same. To test yourself, pick one at random and try to do it.

$\square$

What we have done in the above lemma is to check over the semantic tableau process to make sure that it "works properly" at each step.

Problem 5.11 *Assume the notation used in the lemma above. Suppose $T_{x'}$ was obtained from T_x by picking a statement form $(A \wedge B)$ on the false side of an open branch α of T_x, and splitting α into two subbranches. Show directly that an interpretation σ satisfies the live part of T_x if and only if it satisfies the live part of $T_{x'}$.*

Definition 5.5 *An initial tableau is one in which every statement is alive on every branch.*

Theorem *Let T_{x_0} be an initial tableau. Suppose T_{x_n} is obtained from T_{x_0} by n steps of the semantic tableau process. Then if σ is any interpretation*

σ satisfies T_{x_0} iff σ satisfies T_{x_n} iff σ satisfies live(T_{x_n}).

Proof The claim is that this theorem follows from the previous lemma. We can prove this in two ways: either directly using the induction principle for the natural numbers; or indirectly using proof by contradiction and the well ordering principle for **N**.

Here is the direct proof. We use induction on n. We need to show that the theorem is true when $n = 0$, and that if the theorem holds for a natural number k, it also holds for $k + 1$.

Basis. Suppose $n = 0$. So $T_{x_0} = T_{x_n}$, and clearly any interpretation σ satisfies T_{x_0} if and only if σ satisfies T_{x_n}. Also since T_{x_0} is an initial tableau, every statement is alive on it and thus $live(T_{x_0}) = T_{x_0}$. So σ satisfies T_{x_n} if and only if σ satisfies $live(T_{x_n})$.

Induction step. Suppose the theorem is true for $n = k$. Starting with T_{x_0}, do $k + 1$ steps of the semantic tableau process to get

$$T_{x_0}, T_{x_1}, ..., T_{x_k}, T_{x_{k+1}}$$

Since we suppose that the theorem is true for $n = k$, we have that σ satisfies T_{x_0} if and only if σ satisfies T_{x_k}, and σ satisfies T_{x_k} if and only if σ satisfies $live(T_{x_k})$. At this point we apply the lemma. This tells us that σ satisfies T_{x_k} if and only if σ satisfies $T_{x_{k+1}}$, and σ satisfies $live(T_{x_k})$ if and only if σ satisfies $live(T_{x_{k+1}})$. Thus σ satisfies T_{x_0} if and only if σ satisfies $T_{x_{k+1}}$ if and only if σ satisfies $live(T_{x_{k+1}})$.

□

An indirect proof of the above theorem would begin by assuming that the theorem was false. The well ordering principle for **N** can then be used to imply that there is a smallest number, n, which gives a counterexample to the theorem. We can argue that n cannot be 0, as above. It follows that $n - 1$ is a natural number, and since n was the smallest counterexample, the theorem must be true for $n - 1$. We now apply the lemma to get a contradiction.

Propositional soundness theorem *If A is a statement form and $\vdash A$, then A is a tautology.*

Proof Form T_{x_0}, an initial tableau with A at the top of the false side. We suppose $\vdash A$. So after some number, k, of semantic tableau process steps, we get a terminal tableau T_{x_k}, which is contradictory. Every branch of T_{x_k} has a contradiction on it. So no interpretation, σ can satisfy T_{x_k}. By the previous theorem, no interpretation can satisfy T_{x_0}. But T_{x_0} only had one statement form in it, A in the false side. So there is no interpretation, σ, so that $sat(A, \sigma) = F$. Thus $sat(A, \sigma) = T$ for all interpretations σ. This means that A is a tautology.

Completeness theorem for propositional calculus *If statement form A is a tautology, then $\vdash A$.*

Proof We prove the contrapositive. So we assume that A is not a theorem in the semantic tableau system, and try to demonstrate that A is not a tautology. As before, form initial tableau T_{x_0} by putting A on the false side. Run the algorithm until we get a terminal tableau T_{x_k}. If we suppose this does not give us a proof of A, there must be an open branch α of T_{x_k}. Since T_{x_k} is terminal, $live(\alpha)$ has only proposition names on it, and since α is open, the same proposition name does not occur on both the true and the false side of α. Define interpretation σ_α to satisfy the live part of α. That is, if a proposition name P occurs on the true side of α we let $\sigma_\alpha(P) = T$; if P occurs on the false side of α we let $\sigma_\alpha(P) = F$. How σ_α is defined for proposition names which do not occur on $live(\alpha)$ does not matter. Clearly $live(\alpha)$ can be satisfied. Thus $live(T_{x_k})$ can be satisfied. By the theorem above, $live(T_{x_0})$ can be satisfied. In fact T_{x_0} is satisfied by σ_α. But T_{x_0} had A on its false side. So $sat(A, \sigma_\alpha) = F$. We have found a counterexample to A. So A is not a tautology. Thus if A is a tautology it must be a theorem in the semantic tableau system.

5.9.1 Remarks

What is wrong with the above proof? *We have not yet shown that the algorithm always terminates.* Do you believe that it always does terminate? If so, why? If not, can you find an example in which it does not terminate? One way to make progress with such a question is to apply the same general method of analysis which is used above on statement forms. We imagine a situation in which termination never occurs, and see if it leads to a contradiction.

Suppose, then, that T_{x_0} is an initial tableau with statement forms $A_1, ..., A_n$ on the true side, and statement forms $B_1, ..., B_m$ on the false side. Each step of the semantic tableau process kills off a statement form on a branch, and adds one or two others, and possibly splits the branch into two. Is it possible that no matter how many steps are done the process does not terminate? How much faith do you place in your intuition in this area? If you really know what is going to happen shouldn't you be able to prove it?

So far, we have T_{x_0}, described above. We keep applying the semantic tableau process; if the process does not terminate, we get an *infinite* sequence:

$$T_{x_0}, T_{x_1}, T_{x_2}, T_{x_3}, T_{x_4},...$$

Can you draw any conclusions about the tableau T_{x_n} as $n \to \infty$? Can you define a limiting tableau, $T*$? We will return to these issues later.

5.10 Proof from assumptions, and consistency

Suppose Γ is a set of assumptions and X is a statement form , and we wish to know whether or not X is a logical consequence of Γ. To decide this, we run the semantic tableau algorithm on an initial tableau with Γ on the true side and X on the false side. The algorithm attempts to find a counterexample, i.e. an interpretation which makes Γ true and X false. If it terminates with an open branch, that branch defines a counterexample. Otherwise, if it terminates with all branches closed, we know that there is no counterexample and $\Gamma \models X$.

Problem 5.12 *Assume*

"Louise is lying. If kangaroos are numerous and Louise is lying, then Harriet is lying. If kangaroos are numerous and the dog got out last night and Harriet is lying, then I win my bet. If the dog got out last night then kangaroos are numerous. If Louise is lying then the dog got out last night."

Decide whether or not it is a logical consequence of this that I win my bet.

∎

Let Γ be a set of statement forms, and let A be a statement form.

Definition 5.6 $\Gamma \vdash A$ *means that there is a finite subset, Δ of Γ, so that a semantic tableau started with Δ on the true side and A on the false side ends in contradiction, i.e. with all branches closed.*

Definition 5.7 Γ *is* consistent *if Γ has no finite subset Δ so that a semantic tableau started with Δ on the true side, and nothing on the false side, ends in contradiction.*

∎

5.11 Problems

Advice: learn how to use semantic tableaux if you have not yet done so.

Problem 5.13 *Find a counterexample to the following, or give a proof. In each case, complete the semantic tableau construction, and state how many branches there are in the completed tree. How many are closed? Verify that each branch which is not closed defines a counterexample.*

a) $(((p \to q) \to p) \to q)$
b) $((q \to p) \to (q \to (\neg q)))$
c) $((p \to q) \to ((\neg p) \to (\neg q)))$
d) $((p \to q) \to ((\neg q) \to (\neg p)))$

Problem 5.14 *If we know that either A is true or B is true and we know that either B is false or C is true, and we know that A and C can't both be true, then it must happen that A is true. Either give a formal proof of this, or a counterexample.*

Problem 5.15 *Show whether or not the following set of statements is consistent.*
A and B and C implies that D is false unless E is true. E and not B implies C. A and B are equivalent. C is true.

Problem 5.16 *Prove this or construct a counterexample:*
A and (B or C or D) is logically equivalent to (A and B) or (A and C) or (A and D).

Problem 5.17 * *Show that if $\vdash A$ and $\vdash (A \to B)$, then $\vdash B$ in the semantic tableaux system.*

Problem 5.18 * *Suppose that Γ is a consistent set of statements forms. Let A be any statement form. Show that either $\Gamma \cup \{A\}$ is consistent, or $\Gamma \cup \{(\neg A)\}$ is consistent.*

Problem 5.19 * *Is it possible to have Γ_1 consistent and Γ_2 consistent, but $\Gamma_1 \cup \Gamma_2$ inconsistent?*

Problem 5.20 * *Show that if $\Gamma \cup \{A\}$ is inconsistent, then Γ logically implies $(\neg A)$.*

Problem 5.21 * *Suppose Γ_i is an increasing sequence of finite consistent sets of statement forms, i.e. $\Gamma_i \subseteq \Gamma_{i=1}$ for all i. Show that the union of this sequence is a consistent set of statement forms.*

Problem 5.22 * *Prove the soundness theorem for H. That is, show that $\vdash_H A$ implies that A is a tautology. Hint: First show that the axioms are tautologies, and then use induction on the length of the proof.*

Problem 5.23 * *Let T be a completed tableau and let α be an open branch. Explain how the statement that the alive part of α can be satisfied can be expressed as a conjunction of proposition names and negations of proposition names.*

Problem 5.24 * *An alternative method of finding disjunctive normal form. Given statement form X, put X on the True side of an initial tableau and run the semantic tableau algorithm until termination. Show how $DNF(X)$ can be read off the completed tableau.*

Problem 5.25 * *Define $(A \mid B)$ as $(\neg(A \wedge B))$. Give rules for a semantic tableau system using only this logical operator. Prove the soundness and completeness theorems for the system you have just invented.*

Problem 5.26 ** *The Martians also use the semantic tableau system, but they use different symbols for the logical operators and instead of left and right they write in red and brown to distinguish true and false, but we do not know which colour has which meaning. Is it possible by observing the Martians to decide which symbols are used for which logical operator? (Note: The Martians also use semantic tableaux to test consistency. So you can't determine which colour is false just by observing the colour of the first statement a Martian writes.)*

5.12 Eventual termination, no matter what

Define the *complexity* of a statement form to be the number of logical operators in it. Thus, the complexity of a *proposition name* is 0. $complexity(A \rightarrow B) = complexity(A) + complexity(B) + 1$, etc.

Define the complexity of a branch α in a semantic tableau to be the sum of the complexities of the live statements on the branch.

If one step of the semantic tableau process operates on a branch α to produce another branch α_1, then the complexity of α_1 is strictly less than the complexity of α (since the rules always get rid of at least one logical operator).

This means that every branch of a semantic tableau produced by iteration of the semantic tableau process has length bounded by the complexity of the initial tableau.

So if we have an initial tableau, we can give in advance an upper bound on the length of path which can be produced by the semantic tableau algorithm, no matter how the steps are applied.

■

Problem 5.27 * *Use this fact to show that the semantic algorithm always terminates, given any finite initial tableau. Hint: if the algorithm does not terminate, it must produce an infinite tree. Now consider König's lemma.*

■

5.13 The best way to find CNF

We can now reveal the best way to find CNF. Given statement form X, put it on the false side of an initial semantic tableau. Run the semantic tableau process until termination. Let $\alpha_1, ..., \alpha_n$ be the open branches. These branches show the various ways in which X can be false. So X is true if and only if

α_1 does not happen and ... α_n does not happen.

We can express

α_i does not happen

as a disjunction of literals, and thus we get CNF. (See figure 5.5.)

Problem 5.28 *Explain how to find clausal form, using semantic tableaux.*

5.14 How to finish quickly

The semantic tableau algorithm is highly non-deterministic. At any stage there may be a large number of possible operations on each branch and there may be a large number of open branches. We have said that it does not matter in which order the operations are done. This is true in the sense that the process always eventually terminates, no matter what we do, and the final result, i.e. whether or not the terminal tree is closed, does not depend on what choices are made. On the other hand, some choices will result in termination faster than others. Can we say anything about efficient use of the semantic tableau algorithm? How do we choose what to do?

In general this problem is rather hard. The difficulties here are related to the satisfiability problem.

A statement form, S, is satisfiable if and only if there exists an interpretation v so that $sat(S, v) = \text{T}$.

The famous, or notorious, satisfiability problem is to decide, given a statement form S, whether or not it is satisfiable.

You can probably see a way to solve this problem.

One approach would be the following. Put the statement form, S, to be tested on the true side of an initial semantic tableau and run the process to termination. Then S is satisfiable if and only if there is an open branch in the terminal situation. Any open branch in the terminal tree defines an interpretation which satisfies S.

Thus a good solution to the problem of how to run the semantic tableau algorithm would immediately give us a good solution to the satisfiability problem. This would also immediately solve an intimidating array of other problems in discrete mathematics. (See the discussion in Hopcroft and Ullman [1979].) However we should not be discouraged. Even if we cannot currently see a good solution to the whole problem in front of us, we can at least make some progress with it, and make some useful remarks.

We can say that a large number of branches seems undesirable. So, it seems,

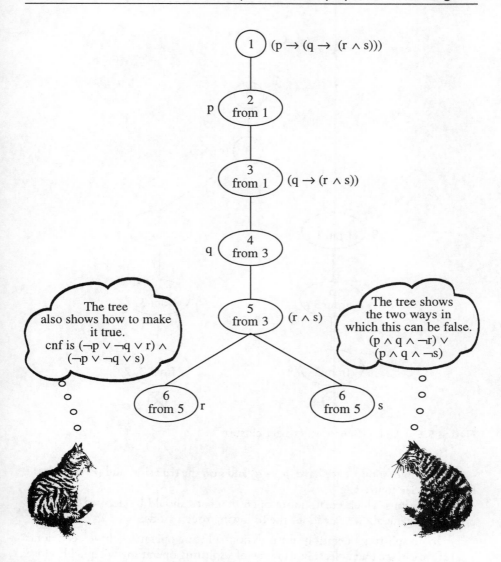

Figure 5.5 $(p \to (q \to (r \wedge s)))$

in general, preferable to do operations which do not create new branches before operations which do create new ones.

So, for example, if we have $(A \to B)$ alive on the true side of a branch, α, and $(C \to D)$ also alive on the false side of the same branch, it would seem reasonable to operate on $(C \to D)$ first since this may close the branch. If we first work with $(A \to B)$, splitting α into two branches α_1 and α_2, we still have $(C \to D)$ alive on both branches. If we discover that α_1 can be closed by operating on $(C \to D)$ on the false side, we may have to do the same thing all over again in order to close α_2.

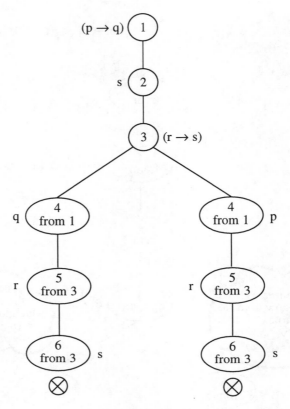

Figure 5.6 An inefficient way to get closure

For example, suppose we have $(p \rightarrow q)$ and s on the true side, and $(r \rightarrow s)$ on the false side. See figure 5.6.

So operations which create more open branches should be delayed as long as possible in general. We can adopt the following rough guide:

1) Do no splitting operations until all non-splitting operations have been done.

2) If we can see that at least one branch of a splitting operation will quickly close, do that splitting operation before others in which we cannot see this.

This still leaves a lot of room for improvement. What we really want here is a way to look at the live part of an open branch and somehow pick the important live statements, which should be operated on with priority. We do not know a satisfactory way to do this in general.

There are, however, some very interesting special cases.

5.14.1 Resolution in semantic tableaux

Suppose Γ is a finite set of clauses and we are trying to find a way to satisfy Γ if possible.

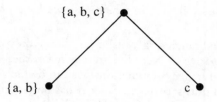

Figure 5.7

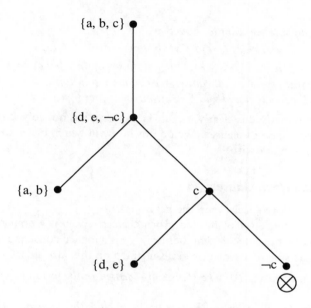

Figure 5.8

Γ is a list of disjunctions of literals. For example, Γ might be:

$\Gamma = ((a \lor (b \lor c)), ((d \lor e) \lor (\neg e)))$

We know that the order in which we write a disjunction is irrelevant. So we may as well consider each clause in Γ as a set of literals:

$\Gamma = (\{a, b, c\}, \{d, e, \neg e\})$

Our semantic tableau rules extend naturally to allow us to split any of these sets, as long as all the clauses are on the true side. For example, see figure 5.7.

The *resolution method* is to do this splitting in such a way that each pair of splits closes one of the possible branches. For example, see figure 5.8.

Given a list of clauses on the true side of a branch, we fix on some literal which occurs in both the positive and negative forms in two of the clauses. We then split that literal off, and get closure on one branch.

A nice feature of this is that we always continue to have a list of clauses on the true side of each open branch. So we can continue recursively.

If we keep on doing this, one of two things must eventually happen.

- Either the tree becomes closed, in which case we have proved that Γ is not satisfiable.
- Or we get some open branch α in which every literal only occurs in one form, either positive or negative in every live statement on the branch. In this case we can stop without further computation! We can define an interpretation σ_α which satisfies α and thus satisfies Γ. Since α has only clauses on it, and these are only on the true side, we can define $\sigma_\alpha(p) = \mathrm{T}$ if and only if p is a proposition name which occurs in α in the positive form. This interpretation makes all live clauses in α true, and therefore makes all the clauses in α true, and therefore satisfies Γ.

Example 5.7 *Suppose we want to show that*

$$((\neg a \vee b) \wedge (\neg b \vee c) \wedge (a \vee \neg c) \wedge (a \vee b \vee c)) \rightarrow (a \wedge b \wedge c).$$

It suffices to show that $\Gamma = \{(\neg a \vee b), (\neg b \vee c), (a \vee \neg c), (a \vee b \vee c), (\neg a \vee \neg b \vee \neg c)\}$ *is inconsistent. Since these are all clauses, we can use resolution.*

We find that the tree is closed and Γ is inconsistent. See figure 5.9

The resolution method is clearly useful. However it has not solved the problem even in the special case of clauses. We do not know in which order to choose the pairs of clauses to work with.

5.14.2 Headed Horn clauses

This case is even more special than the previous one.

Suppose Γ is a finite set of headed Horn clauses, and p is a *proposition name*. Assume that we want to decide whether or not p is a logical consequence of Γ. We put Γ on the true side of a semantic tableau, and p on the false side.

Example 5.8 *See figure 5.10. The clauses are written in the form of implications in this case.*

We have p on the false side and we are trying to close this tableau. So we hope to get p on the true side. Thus we regard p as a goal. *We look for a clause on the true side which has p as a conclusion. We operate on such a clause $(a \rightarrow p)$. We split, and one branch closes immediately. On the other branch, we have a on the false side. So a becomes our new goal.*

We now have two goals, b and c. We look for clauses on the true side with these as conclusions. Try to continue this procedure until the tableau is closed.

We have the following rule:

If the true side of a branch is a set Γ of headed Horn clauses and the false side is a single proposition name, X, regard X as a goal and work on statements in Γ which have X as a conclusion.

Although this is a special case it is rather useful. This is because if we split the conjunctions on the false side the rule may be applied recursively and all the new open branches continue to have headed Horn clauses on the true side and single *proposition name*s on the false side.

Suppose, as above, Γ is a list of headed Horn clauses on the true side of a branch α and the false side has just one proposition name X. What do we do if X is not a

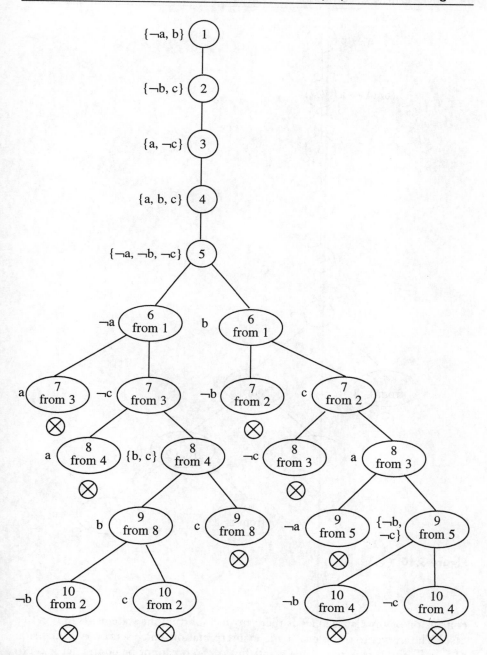

Figure 5.9 The tree is closed and Γ is inconsistent

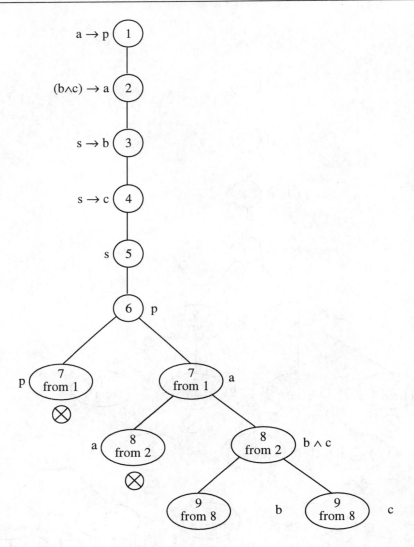

Figure 5.10

conclusion of any clause in Γ? Is there any use splitting the statements in Γ in this case? The answer to this is no. If σ is an interpretation which sets every conclusion of Γ to T, and sets X to F, then σ satisfies α. So α cannot be contradictory. No matter how much we split it, closure will not be obtained.

Thus in this special case we have a way to recognise when there is no use proceeding with the algorithm. We can see in advance what the conclusion will be.

Clearly the semantic tableau algorithm ought to have a computer implementation, and a prime candidate for a first implementation would be the special case in which we are trying to work out the logical consequences of a set of headed Horn clauses. This has been done in Prolog, as will be seen in the next chapter.

5.15 Summary of chapter 5

There are two types of formal reasoning systems, forward chaining and backward chaining. We have given two systems, one of each type, whose purpose is to prove tautologies.

The Hilbert style system, H, has three axiom schemes and uses one rule of inference, modus ponens. A sequence of statement forms is a proof in H if each statement form is either an axiom or follows from earlier statements in the sequence by modus ponens. Proofs in H are difficult to discover and even when you have a proof of a statement the proof does not seem to explain why the statement is true.

In contrast to this, the semantic tableaux system attempts to prove that a statement form X is a tautology by trying systematically to construct a counterexample to X. The construction generates a tree of possibilities. Either a counterexample is produced or the construction becomes blocked by contradictions. In the latter case we say that the tree is closed and we call the closed tree a proof of X.

We have proved soundness and completeness theorems for the semantic tableaux system as applied to statement forms.

The soundness theorem says that if X is provable in the system, then $\models X$.

The completeness theorem says that if $\models X$, then X is provable in the semantic tableau system.

These two theorems mean that we have a formal reasoning system which captures all the semantics of the propositional calculus.

The semantic tableaux method also seems to be a useful tool for reasoning.

The semantic tableaux method is non-deterministic but has the delightful property that you always end up with the right answer no matter what choices you make.

It is currently not understood how best to make the choices in order to terminate quickly. Most people think this problem is extremely difficult. A good solution to it would revolutionise discrete mathematics and make the inventor of it famous among mathematicians and computer scientists.

Chapter 6

Logic programming (simple Prolog)

There are two aspects of any computer program, a procedural aspect and a declarative aspect.

The procedural aspect of a computer program tells a computer how to operate on its inputs to produce its desired output. It is realised as a process which changes state with time. It is often expressed as a list of instructions, with possible tests, branches and loops, telling a computer what to do at each stage.

On the other hand, the declarative aspect of a computer program specifies the desired logical relationship between the objects dealt with by the program. It might, for example, specify some relationship between the input and the output, while tending to avoid the details of how to achieve this logical relationship.

Most programs in most languages are a mixture of procedural and declarative elements. However, certain programming languages tend to emphasise one aspect rather than another. Roughly speaking, C and FORTRAN would be called procedural languages because the emphasis in these languages is on the procedural aspect of programming.

Logic programming, which includes programming in Prolog and a number of related languages, aspires to emphasise the declarative aspect of programming, and to separate it from the procedural aspect. The idea is that the program should be a set of axioms for some field of knowledge. The job of the computer is then to draw logical conclusions from its program.

The declarative aspect of a logic program is the axiom set. The procedural aspect is the way in which the computer draws conclusions from this axiom set.

There is a fairly commonly held declarative ideal in logic programming, which is that the procedural aspect of a logic program, i.e. what is actually done, should be automatically derived from the declarative aspect.

The programmer should not have to be concerned with how the computer actually does its problem solving, according to the extreme declarative ideal; but we will see that in practice this ideal is not fulfilled.

Of course it is admitted in logic programming that this ideal is not fulfilled. However it is often asserted or suggested (see Lazarev (1989), in the references in chapter 13 for example) that this situation is temporary, or somehow about to be overcome except for minor details. My view is that this is definitely, permanently wrong. The procedural aspect of a logic program must always be taken into account.

So in my opinion the thing I am calling the extreme form of the declarative ideal is not an ideal at all, but a mistake.

I hope, at least, that you will agree that it is possible to use logic programming without believing in the desirability of complete separation between the procedural and declarative aspects of programming.

Prolog is a typical logic programming language. There are two important ideas in Prolog, predicates and lists. We will first discuss predicates.

6.1   Predicates

In logic, or in Prolog, a property or relation is called a *predicate*.

Examples of predicates:

X is red
X is prime
X is a parent of Y
$X < Y$
$X \equiv Y$ modulo Z
X is a number so that if Y and Z are any integers then $| e^Y - Z | < X$
$U + V = W$.

Predicates can have any number of arguments. A predicate with one argument is a property. For example the predicate

X is red

asserts a property, redness, of its argument, which is represented by the variable X.

Predicates of more than one argument are relations. For example the predicate

X is a parent of Y

is a predicate which asserts a relation, parenthood, between its two arguments.

Usually a predicate is described by a statement with variables in it. We intend to talk about translations of predicates from one language to another, so it seems best to say that a predicate is the meaning of a statement with variables in it, rather than to say that a predicate is such a statement.

We consider the *truth values* to be True and False, which we abbreviate T and F, as before.

When appropriate values are substituted for the arguments of a predicate, the predicate evaluates to one of the truth values. The truth value of a predicate is a function of the values given to its arguments. Having decided this, we get the following mathematical definition for this fundamental idea.

Definition 6.1 *A predicate is a function whose codomain is the set of truth values,* $\{T,F\}$.

In life and in mathematics and in computing, there are many predicates whose arguments range over essentially different domains. These are called multi-sorted predicates. In Prolog, however, we will consider only predicates all of whose arguments range over the same domain. There is only one intended domain in any Prolog program, but it may contain objects which are quite dissimilar, from a human point of view.

Let D be some domain. An n-tuple from D is a list of n elements from D. Two n-tuples are the same if and only if they have the same elements in the same order. D^n is the set of all n-tuples from D.

A *predicate of arity n with domain D* is a function $p(X_1, ..., X_n) : D^n \to \{T, F\}$. So the arity of a predicate is the same as the number of its arguments.

If p is a predicate of arity n over D, and $(a_1, ..., a_n)$ are elements of D, then $p(a_1, ..., a_n)$ will tell us whether or not p is true of $(a_1, ..., a_n)$. In fact $p(a_1, ..., a_n) = $ T if and only if the predicate p is true of $(a_1, ..., a_n)$.

For example, the arity of

X is red

is one. We will often write the predicate name first and put the arguments in brackets to the right. So we might write this as

red(X)

and presumably, if the domain is considered to be all physical objects,

red(cherry) = T.

Similarly, we can write $X < Y$ as $less(X, Y)$. The arity is two, the domain might be the integers, and presumably $less(10, 2) = $ F.

There are, incidentally, predicates of arity zero. These are constant functions whose codomain is the truth values.

We will consider that predicate names of arity zero are the same as *proposition names*.

6.2 Predicates, facts, constants, variables in Prolog

In the following, a "character" is either a letter or a digit.

A *constant* in Prolog is either a number, such as "776", or a string of characters beginning with a lower case letter. So, for example, "jane" is a constant, but "Jane" is not a constant.

A *variable* in Prolog is a string of characters beginning with an upper case letter.

A *term* in Prolog can be either a constant or a variable. For the moment, this is all the terms we will consider. There are other types of terms, which will be discussed later. So the following are terms:

X, unless, Y, Dogsbreakfast

three variables and one constant.

Predicate names in Prolog are strings of characters beginning with lower case letters.

You should try to keep in mind the distinction between predicates, which are semantic things, functions whose codomain is {T, F}, and predicate names, which are defined by syntax.

Predicate expressions are usually written as predicate names followed by a list of terms enclosed in brackets. For example

red(cup)

says that some particular object, called "cup" is red.

Prolog has a few built-in predicates, whose names are already determined. Except for these, however, we can invent predicate names to suit ourselves. Of course it is necessary to use whatever names we invent in a consistent manner. Suppose, for example, we wish to write some axioms for motherhood. We might begin by asking ourselves: what is the arity of motherhood? We seem to need a predicate of arity 2, which says that one person is the mother of another. We could decide to write this as

qqqqqzsz(A,B).

However, this will be hard to remember, and it seems better to use a more natural name. We could call our predicate

mother(A,B).

This is clearly meant to say either that A is the mother of B, or vice versa. Obviously, we have to determine which we mean. So we have to invent some convention to determine, in our own minds, the order of the arguments. We might decide, for example, that mother(A,B) should mean that A is the mother of B. Having set up this convention, we have to hold to it.

A *fact* in Prolog is a predicate expression in which all the terms are constant. For example

mother(louise, mabel)

is a fact. To say that this is a fact does not, in this context, imply that we think it is true. It may be true or it may be false. A fact, in this context, is an expression which has the form

predicate-name(constant,..., constant).

To give another example,

likes(joe, alice)

which is intended to say that joe likes alice, is a fact.

A predicate of arity zero is written as

P

As mentioned previously, these play the same role in Prolog as *proposition name*s in the propositional calculus.

6.3 Programs in Prolog

A Prolog program may be regarded as a set of axioms for some field of knowledge. When the program is consulted we ask whether some statement is a logical consequence of the axioms. If the statement has variables in it we ask for assignments of values to the variables so that the statement is a logical consequence of the axioms.

A Prolog program consists of a list of statements, with full stops at the end of each. Example:

---

mortal(X) :- human(X).
featherless(socrates).
bipedal(socrates).
animal(socrates).
human(X) :- featherless(X), bipedal(X), animal(X).

As mentioned above, terms starting with upper case letters, such as X, are variables, and other names such as socrates are constants. human(X) is a predicate expression with variable X, meaning X is human. Note that predicate names, such as human, mortal, featherless, should start with lower case letters.

In Prolog, the sign :- is interpreted as "if". So the first line in the example program above means X is mortal if X is human, for all X. The next three lines say that socrates is a featherless bipedal animal. The comma , is interpreted as "and", so the last line says that X is human if X is a featherless bipedal animal, for all X.

Among the five statements in the above Prolog program, the statements on lines 2, 3, 4 are facts. The other statements are called rules. A *rule* in Prolog, in general, is a statement of the form

   p :- q1, q2, ..., qn.

where p, q1, q2, ..., qn are predicate expressions. The meaning of this rule is that p is true whenever all of q1,..., qn are true.

Statements in Prolog are only of two types, either facts or rules. Prolog statements are also called *clauses*.

In a rule, such as

   mortal(X) :- human(X).

the left hand side is called the conclusion. A rule is supposed to state a truth and also show a possible way to prove the conclusion. So, for example,

   human(X):- featherless(X), bipedal(X), animal(X).

expresses the truth that any featherless bipedal animal is human, and also tells us that if we have an X and want to show

   human(X)

we can do this by checking

   featherless(X), bipedal(X), animal(X).

Note that different occurrences of a variable in a single rule must refer to the same object. If we have the above rule and we want to prove

   human(fred).

we need to check

   featherless(fred), bipedal(fred), animal(fred).

On the other hand, occurrences of the same variable in different rules are not linked at all. The program given above would have the same meaning if the first line were changed to

   mortal(Y):- human(Y).

Exercise: You can create a Prolog program with any editor. Try this.

Once a program has been written, we may wish to ask questions about its logical consequences. This process is called consultation and is done with a Prolog interpreter and/or compiler.

The reader should at this point discover how to get access to some version of Prolog.

Suppose you have written a Prolog program. Give whatever local command is necessary to run Prolog.

Once Prolog is running, type

[file].

if file is the name of the program you have written. You can then ask questions, and you should get logical consequences of the facts and rules you have given. For example if you ask mortal(socrates). after reading in the above example, it should (after thinking for a while) say yes. To get out of Prolog type

halt.

Note that a full stop is necessary after each statement.

Now, try to create a program and consult it.

6.3.1 Programs with just facts

According to what was said above, a Prolog program is a list of statements, which are either facts or rules. In particular, a list of facts is a Prolog program. Suppose, for example, we had a list of facts of the form

criminal(X)

meaning that X is a criminal

locate(X,City, Date)

meaning that X is known to have been in City on Date, and

associate(X,Y)

meaning that persons X and Y are associates.

We could just list all our facts in a program. For example,

---

criminal(bigred).
criminal(boxcarjoe).
criminal(eaglehat).
locate(bigred,ny,july3).
locate(bigred,sf,june4).
associate(bigred,boxcarjoe).
locate(boxcarjoe,milan,june5).
etc.

We store this in some file. We then call Prolog. We read in the file with

['filename'].

We can then ask questions. If we ask, for example,

criminal(bigred).

we get the answer

yes.

We can also ask questions with variables, such as

criminal(X).

In this case we would get the first criminal

X = bigred.

In general, given a query with variables in it, Prolog attempts to find values of the variables which make the query true. If we want another example, we type

;

and we get the next crook, boxcarjoe. If we type ; again we get the next one. When the list is exhausted, we get answer

no.

We can also ask compound queries. Suppose, for example, we are concerned to discover a criminal associate of bigjoe who was in Milan on some date. We ask

associate(bigjoe,X), criminal(X), locate(X,milan,Date).

and we will get an answer such as

X=boxcarjoe, Date=june5.

6.3.2 Why not just give all the facts?

We can represent any situation, as above, by just writing down all known facts about it. There are many situations, however, in which this does not seem to be a sensible approach. Consider, for example, the information in figure 6.1.

Suppose we are interested in predicates such as

father(X,Y), mother(X,Y), male(X), female(X),

sister(X,Y), brother(X,Y), grandfather(X,Y),

grandmother(X,Y), uncle(X,Y), aunt(X,Y).

We would have to write a very long list of facts to represent the fairly simple data structure given above. Also, if we found that part of the family tree was incorrect, we would discover that a small change in the data structure would result in many changes in the program. Obviously, what is wrong with just giving the facts is that some of the facts are logical consequences of others. So we should define some of the predicates in terms of others, using rules.

6.3.3 How to write simple Prolog

Suppose we have a situation which we wish to describe in Prolog. We first decide what are the important predicates in the situation. We then think about the predicates to try to see which ones can be defined in terms of the others. We should arrange the predicates in a hierarchy of complexity, with complex predicates defined in terms of simpler ones. Usually there are many different ways to do this! If possible, all the facts should be entered using the simplest predicates. If possible, the simplest predicates should be logically independent, so that no single piece of information is held in two different ways. These are *desirable* features, which can't all be realised in every case. So writing a Prolog program is a problem in design, and different people will have different solutions, and some solutions will be simpler and more elegant than others. There may not exist any perfect solution.

In general, it is best to put the facts before the rules in a Prolog program. It is best to put definitions of relatively simple predicates before definitions of relatively complex predicates. In other words, the order of the program should reflect, if possible, the hierarchy of complexity which you are using. This usually makes the

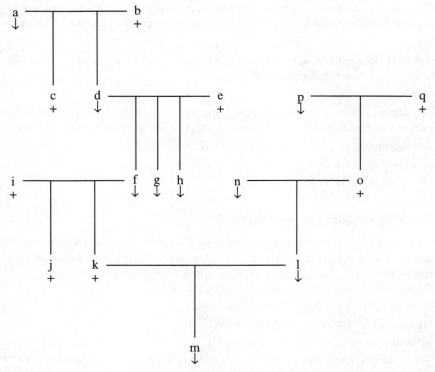

Figure 6.1 A large amount of information is contained in this excellent data structure. You can see, for example, that f and g are brothers, and g and h are uncles of k.

program easier to read for a human being. And in some cases, as we will see, it may also improve the computational behaviour of the program.

Exercise: defining a family tree in Prolog

Imagine a small community where everyone is related to everyone else in several different ways. We wish to express the relationships in a Prolog program.

Some of the predicates we might be concerned with here are:

parent(X,Y), father(X,Y), mother(X,Y),

male(X), female(X), sister(X,Y),

grandfather(X,Y), aunt(X,Y), cousin(X,Y).

Evidently there are many logical relationships, for example:

parent(X,Y) :- mother(X,Y).

parent(X,Y) :- father(X,Y).

grandfather(X,Y) :- father(X,Z),

parent(Z,Y).

The problem is to decide which are the basic predicates, and then to build up definitions of the more complex predicates in terms of the simpler ones.

To begin with, suppose we took the above definition of parent in terms of father and mother, and of grandfather in terms of father and parent. Suppose we added some facts to the program given above.

```
father(jud,rubel).
father(rubel,jubel).
parent(jubel,marx).
parent(rubel,jed).
father(jubel,lu).
parent(marx,mabel).
parent(X,Y) :- mother(X,Y).
parent(X,Y) :- father(X,Y).
grandfather(X,Y) :- father(X,Z),
parent(Z,Y).
```

If the above sample were consulted with
grandfather(rubel, lu).
the answer should be
yes.

We can also have questions with variables in them, e.g.
grandfather(X,Y).
In this case, Prolog will try to find values of X and Y which make this true. It might reply
X=jud, Y=jubel.
If you then type
;
you get another possibility such as
X=rubel, Y=marx.
By giving more semicolons, you should get all the possibilities, one after the other.
You can also have compound queries, such as
grandfather(X,Y), parent(Y,lu).
And again all the possibilities should be generated, e.g. X=jud,Y=jubel.

Example: tree recognition

Suppose we wish to have a program which will identify trees. The idea is to describe features of a tree, and hope that the program will identify it. The first step here is to look at a book about identifying trees, and see what predicates are involved.

It may be that we do not need any rules here, but that all the information can be given by a list of facts. For example, we might find predicates of arity one, such as simple-leaf(X), or lobed-leaf(X), and predicates of arity 2, such as autumn-colours(X,Y); and we might then have facts such as:

---

simple-leaf(beach).
simple-leaf(elm).
lobed-leaf(maple).
lobed-leaf(sycamore).
autumn-colours(red,maple).
autumn-colours(brown, sycamore).

If we want to find a tree with a lobed leaf, we ask the question:
    lobed-leaf(X).
and we might get the answer:
    yes. X=maple.
If we want another possibility, we type
    ;
and we might get
    yes. X=sycamore.
If we see a tree leaf, lobed and red in autumn, we could say:
    lobed-leaf(X), autumn-colours(red,X).
and we might get the answer
    yes. X=maple.
Evidently this technique can be used quite nicely for finding information in a large data base.

6.4 The Herbrand Universe of a simple Prolog program

Before we write a Prolog program we have in mind an application. We intend that the statements we write in the program are true of the application. We also hope for a soundness and completeness property for the responses of Prolog to our queries. That is, we would hope that if Prolog says some statement, S, is true, then it is actually true. Also, within certain limits, we would hope that if we ask S and if there is a way to make S true then Prolog will discover this. Clearly, however, Prolog can't read our minds. Prolog does not have any information about the application other than what we tell it.

The most we can expect is that Prolog might be sound and complete (within some limits) for the simplest possible interpretation of the program which it has. The Herbrand universe associated with a Prolog program is intended to be such a smallest and simplest interpretation.

So far we are considering simple Prolog programs in which the terms are all either variables or constants.

Suppose we are looking at a program with n constants $c_1, ..., c_n$, and k predicate names $p_1, ..., p_k$. The Herbrand universe for this program will consist of a domain of n objects, one for each constant, and k predicates, one to interpret each predicate name.

For programs of the type we are considering, Prolog does not need to consider any objects other than those named by the constants. Also it will only assume a predicate is true if its truth is a logical consequence of the program. (At this stage, we are not able to give a precise definition of this notion of logical consequence. We can only say that Prolog will only affirm that a predicate is true if it is forced to do so by the facts and rules in its program.)

If the constants of our program are as above, then the domain of the Herbrand universe will be the constants

$$D = \{c_1, ..., c_n\}$$

Let P be a predicate name. We will use the notation **P** to stand for the predicate which, in the Herbrand universe, interprets the predicate name P. So if the predicate names are as above, the Herbrand universe consists of domain D together with predicates $\mathbf{p_1}, ..., \mathbf{p_k}$ defined over D.

We bundle all this together in one notation:

Herbrand universe $= (D, \mathbf{p_1}, ..., \mathbf{p_k})$

We previously defined a type to be a set together with a list of functions associated with the set. A Herbrand universe $(D, \mathbf{p_1}, ..., \mathbf{p_k})$ is, therefore, a special kind of type. For a Herbrand universe associated with a simple Prolog program, the functions are all predicates.

As mentioned above, the predicates are assumed to be false unless they are forced to be true by the program. The Herbrand universe has every predicate false unless proven otherwise.

Note that there is only one domain in the Herbrand universe. All the constants are treated as being of the same type. In fact everything in Prolog is assumed to be of the same type. So, for example, in the tree recognition part-program given above, the Herbrand universe would have domain

D = {beach, elm, maple, red, sycamore, brown }

Prolog does not know that "red" and "beach" are understood by us to be in different categories.

The predicates in this Herbrand universe are defined exactly by the list of facts, because the program did not have any rules. So in this case a predicate is true for certain arguments if and only if the program says it is.

Let $H(\mathbf{P})$ be the Herbrand universe for a Prolog program **P**.

Let $S(X_1, ..., X_n)$ be a possible Prolog query, i.e. a list of predicate expressions involving the variables $X_1, ..., X_n$.

We will say that Prolog, with program **P**, solves $S(X_1, ..., X_n)$ if, given this as query it eventually terminates and gives some values to the variables, say $X_1 = a_1, ..., X_n = a_n$.

The soundness property for Prolog with program **P** would have two parts

Level 1 soundness: if Prolog solves $S(X_1, ..., X_n)$ with solution $(a_1, ..., a_n)$, then this instantiation of the variables actually makes $S(X_1, ..., X_n)$ true in the Herbrand universe $H(\mathbf{P})$

Level 2 soundness : If Prolog, given $S(X_1, ..., X_n)$ as query, eventually stops and says

no

then there is no possible instantiation of the variables which makes $S(X_1, ..., X_n)$ true in the Herbrand universe.

The completeness property for Prolog, with program **P** would have two parts as follows.

Level 1 completeness: Prolog, given query $S(X_1, ..., X_n)$, should eventually terminate.

Level 2 completeness: Prolog, given query $S(X_1, ..., X_n)$ and a sequence of semicolons, should eventually list all possible instantiations of the variables which make the query true in the Herbrand universe.

Unfortunately, however, these properties do not hold in all cases. We do have the level 1 soundness property for Prolog, but all the other properties frequently fail. It is up to us to write programs in Prolog which do have the soundness and completeness properties, if possible.

In order to have any chance of doing this, we need to understand in detail how Prolog works.

6.5 How Prolog works, part I: backtracking

What Prolog does can be understood in terms of semantic tableaux. (Prolog does not use the full semantic tableau algorithm. It tries to make short cuts which take advantage of the special form of its statements, which are all headed Horn clauses. We will see that these short cuts cause some problems.)

Given a program and a query, q, Prolog tries to prove that q is a logical consequence of the program. We can simulate the activities of Prolog by putting the program on the true side of a semantic tableau, and the query, q, on the false side, and applying the techniques we know.

The situation is made more complicated and also more interesting by the fact that there may be variables in both the program and the query. To begin with, however, we will consider statements without variables, i.e. without upper case letters. Consider, for example, the following program.

---

p:- a,b.
p:-c,d.
a:- c,e.
c.
e.
d.

(In case you are wondering, the Herbrand universe for this sets every one of these propositions false unless it is forced to be true by the program.)

Suppose the query is p,c. We will write the tableau as a tree using Prolog notation for the logical operators.

Conjunction on the false side leads to a split, so after one application of the rules we have the situation shown in figure 6.2.

In order to get a contradiction, it will be necessary to close all the branches. Prolog always works from left to right. So it starts with the left most open branch.

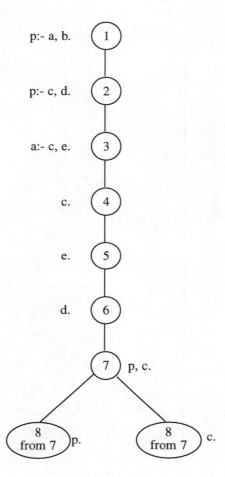

Figure 6.2

Since Prolog only works with headed Horn clauses, all the open branches will have the same true side, i.e. the original program. Also Prolog only looks at the leaves of the false side. The statements on the leaves on the false side of open branches are considered by Prolog to be *goals*. Prolog starts, then, with the left most goal. In the case above, this would be p.

Once it has picked its goal, Prolog starts at the top of the program and attempts to match the current goal with a left hand side of a rule or with a fact.

In this case it matches the goal p with the left hand side of

p:- a,b.

in line 1. The right hand side of the matching rule gives Prolog new goals. See figure 6.3.

(Check that this is just what would have happened if we had been working with the equivalent statement forms in the statement form notation. $(a \wedge b) \rightarrow p$ would

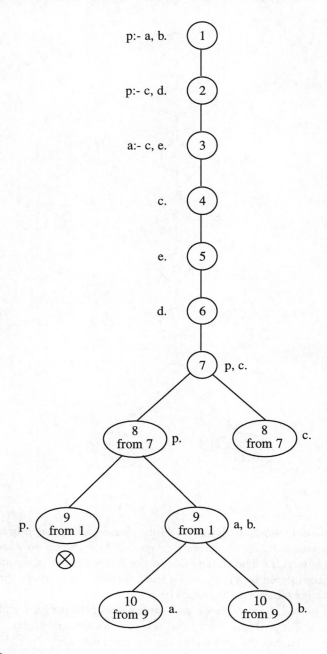

Figure 6.3

have split and the branch on which p was true would have immediately been closed, leaving the above tree.)

Prolog begins again with its left most goal, in this case

a.

Again it finds a match with the left hand side of a rule

a:- c,e.

so c and e become new goals. See figure 6.4.

Prolog's goal is now b. It tries to match this and fails. *(In general, if Prolog has a goal, q, and gets to the end of the program with no match with either a fact or the left hand side of a rule, we will say it has failed to satisfy q.)*

When failure occurs, Prolog backtracks to the last goal which was matched. In this case the last goal is e. Prolog tries to find another way to satisfy e, by looking lower in the program. It fails again, and backtracks again, this time to c, where, once again it fails to find another match. It then backtracks to a, trying to find another match and fails again. It now backtracks to p. It remembers that p was matched at line 1. It looks below line 1 for another match, and succeeds at line 2. Prolog deletes that part of the tree over which it has backtracked. Therefore the new situation is as shown in figure 6.5.

All branches are closed, so Prolog says

yes.

This means that p,c is a logical consequence of the program.

So far we have the following

1) All the open branches of the tableau have the same true side, which is the original program. (This is because a Prolog program consists of headed Horn clauses, and is not true for semantic tableaux in general.)

2) The leaves of the open branches on the false side are called goals. Prolog always works on its left most goal.

3) Prolog tries to close the branch of its current goal by matching the goal with a fact or a left hand side of a rule in the program.

4) When Prolog has scanned to the end of the program without matching its current goal, it backtracks to the last goal which was matched, and looks for an alternative match, below the place in the program where the last match was found. If this fails, Prolog backtracks again. As Prolog backtracks it deletes the proof tree.

5) If Prolog succeeds in closing the proof tree, it says yes.

6) If the program terminates with an open branch, Prolog says no.

Like most entities in computing, Prolog is an odd mixture of fundamental insights and arbitrary conventions. The most obtrusive arbitrariness here lies in the particular search strategy which Prolog adopts. This can get it into trouble, even with headed Horn clauses and no variables. If one of us were given assumption

p:- p.

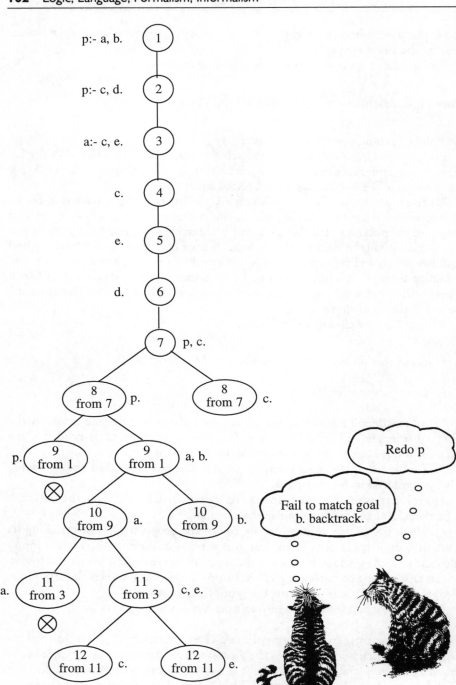

Figure 6.4

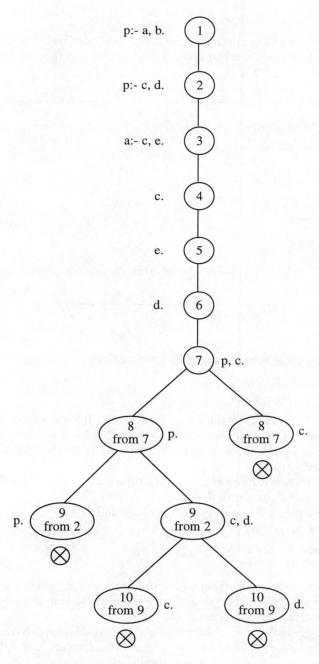

Figure 6.5   Match *p* with the left hand side of line 2

and question

p

we would split the tableau, find one open branch and stop. But Prolog takes p as its goal, matches it with the left hand side of p:-p., finds p as a subgoal, and continues forever.

Problem 6.1 *Draw a tree to show what Prolog does with program*

---

dog:- cat.

cat:- dog.

cat.

---

and query

cat,dog.

Problem 6.2 * *Make some polite suggestions to designers of an improved version of Prolog.*

6.6 How Prolog works, part 2: unification

We define a *substitution* to be a list,

$$\alpha = \{(X_1, T_1), (X_2, T_2), ..., (X_n, T_n)\},$$

where $X_1, ..., X_n$ are variables and $T_1, ..., T_n$ are terms. If S is any Prolog expression, and α is a substitution, we apply the substitution α to S by simultaneously replacing all the variables in the substitution by their corresponding terms, within S. The result is denoted S_α.

If P and Q are two expressions, and α is a substitution, we will say that P and Q are *unified* by α if P_α is identical with Q_α.

For example parent(X,jo) and parent(Y,Z) are unified by

{ (Z,jo), (X,W), (Y,W) }

They would also be unified by

{(Z,jo), (X,lulu), (Y,lulu) }.

The second substitution assumes that X and Y are both lulu, which is not necessary to get unification. So, in this sense, the second of these unifying substitutions is making an unnecessary assumption.

In order to get unification in the example above, we do need to have X and Y the same, and Z has to be jo. The first substitution above does achieve unification, but without adding any unnecessary information to the situation.

Suppose α is a unifying substitution for two predicate expressions or terms, P and Q; so

$$P_\alpha = Q_\alpha = R$$

for some R. We will call α a *most general unifier* for P and Q if any other unifier can be obtained by α followed by some other substitution, γ; that is, if

1) α is a unifier of P and Q, i.e. and $P_\alpha = Q_\alpha = R$ for some R, and
2) whenever β is any other unifier of P and Q, so that $P_\beta = Q_\beta = S$, for some S, then there exists a substitution γ so that
$$S = R_\gamma$$

Example 6.1 $\alpha = \{(Z, jo), (Y, W), (Z, W)\}$ *is a most general unifier of parent*(X, jo) *and parent*(Y, Z). *The result of unification is parent*(W, jo). *Another unifier is* $\beta = \{(Z, jo), (Y, lulu), (X, lulu)\}$. *Notice that* α *followed by* $\gamma = \{(W, lulu)\}$ *gives the same result as* β.

Prolog works by pattern matching and substitution. Consider the family tree example. When given a question, such as

grandfather(jud, Y)

Prolog considers this as a goal. It tries to satisfy the goal by matching it either with a fact in its program or with a left hand side of one of its rules. The matching is done by finding a substitution which makes the goal the same as the fact, or the left hand side of a rule, i.e. by finding a substitution which unifies the goal with either a fact or the left hand side of a rule. A most general unifier is always used.

We can now return to a description of Prolog's behaviour.

We suppose, as before, that Prolog is given a program $\text{prog}(X_1, ..., X_j)$, and a query $q(Y_1, ..., Y_k)$. Prolog attempts to find values of the variables in the query $Y_1, ..., Y_k$ so that
$$q(Y_1, ..., Y_k)$$
is a logical consequence of the program. In terms of quantifiers, Prolog is trying to show
$$(\forall X_1)...(\forall X_j)\text{prog}(X_1, ..., X_j) \rightarrow$$
$$(\exists Y_1)...(\exists Y_k)q(Y_1, ..., Y_k)$$

As before, we will simulate what Prolog does using semantic tableaux. Here is an example.

Example 6.2

---

cat(bags).
cat(felix).
bird(harold).
hunt(X,Y) : - cat(X), bird(Y).

Suppose we ask the question:

hunt(felix, harold).

Prolog matches this goal with the left hand side of the first rule, using unifying substitution $\alpha = (X, felix), (Y, harold)$. *It then has two subgoals*

cat(felix), bird(harold).

It satisfies these from left to right, and eventually says "yes".
In this case there were no variables in the query. If we had asked

hunt(felix,W).

Prolog would have eventually said

yes, W=harold.

You can see what Prolog is doing, step by step, by turning on the trace. This is done as follows:

trace, hunt(felix,harold).

It may happen that the same variable is used in two different statements in a program. In order to prevent clashes in the substitutions, most versions of Prolog will begin by renaming the variables. So you will find that new, perhaps peculiar variable names are used in trace.
The trace can be turned off by calling

notrace.

Now consider the situation in more detail. As before we simulate what Prolog does using semantic tableaux. To begin with, Prolog puts the program on the true side of a tableau and the query on the false side, renaming the variables to try to avoid confusion.

Consider, for example,

---

p(a,f).
p(e,f).
p(e,g).
p(g,h).
de(X,Y) :- p(Y,X).
de(X,Z) :- p(Z,Y), de(X,Y).

---

with query

de(f,X), de(h,X).

The variables are renamed and the program is put on the true side and the query on the false side of a tableau.

p(a,f).
p(e,f).
p(e,g).
p(g,h).
de(X,Y):- p(X,Y).
de(A,C) :- p(C,B), de(A,B).
goal: de(f,W), de(h,W)

Note that the variable W on the false side of the two branches refers to the same object. We now start with the goal on the left most open branch, as before. In this case it is de(f,W). As before, we try to match this with facts or left hand sides of rules starting at the top of the program. The main thing to understand here is

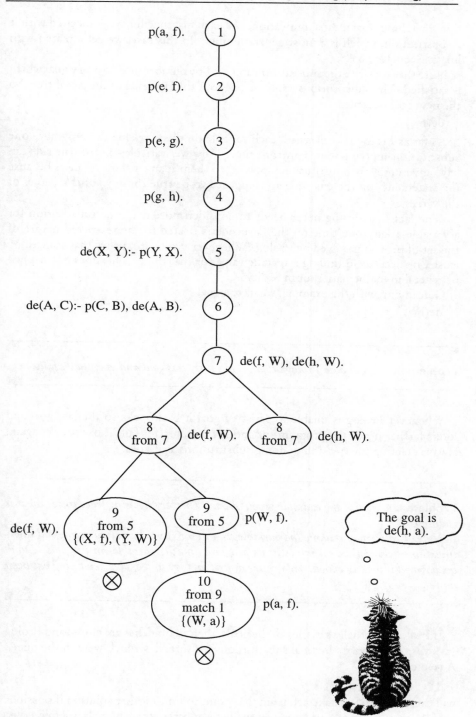

Figure 6.6

this: matching now means unification, and each match will have associated with it a substitution, which is a most general unifier. In this case, we get a match with line 5. See figure 6.6.

Note that we write the substitution and the line number next to every goal which is satisfied. The substitutions apply throughout the false side of the proof tree. So the new goal becomes

   de(h,a)

As far as Prolog is concerned, each variable on the false side can only have one substitution applying to it at any one time. However variables on the true side can have any number of substitutions applying to them at any instant. (This is because the statements on the true side are supposed to be true for *any possible values* of the variables.)

(The fact that Prolog never needs to consider more than one substitution for a variable at any one time on the false side is related to the restricted nature of the set of problems solved by Prolog. Whenever Prolog can prove that something exists, it succeeds in finding a specific value for that thing. This does not happen in general in mathematics, or in reality.)

Continuing with the example, we have a goal

   de(h,a).

Problem 6.3 *Show how Prolog attempts to satisfy this goal and eventually fails.*

Whenever Prolog is unable to satisfy a goal it backtracks to the last goal and looks farther down the program for another match. If it fails it backtracks again, always deleting the tree and undoing substitutions as it goes.

Problem 6.4 *Finish the example given above. Then try it, using trace to see what it is doing.*

Note: Prolog may rename the variables in order to avoid creating accidental identifications between the variables in its program and the variables in its goals. Don't be alarmed if the trace looks unfamiliar at first, but try to see what renaming has been done.

If Prolog eventually satisfies all the goals, then all branches are closed and Prolog says yes, and reports the final substitutions for variables which were in the query. A semicolon

   ;

will cause Prolog to backtrack from that point to find another solution if possible.

If the whole intricate process eventually terminates with a branch still open (i.e., with a goal unsatisfied) Prolog just says no

In fact, Prolog really has nothing more to say about this issue. Because of the way the backtracking is done the whole tree and all the substitutions have been deleted except for the original program and the original query.

6.7 Equality and Inequality

Prolog has a built-in equality predicate, which is written

X = Y

When Prolog encounters a goal X = Y, where X and Y are terms, it attempts to unify X and Y. The goal succeeds if the unification succeeds, and in this case the unifying substitution is applied to X and Y.

The built-in predicate

X \= Y

succeeds exactly if X=Y fails. On the other hand,

X \= Y

fails just in case X = Y succeeds.

For example, we might say that X is a brother of Y if X and Y have the same parent, but X and Y are not the same, and X is male. We could write this as follows

---

brother(X,Y) :- parent(Z,X), parent(Z,Y), X \= Y, male(X).

Prolog is not able to unify two different constants. So

cat=dog

will fail. On the other hand

X=dog

will succeed, and result in instantiating X to dog. Thus

cat \= dog

will succeed, and

X \= dog

will fail. The important point to understand here is that when given the goal

X \= Y

Prolog tries to unify X and Y. The goal will fail if the unification succeeds.

One way to understand the X=Y predicate in Prolog is to think how it might be defined if it were not already present.

Suppose we were considering a binary predicate

same(X, Y)

and all we wanted to assume about this predicate was that it is reflexive, that is, that same(X,X) is true for all X. We could define the predicate with the one line program:

---

same(X,X).

If Prolog is given a query

    same(A,B).

it will try to unify A and B. In fact this predicate will behave just like the equality predicate mentioned above.

Prolog also has a stricter predicate for equality, which is written

    X = =Y

This means that X and Y are already the same, on the basis of the current substitutions in force, without doing any additional unification.

So if X is uninstantiated

    X = =cat

will fail, as will, of course

    dog= =cat.

The strict equality can also be negated.

    X \ = = Y

succeeds just if

    X = =Y

fails, and fails just if

    X= =Y

succeeds.

6.8 Circular definitions and recursion

You are lost in the country and you ask someone how to get to the old Stanley place. "You go down Stanley road," you are told. So you ask: How do you get to Stanley Road? "It goes right past the old Stanley Place," you are told.

This type of muddled definition or description will be called circular. The person who has given it actually has the information which is wanted, and has in fact said something possibly useful, but it is not sufficient to find what we want. Compare that with the following, possibly from an obscure nineteenth century anthropological work.

"If the relation Kram holds between a man and woman they are not allowed to marry. Kram holds between a man and woman if they share the same mother. Kram also holds between a man and woman, if Kram holds between the mother of the man and the father of the woman. Kram never happens for any other reasons."

This definition might at first sight seem to be circular. Kram is defined in terms of another instance of Kram. If you look at it carefully, however, you will see that the explanation is arranged quite subtly to give us just the right amount of information to let us know what Kram is. All the information has been conveyed in a very compact way in this definition.

It is quite common for concepts to be self-referential. A predicate at one set of arguments is defined in terms of itself, but with other instances of the arguments. This is a powerful technique but is obviously easy to misuse. The problem is that a person attempting to apply the definition may be sent off into considering an infinite loop of possibilities. A definition or description which is self-referential but eventually terminating is called recursive. On the other hand, a muddled self-referential definition will be called circular.

Consider a definition of $n!$. We could say that $0! = 1$. Also, $(X')! = (X' * (X!))$. This recursive definition gives us an algorithm to calculate $n!$ for any natural number n. We get

$$7! = 7 * 6! = 7 * 6 * 5! = 7 * 6 * 5 * 4! = 7 * 6 * 5 * 4 * 3! = 7 * 6 * 5 * 4 * 3 * 2! =$$
$$7 * 6 * 5 * 4 * 3 * 2 * 1! = 7 * 6 * 5 * 4 * 3 * 2 * 1 * 0! = 7 * 6 * 5 * 4 * 3 * 2 * 1.$$

In terms of Prolog, we will say that a rule is *recursive* if the same predicate appears on both the left and right hand sides. Of course the arguments on the two sides may be different. In fact if the arguments are not different, the rule is obviously circular, i.e. muddled.

Suppose, for example, that we have a Prolog program in which parent(X,Y) is defined. We want to define "Z is a descendent of X"; this should mean that either X is a parent of Z, or X is a parent of a parent of Z, or X is a parent of a parent of Z or ....

We can express this recursively as follows.

---

descendent(Z,X) :- parent(X,Z).
descendent(Z,X) :- parent(X,Y), descendent(Z,Y).

6.9 The cut, and negation

Before reading this section, you should be sure that you understand the idea of backtracking, which was explained above.

Example 6.3

---

q(a).
s(a).
p(X) :- q(X), r(X).
p(Y) :- s(Y).

Suppose we ask
p(a).
Prolog will find a match with the first rule, using $\alpha = \{(X, a)\}$. *It then has subgoals*
q(a), r(a).
It satisfies $q(a)$, *but then fails to satisfy* $r(a)$. *So it backtracks, and discards the substitution* α; *it gives up on the first rule and tries the second. It matches, with substitution* $\{(Y, a)\}$, *and gets subgoal* $s(a)$, *which it satisfies. So it says "yes".*

Prolog's search for ways to satisfy its goal is like the exploration of a maze. The process of backtracking is like the retracing of steps in a maze, after a dead end has been found.

Backtracking may be inhibited by writing

!

The instruction ! is called a cut. An example of how this is used would be:

p :- q1, !, q2

This statement would tell Prolog that if it is trying to satisfy p and has got as far as q1, it can't backtrack in order to satisfy p. The only way to satisfy p is then to satisfy q2.

Continuing with the maze analogy, the cut is like a one way door in the maze of possibilities. Notice that this has absolutely no axiomatic analogy. There is no such thing as a cut, or anything like a cut, in a set of axioms. With the appearance of the cut, Prolog blatantly diverges from its original idea. Nevertheless, the cut is interesting and useful.

Example 6.4

---

a :- b,c.
c:- d,!,e.
c:- f.
a:- d,f.
b.
d.
f.

The goal

c

will fail, but the goal

a

will succeed.

We can understand the cut more fully by returning to semantic tableaux. As a goal, the cut always succeeds immediately. A branch with

!

at the leaf on the false side is just declared to be closed. As a predicate then

!

is like

True.

So a cut has no effect until a situation arises in which Prolog tries to backtrack through the cut. The cut then comes into effect. Normally Prolog would backtrack to the last goal, deleting the tree and the substitutions as it goes; this usually means reconsidering the branch immediately to the left of the current one. In the presence of the cut, however, Prolog backtracks *up* the tree to the parent goal, deletes the parent goal and the whole subtree of subgoals below it, and backtracks from there, as if no match for the parent goal could be found in the whole program.

Example 6.5 *Suppose, for example, we defined*

```
brother(X,Y):- father(Z,X), father(Z,Y), male(X), X \= Y.
brother(X,Y) :- mother(Z,X), mother(Z,Y), male(X), X \= Y.
```

Suppose you are trying to decide whether or not
brother(a,b)
and you already know that a and b have a common father. You need now to check that a is male and not the same as b. We know however that there is no use looking for another common father, or in looking for a common mother, since that will still leave us with the same subgoals. So we can add cuts which speed up the computation without changing its results.

```
brother(X,Y):- father(Z,X), father(Z,Y), !, male(X), X \= Y.
brother(X,Y) :- mother(Z,X), mother(Z,Y), !, male(X), X \= Y.
```

This is what we might call an innocuous cut, since we believe it never can change the results of a computation. There are, however, other uses of the cut which are not innocuous in this way.

6.9.1 The cut and fail combination

There is a predicate
fail
which is always false.

It is clear that with cut and fail we can, in effect, build mazes with traps in them. This can be used to express a sort of logical negation. For example:

```
p :- q, !, fail.
p.
```

This means that if q can be satisfied, p must fail. On the other hand, if q cannot be satisfied, p is true. In this situation, p means that Prolog can't prove q. We could think of p as
$not \vdash_{Prolog} q$.
For example, Prolog has a built-in equality predicate, written
X == Y.
We can use this, together with the cut and fail combination, to define inequality, as follows.

```
notequal(X,Y) :- X == Y, !, fail.
notequal(X,Y).
```

Another way of thinking of the above is that we take inequality to be true by default; it will be false only when we can prove equality.

To give another example, we could define femaleness as the negation of maleness, or vice versa

```
female(X) :- male(X), !, fail.
female(X).
```

Note that the whole effect is ruined if we change the order of the statements in a Prolog program of this kind. So the meaning of such a Prolog program depends on the order of the statements in it.

Another annoying feature of the cut is that it interferes with the capacity of a Prolog program to generate a list of substitutions which satisfy a given condition. This is because the

```
;
```

depends on backtracking, which may be inhibited. For example, the above program will not generate a list of females. It can only be used to test whether or not a known individual is female.

To make the example even more annoying, consider

```
female(X) :- male(X), !, fail.
female(X).
female(louise).
male(john).
```

If this program is given query
```
female(X).
```
it will incorrectly say no.

■

6.10 Simple Prolog problems

Problem 6.5 *Finish the family tree example, which is started above, containing information about real or imaginary people over a number of generations. Define at least ten predicates, and include at least thirty facts. As well as a program,* draw a family tree *for your community. This is a picture of the Herbrand universe for your program.*

Problem 6.6 *Assume we can define Prolog predicates*
   formula(X),   *imp*(X, Y, Z),   *and*   *neg*(X, Y),
which mean X is a formula of the Hilbert style system H, Z is $(X \rightarrow Y)$, *and Y is* $(\neg X)$, *respectively. Write Prolog rules defining predicates axiom*(X), *and theorem*(X), *meaning X is an axiom of H, and X is a theorem of H, respectively. Do you expect these definitions will work, and why or why not?*

Problem 6.7 * *The classification of animals tree which was given at the beginning of this book has classes of animals on the nodes, and the arrows were labelled with properties which were true of all the animals in the subtree below the arrow. Express the information in the tree in a Prolog program.*

The query

bagshaped(X).

should generate a list of all known classes of bagshaped animals, and also all known individual bagshaped animals. Make some extensions to the tree, and put these in your program.

■

6.11 Summary of chapter 6

A Prolog program is a compact way to represent information about a situation.

A predicate is a function whose codomain is the truth values. Prolog is concerned with representing logical relationships between predicates by rules and facts.

A fact is a single predicate expression.

A rule is an implication, written in the form

p :- q1, q2, ..., qn.

where p, q1, q2,..., qn are all predicate expressions. The rule

p :- q1,q2,..., qn.

means that p is true whenever all of q1,q2,..., qn are true.

From a procedural point of view, such a rule says that in order to find values which make p true, we should search for values which make q1, q2,..., qn true.

In order to create a Prolog program about a situation, do the following.

- Decide what are the important predicates.

- Arrange the predicates in a hierarchy of complexity.

- Define more complex predicates in terms of simpler ones, using rules.

- Enter facts about predicates which are as simple as possible. Put the facts at the top of the program.

When given a program and a query, Prolog computes as follows. It puts the program on the true side and the query on the false side of a semantic tableau. Prolog now tries to find a substitution which will lead to the tree being closed. (The substituted values must then make the query true.)

Prolog always works on the left most open branch. Prolog takes as goal the predicate expression on the frontier of the false side of this left most open branch. Suppose this is *G*. Prolog goes through the program line by line, starting at the top, trying to find a unifying substitution between *G* and either a fact or the left hand side of a rule.

If a fact is found, Prolog closes the branch by adopting the most general unifying substitution α. α is then applied to the whole false side of the tree and Prolog continues with its next goal.

In case Prolog unifies its goal *G* with *H*, the left hand side of a rule

H :- Q1,..., Qk

Prolog splits the branch with goal G into branches labelled with Q1,..., Qk, the predicate expressions on the right hand side of the rule. The most general unifier α is found between G and H, and α is then applied to the whole false side of the tree.

If some goal is impossible to match, Prolog backtracks to the last match which was done previously and tries to redo this by finding a match lower in the program.

If the tree eventually becomes closed, Prolog says

yes

and returns the final substitution for the variables in the query.

If the process terminates with an open branch, Prolog says

no.

This means that Prolog has not been able to find a substitution for the variables in the query which make it a logical consequence of the program.

Chapter 7

Using function symbols and lists in Prolog

So far our terms in Prolog have only been constants and variables. There have not been any function symbols. The Herbrand universes of the programs we have considered so far have all been finite, having just one object for each constant used. By looking at the finite Herbrand universes, we have been able to have a very clear idea of what Prolog ought to do. The situation changes dramatically as soon as function symbols or lists are introduced. As soon as the set of terms is increased in this way, all the minimal models become infinite and at least as complicated as the natural numbers. Also the expressive power of Prolog increases correspondingly.

7.1 Lists, member(X,Y), append(X,Y,Z)

A list is a type of data structure. It is supposed to represent a set whose elements are arranged in some order.

We assume that there is such a thing as the empty list. This is denoted by [ ]. [ ] is a peculiar object but it is evidently necessary.

We can now give a recursive definition of a finite list.

Basis: [ ] is a finite list

Recursive step: A non-empty finite list L consists of an object called the head of L together with a arrow to another finite list called the tail of L.

Nothing will be called a finite list unless it is so as a consequence of the above two statements.

In Prolog all lists are finite.

In Prolog a list is written as a finite sequence of terms

$$[t_1, t_2, ..., t_n]$$

separated by commas and proceeded by a [and followed by a].

The terms $t_1, t_2, ..., t_n$ in list $[t_1, t_2, ..., t_n]$ are called the components of the list. The components of a list may also be lists.

Examples of lists

[a,b,c] is a list with three components.

[[cat,X],Y] is a list with two components. The first component is also a list.

[[the, quick, brown, fox], [jumped], [over, the, lazy, dog]] is a list with three components.

The *head* of a list $[t_1, t_2, ..., t_n]$ is the first component, t_1. The *tail* is the rest of the list, $[t_2, t_3, ..., t_n]$.

We use $[X \mid Y]$ to denote the list with head X and tail Y.

$[X \mid Y]$

is usually read as "X cons Y".

More examples

[a,b,c,d] has head a and tail [b,c,d].

[[a,a],[b,c],d] had head [a,a] and tail [[b,c],d].

[a | [b,c]] = [a,b,c]

[cat,cow,pig] = [cat | [cow,pig]] = [cat | [cow | [pig]]] = [cat | [cow | [pig | [ ]]]].

Prolog represents lists internally as built up from the cons operation.

[p, imp, [q, imp, p]] is a list with three components. It is not the same list as [[q,imp,p], imp, p], i.e. order is important in lists. A list may also have repeated components. So [a,a,b] is not the same as [a,b].

Predicates involving lists are usually defined by recursion. For example,

---

samelength([ ], [ ]).

samelength([X | List1], [Y | List2]) :-samelength(List1,List2).

First the predicate is defined in the simplest case, when both lists are empty. Then if we are given two lists, neither of which is empty, we chop off their heads, and compare the lengths of the tails.

Most versions of Prolog have built-in predicates

member(X,Y)

and

append(X,Y,Z).

The predicate member(X,Y) is true if and only if Y is a list and X is a component of Y. If our Prolog does not have member(X,Y) already defined, we can define it as follows:

---

member(X, [X | Z]).

member(X, [W | Z]) :- member(X,Z).

The idea here is: X is a member of Y if X is the first component of Y. Otherwise check to see if X is a member of the tail of Y.

The predicate append(X,Y,Z) is true if X, Y, and Z are all lists, and the list Z is obtained by appending list Y to list X.

We could give a recursive definition. The idea here is first to think of the simplest possible case: append(X,Y,Z) is true if X is empty and Y and Z are the same. We then express a more complicated case in terms of simpler cases. Suppose X is not empty, but the head of X is the same as the head of Z. We chop off these two heads and continue recursively.

---

append([ ], Y, Y).
append([X | Y], Z, [X | W]) :- append (Y,Z,W).

Exercise. Try to see what Prolog actually does when given a question such as:
append([cat],[dog,horse],[cat,dog,horse]).

7.2 General terms in Prolog

Define a *function name* in Prolog to be a string of characters starting with a lower case letter. We can now give a complete recursive definition of terms in Prolog.

1) A constant or a variable is a term.
2) If f is a function name, and $t_1, ..., t_n$ are terms, then $f(t_1, ..., t_n)$ is a term.
3) [ ] is a list.
4) If T_1 is a term and T_2 is a list, then $[T_1 \mid T_2]$ is a list.
5) If $T_1, ..., T_n$ are terms, then $[T_1, ..., T_2]$ is a list.
6) Every list is also a term.

Every term has a corresponding parse tree.

7.3 Unification revisited

The definitions of substitution, unifier, and most general unifier are verbally just the same as before but the ideas are more complicated, since the notion of term has been extended.

A substitution, α, can be written in the form

$$\alpha = \{(X_1, S_1), ..., (X_n, S_n)\}$$

where $X_1, ..., X_n$ are variables and $S_1, ..., S_n$ are terms.

If T is a term and α is a substitution, written as above, then T_α is the term obtained from T by simultaneously replacing each variable X_i by the corresponding term S_i, for $i = 1, ..., n$, according to α.

A *unifier* of two terms, T and S, is a substitution, α, so that $T_\alpha = S_\alpha$. A most general unifier of two terms T and S is a substitution α which is a unifier, and which also has the property that any other unifier β can be obtained from α by a further substitution. That is, if $T_\beta = S_\beta$, then there must exist a substitution γ so that

$$(T_\alpha)_\gamma = T_\beta$$

and

$$(S_\alpha)_\gamma = S_\beta$$

A good intuitive way to begin to understand the most general unifier of two terms is by thinking of the parse trees. To get a most general unifier of two terms, say t_1 and t_2, you superimpose the two parse trees, and then make the minimum substitution to make the two trees equal. Of course if the two parse trees can't be superimposed without conflict, the two terms have no unifier.

Example 7.1 *Suppose we wish to unify*

$$f(X, g(U, h(U, s), U))$$

and

$$f(g(U, V, s), g(W, Y, t))$$

We see that X must be the same as $g(U, V, s)$, and $g(U, h(U, s), U)$ must be the same as $g(W, Y, t)$. Thus W and U must be the same, and Y must be $h(U, s)$, and U must be t. So we end up with

$$\alpha = \{(U, t), (Y, h(t, s)), (W, t), (X, g(t, V, s))\}$$

Example 7.2 *Prolog internally represents lists as built up using the [X | Y] notation. Thus Prolog will unify [X | Y] with [one, two, three] to get most general unifier $\{(X, one), (Y, [two, three])\}$*

7.3.1 More about substitution

Before discussing the unification algorithm in detail, we need to think about composition of substitutions.

Let α and β be substitutions, and let T be any term. We have defined T_α and T_β.

Suppose we first apply α to T to obtain T_α and then apply β to T_α. The result will be $(T_\alpha)_\beta$.

Is $(T_\alpha)_\beta$ obtained from T by some substitution, say γ, and if so, how can we find γ?

Theorem *Suppose*

$$\alpha = \{(X_1, S_1), ..., (X_n, S_n)\}$$
$$\beta = \{(Y_1, A_1), ..., (Y_j, A_j), (Z_1, B_1), ..., (Z_k, B_k)\}$$

where $\{Z_1, ..., Z_k\} \subseteq \{X_1, ..., X_n\}$ and $\{Y_1, ..., Y_j\} \cap \{X_1, ..., X_n\}$ is empty. Then $(T_\alpha)_\beta = T_\gamma$, where

$$\gamma = \{(X_1, (S_1)_\beta), ..., (X_n, (S_n)_\beta), (Y_1, A_1), ..., (Y_j, A_j)\}$$

Problem 7.1 * *Prove the above theorem in the simplest case, that is, when T is a variable show that $(T_\alpha)_\beta = T_\gamma$.*

Problem 7.2 * *Finish the proof of the theorem above, using induction on the complexity of the term T.*

We may consider a substitution as a function whose domain and codomain is the terms. We will write α followed by β as $\alpha \circ \beta$, and this will be called the *composition* of β and α. So we have

$$(T_\alpha)_\beta = T_\gamma, \text{ where } \gamma = \alpha \circ \beta.$$

Warning: we are writing composition here in such a way as to be consistent with the order of application. So $\alpha \circ \beta$ means first do α and then do β. Many authors write this the other way around. That is because many functions are written in prefix form. However we are writing substitution in postfix form. As an experiment to see what happens when you use a confusing notation, try writing a proof of the correctness of the unification algorithm with the composition notation in the conventional order. This should convince you that, at least in this case, composition should be written in order of application.

Problem 7.3 *Let α_0 be the empty substitution.*

$\alpha_0 = \{\}$.

Show that for any substitution β,

$\alpha_0 \circ \beta = \beta \circ \alpha_0 = \beta$

Problem 7.4 * *Show that if α, β, γ are substitutions, then*

$\alpha \circ (\beta \circ \gamma) = (\alpha \circ \beta) \circ \gamma$

Problem 7.5 *Show that in general*

$\alpha \circ \beta \neq \beta \circ \alpha$

Problem 7.6 * *We will say that a substitution α is* idempotent *if $\alpha \circ \alpha = \alpha$. Give a simple condition which implies idempotence.*

Problem 7.7 *Show that if any two terms have a unifier they have an idempotent unifier.*

7.3.2 The unification algorithm

This will apply to two lists of terms $(S_1, ..., S_n)$ and $(T_1, ..., T_m)$. The algorithm will either produce a most general unifier of these two lists, or it will fail. It should fail if and only if no unifier is possible.

The algorithm will be described recursively.

Basis This is a collection of simple cases. To begin with,

$unify((S_1, ..., S_n), (T_1, ..., T_m)) = fail$

if $n \neq m$. Another easy case occurs when $(S_1, ..., S_n)$ and $(T_1, ... T_m)$ are already equal. In this case no unifier is necessary. We let

$unify((S_1, ..., S_n), (T_1, ..., T_m)) = \{\}$, the empty substitution.

Another simple case occurs when $n = m = 1$, and one of S_1 or T_1 is a variable, say X. This case is symmetric in S_1 and T_1. So without loss of generality, assume $S_1 = X$. We have already dealt with the earlier simple cases, so we can assume that T_1 is not X.

We check to see if X occurs inside T_1. If it does than no unification is possible, since, for any substitution α, $(S_1)_\alpha$ is strictly smaller than $(T_1)_\alpha$. In this case, $unify((S_1), (T_1)) = fail$.

The other possibility is that X does not occur in T_1. In this case

$unify((S_1), (T_1)) = \{(X, T_1)\}$.

Recursive step There are several cases in the recursive step. First suppose that $n = m$ and n and m are greater than one.

We are trying to unify

$$(S_1, ..., S_n)$$

and

$$(T_1, ..., T_n)$$

We first find $unify((S_1), (T_1))$. If this fails, then $unify((S_1, ..., S_n), (T_1, ..., T_n))$ also fails. Suppose, however, that unification of S_1 and T_1 succeeds, with most general unifier α. Thus $(S_1)\alpha = (T_1)\alpha$.

We apply α to the rest of the list and continue recursively. That is, we find

$$unify((S_2, ..., S_n)\alpha, (T_2, ..., T_n)\alpha)$$

If this fails, we return $unify = fail$. If this succeeds with most general unifier β, then

$$unify((S_1, ..., S_n), (T_1, ..., T_n)) = \alpha \circ \beta,$$

the composition of β and α.

Finally, suppose $n = m = 1$. In this case, we want to unify S_1 and T_1. We can suppose that neither is a variable, since this case was dealt with earlier. If one of them is a constant, then $unify = fail$. So suppose that neither is a constant.

It must happen that both S_1 and T_1 are compound terms obtained by application of a function symbol to argument lists.

$$S_1 = f(A_1, ..., A_j)$$
$$T_1 = g(B_1, ..., B_k)$$

If f and g are not the same, then unification fails, and we return $unify = fail$. If f and g are the same, then we call the unification algorithm recursively on the argument lists. That is,

$$unify((S_1), (T_1)) = unify((A_1, ..., A_j), (B_1, ..., B_k))$$

$\square$

It is claimed that:

Theorem

1) The unification algorithm, as given above, always eventually terminates.

2) If the algorithm terminates with a unifier this unifier is a most general unifier.

3) If the algorithm terminates and tells us that there is no unifier, then there is no unifier.

It is not *obvious* that any of these claims are true. The reader is invited to try the algorithm on a few cases to see if it works. This may or may not inspire confidence.

Exercise. Try to prove the first claim above, that the algorithm terminates, using the fact that every time a substitution is applied the number of distinct variables in the problem decreases by one.

Please stop to think about this.

If you attempted the above exercise carefully, you will see that there is a difficulty.

When we try to unify $(S_1, ..., S_n)$ and $(T_1, ..., T_n)$, we begin by trying to unify S_1 and T_1. But this may not reduce the number of variables, although it has reduced the size of the problem. The same remark applies to the next recursive call.

So we have: each recursive call either reduces the number of variables in the problem or reduces the size of the problem, where size is measured by counting the number of symbols in the input.

If we keep making recursive calls, the number of variables must eventually be reduced, since each call which does not reduce the number of variables decreases the size and the sizes are well ordered.

In order to finish the correctness proof we can reason as follows.

We use proof by contradiction.

Suppose the algorithm were incorrect in some cases. Then there would exist a minimal number d so that the algorithm is incorrect for some problem with d distinct variables. (Since we say that d is minimal, it follows that the algorithm is correct for problems with less than d distinct variables.) Among problems with d distinct variables, there must be some problem with minimal length, say k, on which the algorithm is incorrect.

Now consider a problem

$$unify((S_1, ..., S_n), (T_1, ..., T_m))$$

on which the algorithm is incorrect, and which has only d distinct variables, and minimal length k. This is, so to speak, a counterexample to correctness of minimal complexity.

Now apply the algorithm to this problem. By assumption, the result is incorrect. So none of the base cases can apply. Thus $n = m$. The $n = 1$ case is also not possible.

Suppose $n > 1$.

The problem $unify((S_1), (T_1))$ is simpler than our minimal problem. So the algorithm must be correct on this subproblem. Suppose it produces a most general unifier, α. The next recursive call is

$$unify((S_2, ..., S_n)\alpha, (T_2, ... T_n)\alpha)$$

which has less than d variables. So the algorithm is again correct on this subproblem. Suppose we get most general unifier β.

$\alpha \circ \beta$ is certainly a unifier for $(S_1, ..., S_n)$ and $(T_1, ..., T_n)$.

Is $\alpha \circ \beta$ a most general unifier for $(S_1, ..., S_n)$, and $(T_1, ..., T_n)$? If so, we have a contradiction. (And should therefore be pleased.)

The proof now turns on the following.

Suppose ϵ is any other unifier. We have $(S_1)_\epsilon = (T_1)_\epsilon$. We know that α was a most general unifier for S_1 and T_1. Thus there must exist a substitution γ_1 so that $\epsilon = \alpha \circ \gamma_1$. We have

$$(S_2, ..., S_n)_\epsilon = (T_2, ..., T_n)_\epsilon = (S_2, ..., S_n)_{\alpha \circ \gamma_1} =$$
$$(T_2, ..., T_n)_{\alpha \circ \gamma_1} = ((S_2, ..., S_n)\alpha)_{\gamma_1} = ((T_2, ..., T_n)\alpha)_{\gamma_1}.$$

Of course β is a most general unifier for $(S_2, ..., S_n)\alpha$ and $(T_2, ..., T_n)\alpha$. So there must be a substitution γ_2 so that $\gamma_1 = \beta \circ \gamma_2$. It follows that $\epsilon = \alpha \circ \beta \circ \gamma_2$, as required. We have demonstrated that $\alpha \circ \beta$ is a most general unifier.

We have a contradiction. Thus the algorithm is correct in all cases.

$\square$

7.4 Sorting

Prolog has built-in predicates $X = < Y$ and $X < Y$ which have the usual meaning as applied to numbers. We will say a list of numbers is monotone non-decreasing if every number in the list is less than or equal to the next number, if any, in the list. We can define this as follows:

---

mnd([X]).
mnd([X | [Y | Z]]) :- X =< Y, mnd([Y | Z]).

There is an algorithm called bubble sort, which takes a list, X, of numbers and rearranges it to get a monotone non-decreasing list, Y. If the first list, X, is already monotone non-decreasing, then bubble sort does nothing and Y is the same as X. On the other hand, if X is not already monotone non-decreasing, bubble sort finds a pair of numbers in X which is out of order, swaps them to get list Z and then applies bubble sort recursively to Z.

Problem 7.8 *Let* $bubble(X, Y)$ *mean that* X *is a list of numbers and* Y *is a monotone non-decreasing list which is obtained from* X *by bubble sort.*

  Define $bubble(X, Y)$ *in Prolog without using the cut or negation. (Hint: if a list* X *is not in order, there is an adjacent pair of numbers in the list which is out of order.)*

  If you give it a specific list X, *and leave* Y *as a variable, it should return a sorted list. For example*

  $bubble([3, 5, 4], Y)$

should get the response $Y = [3, 4, 5]$.

This example shows how an algorithm, such as bubble sort, can be expressed in a declarative style. However it should be clear that a solution to the above problem actually relies on knowledge of how Prolog behaves. So the distinction between procedural and imperative styles tends to break down when examined.

  A solution to the above problem may look like a list of axioms for the predicate $bubble(X, Y)$, but it is also a detailed specification of Prolog's behaviour.

7.5 Equivalence relations; and how to find your way out of a labyrinth

A labyrinth is defined by a data structure with finitely many nodes and finitely many arrows. We will say that if an arrow goes from node X to node Y then it is possible to go either from X to Y or from Y to X in one step.

  The labyrinth problem is to decide, given two nodes Z and W, whether or not there is a path from Z to W, and if there is such a path to find it.

  A slightly harder problem we will call the labyrinth problem with monsters. In this case we are given a labyrinth, and a subset A of nodes which we wish to avoid.

The problem is, given two nodes, to decide whether or not there is a path from one to the other which does not go through any node in the subset A.

Both these problems are extremely ancient. The main difficulty is that although the labyrinth is finite, it seems possible that in the search for a path we might go around in circles forever.

In the following, we will make a series of attempts to solve this problem. None of the proposed solutions are correct, except possibly the last one. This section traces the evolution of a process of development of a solution to this problem. To fix ideas, we will work on the following example. Write down the letters of the alphabet in lower case, from a to z. Put an arrow from one letter to another if there is a word starting with the first letter and ending with the second in this paragraph. So, for example, there is an arrow from i to n because of the word "In", and an arrow from t to e because of the word "the", and an arrow from f to g because of "following", and an arrow from w to e because of "we", and an arrow from w to l because of "will", etc.

7.5.1 First attempt

To begin with, we will represent the immediate connections by a list of facts. This is:

```
c(i,n).
c(t,e).
c(f,g).
c(w,e).
c(w,l).
etc.
```

A binary relation on a domain D is the same as a predicate of arity 2 defined over D.

An *equivalence relation* on a domain D is a binary relation $r(X, Y)$, defined over D so that the statements

1) r is reflexive, i.e.

$r(X, X)$

2) r is symmetric, i.e.

$r(X, Y) \rightarrow r(Y, X)$

3) r is transitive, i.e.

$(r(X, Y) \wedge r(Y, Z)) \rightarrow r(X, Z)$

are true over D. This means that these statements are true for all possible values of the variables X and Y in D.

There is a path from a node X to another node Y if and only if we can prove $r(X, Y)$ from the axioms for an equivalence relation, and

$(\forall X)(\forall Y)(c(X, Y) \rightarrow r(X, Y))$

and the above list of facts. Therefore we might try to solve the labyrinth problem with the following program.

---
facts as above
r(X,X).
r(X,Y) :- r(Y,X).
r(X,Z) :- r(X,Y), r(Y,Z).
r(X,Y) :- c(X,Y).

However this will certainly not work in Prolog.

Prolog, given these axioms and a few facts, will just go into an infinite loop. For example, trying to decide r(a,b), Prolog might choose the second of the two rules, and take as subgoal r(b,a); in trying to satisfy this, it might again use the second rule, and find r(a,b) as a subsubgoal, etc.

The fact that Prolog falls on its face when given one of the simplest axiom systems in mathematics shows that Prolog does not fulfil its ideal of directly representing logic. On the other hand, the fact that Prolog gets mixed up here can also be seen as a criticism of the usual way of doing mathematics. The standard definition does not really give us an effective definition of an equivalence relation.

Although the first attempt does not work, it seems that we have learned something.

7.5.2 Second attempt

We have a problem with saying directly that r(X,Y) is symmetric. It would not have been necessary to say that r(X,Y) was symmetric if all the arrows originally went in both directions. If that were true, then r(X,Y) would turn out to be symmetric, since it is defined symmetrically from c(X,Y).

So we could avoid having to say that r(X,Y) is symmetric just by putting all the arrows in twice. A better solution is just to say that r(X,Y) is to be true if either c(X,Y) is true or c(Y,X) is true.

So we get the following:

---
facts as above
r(X,X).
r(X,Z) :- r(X,Y), r(Y,Z).
r(X,Y) :- c(X,Y).
r(X,Y) :- c(Y,X).

Problem 7.9 *Why does this not work?*

7.5.3 Third attempt

It seems we should put the recursive step last. So we get

---

facts as above
r(X,Y) :- c(X,Y).
r(X,Y) :- c(Y,X).
r(X,X).
r(X,Z) :- r(X,Y), r(Y,Z).

This is an improvement. It sometimes works and sometimes does not work.

Problem 7.10 *Give an example in which the above program does not work.*

7.5.4 Fourth attempt

It seems that we need to keep track of the path and avoid going in loops. We can use a variable
  Route
to be the path of intermediate steps between the start and the finish.
  The predicate
  path(X,Y,Route)
will mean that Route is a path of intermediate steps which goes from X to Y.
  Take out the recursive step in the program above, and replace it with:

---

path(X,Y,[ ]):- r(X,Y).
path(X,Y,[Z | Route]):- r(X,Z), nonmember(Z,Route),
                          path(Z,Y,Route).
nonmember(X,R) :- member(X,R), !, fail.
nonmember(X,R).

Problem 7.11 *What does the above program do?*

Problem 7.12 *What happens if we change the definition of*
  nonmember(X,Y)
as follows.

---

nonmember(X,[ ]).]
nonmember(X, [Y | Z]) :- X \=Y, nonmember(X,Z).

7.5.5 Fifth attempt

Define

path(X, Z, Route, Avoid)

to mean that Route is a path of intermediate steps which goes from X to Z but avoids going through any element in the list Avoid.

The definition is:

---

path(X, Z, [ ], Avoid) :- r(X,Z).
path(X,Z, [A | B], Avoid) :- r(X,A), nonmember(A, Avoid),
path(A, Z, B, [A | Avoid]).
nonmember(X,Y) :- member(X,Y) , !, fail.
nonmember(X,Y).

Then to find a route, for example, from a to z, we ask:

path(a, z, Route, [ ]).

Prolog will give us the route if there is one, and will inform us if there is none.

Problem 7.13 *Do you believe the above claim? What would it mean to say that the path finding program was correct? Try to state this carefully. Note that if we ask*

path(a,z,Route,A)

the program will fall on its face. How does it fall on its face? The area to be avoided must be set initially to a constant. Once you have decided how to state correctness, try either to prove or disprove it.

Would you be worried if your life depended on the correctness of a four line program written by an expert?

Problem 7.14 *Find a route from the entrance to the exit of the labyrinth shown in figure 7.1.*

Problem 7.15 *Try moving the innocuous statement*

r(X,X).

around in the program. Try listing all possible paths from one point to another. On the basis of this, criticise the above program.

7.5.6 Sixth attempt

Please write this yourself. If you are happy with this, try to solve the labyrinth problem with monsters (above).

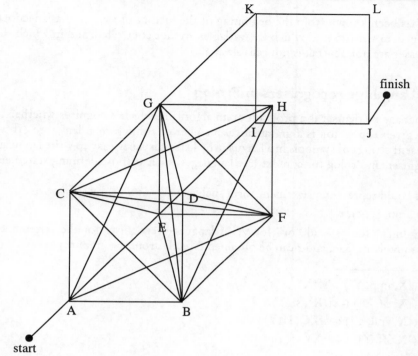

start

Figure 7.1

7.5.7 Testing and proof

The series of examples above is supposed to convince you that there can be short programs which look right to begin with but do not work. Also, there is no way to prove that a program is correct by testing it. All a test can do is reveal that a program is wrong.

Also it is quite possible for an experienced and conscientious person to believe that an incorrect program is correct.

When you write a program and believe that it is correct, that belief should contain at least a vague idea for a proof of correctness. It seems that the only way to make any progress with this situation is to work toward making these vague ideas about correctness more explicit. It is usually quite difficult even to state clearly what we mean by correctness.

Problem 7.16 *If you think the program above, which you wrote, is correct, try to say why it is correct. If you are not able to say why it is correct, but you think it is correct, can you offer any justification to support your assertion? Can you at least say what correctness would be in this case?*

It has been known from the beginning of the history of science that anecdotal evidence, in situations in which the variables are not controlled, and in which the witnesses are not neutral, is not reliable at all.

7.6 Language recognisers in Prolog

A language recogniser is a program or an algorithm which recognises whether or not a given expression is a grammatical member of some formal language. If we represent strings of symbols in a language by lists, it is fairly easy to write language recognisers in Prolog for context free languages, such as those defining statement forms.

We could represent a statement form such as $(p \rightarrow (q \lor r))$ by a list

[p, imp, [q, or, r]]

using "imp" for $\rightarrow$, and "or" for $\lor$. A language recogniser for the statement forms involving p, q, and r can be obtained directly from the grammar.

---

sf([X, imp, Y]) :- sf(X), sf(Y).
sf([X, or, Y]) :- sf(X), sf(Y).
sf([X, and, Y]) :- sf(X), sf(Y).
sf([X, iff, Y]) :- sf(X), sf(Y).
sf([neg, X]) :- sf(X).
sf(X) :- member(X, [p,q,r]).

The number of *proposition name*s can be increased just by adding to the list in the last line. If we really need infinitely many *proposition name*s, we could include

sf(X) :- atom(X).

using the built-in Prolog predicate atom(X), which will return true for any sequence of characters beginning with a lower case letter.

The above Prolog program will not only recognise grammatical statement forms in variables p, q, r, but it will also generate them. For example, if we ask a question

sf(X).

Prolog will find an X which is a statement form. Presumably it will say

yes. X=p.

If we say

;

we will get another grammatical statement form, presumably q, and if we continue to request more, we will get r, [p, imp, p], etc.

So this program appears both to generate and also to recognise statement forms.

Most context free languages can be dealt with in this way. (Some extra difficulty may occur when the grammar allows erasure of some grammatical symbols, i.e.

V := λ

or when the rewrite rules contain a loop.)

7.7 Kitchen table propositional theorem prover

We can also implement the semantic tableau method, as so far described, in Prolog.

In the following, A is supposed to be the set of statements in the true side of a semantic tableau, and D is supposed to be the set of statements on the false side. The predicate contra(A,D) means that if the construction is started with initial tableau (A,D), all branches will end in contradiction.

```
contra(A,D) :- member(X,A), member (X,D).
contra(A,D) :- remove(A,[neg,X ],A1),contra(A1,[X | D]).
contra(A,D) :- remove(D, [neg,X ],D1), contra([X | A],D1).
contra(A,D) :- remove(D, [X,imp,Y ],D1), contra([X | A ], [Y | D1]).
contra(A,D) :- remove(A, [ X,imp,Y ],A1), contra(A1,[X | D ],
                            contra( [Y | A1 ],D).
remove(List,Item,Shorterlist) :- append(A, [Item | B ],List),
                            append(A,B,Shorterlist).
```

The six lines of this program are supposed to correspond to the semantic tableau rules for negation and implication. You will need to add some more rules for other logical operators. To try to prove $(p \rightarrow p)$ you would query: contra([ ],[[p, imp ,p]]), and hope to get the answer yes. Since the semantic tableau system was sound and complete, this program is also a sound and complete formal system for the propositional calculus.

As it stands this kitchen table theorem prover does a lot of unnecessary backtracking. You may wish to add some cuts to speed things up. Another idea is arranging the statements so that the branching is done as late as possible. You may also want to use some write statements, to see what is happening.

Note that although Prolog is defined only using implication and conjunction in a very special form, we have obtained a complete theorem prover for the propositional calculus inside Prolog. In a sense this is a triumph. We have encapsulated almost everything we know about the propositional calculus in a few lines of code.

■

7.8 Problems

Problem 7.17 *What is the relation between the assertion and denial lists which occur in the theorem prover above, and the branches which occurred in the semantic tableau algorithm?*

Problem 7.18 *Explain what Prolog will do with*
contra([p],[[q,imp,p]]).

Problem 7.19 *Suppose the propositional theorem prover is given*
contra([],[[[p,imp,q],imp,[q,imp,r]]])
Following what Prolog is doing, find the first subgoal

contra(A,D)

which fails. This means that there are only variables left in the live part of the branch, and that the same variable does not occur on both sides. Check that this gives a counterexample. What does Prolog do next? Modify the code, using cuts, so that as soon as Prolog finds a counterexample, it stops the computation and prints the counterexample.

To get something printed on the screen, you can use the built-in

write(X)

which will write whatever term X is bound to. For example

write(A, 'are true')

will print the current list of assertions followed by the text "are true".

Problem 7.20 *Write a Prolog program which will check whether or not an expression represents a grammatically correct formula of L_N, the language of first order single sorted arithmetic. (Such a program is called a language recogniser.) Then translate the following statements into L_N, give them to your language recogniser, and see if you were correct, at least grammatically. If not, rewrite your translations, correcting the grammar. You can save yourself some time by telling your language recogniser to report errors as it finds them.*

a) X is prime.

b) X can be written as the sum of three squares in just one way.

c) Some linear combination of X and Y cannot be written as the sum of two squares unless Z is even.

d) X is congruent to Y modulo Z.

e) There are infinitely many prime numbers.

f) There are infinitely many prime numbers P such that P+2 is also prime.

g) There are only finitely many prime numbers P so that P+2 is also prime.

Problem 7.21 *Implement the propositional theorem prover which was described above, and apply it to formulae of L_N. As a result you should be able to prove all tautologies in L_N, a tautology being a formula obtained by substitution from a statement form tautology.*

Problem 7.22* *Invent some axioms, which seem correct to you, and add them to your theorem prover so that you can prove some statements which are true in the normal sense of the word about the natural numbers, but which are not tautologies. Try to make your theorem prover as good as you can, in a couple of hours of work.*

Try your theorem prover on f) and g) in the above list.

What does "true in the normal sense" mean in the above? Is everything which your theorem prover proves true in the normal sense? Do you think there are any statements which are true in the normal sense but which are not consequences of your theorem prover? Please think quite hard about this and explain your opinion, using common sense arguments. We will return to this later.

Problem 7.23 *Give a recursive definition of finite tree and translate this into Prolog.*

Problem 7.24 *Write a Prolog program which finds conjunctive normal form for a statement form, represented as a list. Use the rewriting method rather than the truth table method. cnf(X, Y) should be true if X is a list corresponding to a statement form* *and Y is obtained by applying a sequence of rewrite rules, according to some priority, starting with X, and Y is in conjunctive normal form. This problem is solved, in ML, in the book by Paulson (1992), in the references in chapter 13). Your program will probably not successfully test whether or not Y is a possible conjunctive normal form for X; however given X the program should compute Y which is one of the possible conjunctive normal forms for X.*

This problem convinces me that pure declarativeness should not be taken as an ideal feature of programming. The predicate

Y is a possible conjunctive normal form for X

is much harder to describe than the conjunctive normal form algorithm.

In general it quite often happens that the set of solutions to some problem is quite complicated, but a particular solution can be found relatively easily by performing a certain sequence of operations.

There is a saying that there are two types of mathematicians, Greek and Babylonian, Greek ones being concerned with finding essential relationships in reality, and Babylonian ones being concerned with calculations. In my opinion this is a false distinction; and attempting to make a sharp distinction between procedural and declarative programming is equally flawed.

■

7.9 Input and output in Prolog

When Prolog is running it will have at each instant a current input stream, which is initially from the keyboard, and a current output stream, which is initially the display.

We can switch streams as follows. Suppose X is instantiated to a filename. Then

tell(X)

switches the current output stream to X. The first time this goal occurs a new file with name X is created.

Similarly

see(X)

switches the current input stream to X.

Prolog has built-in predicates

write(X)

and

read(X)

which write to and read from the current input and output streams.

7.9.1 write(X)

If a variable X is instantiated to a term, then write(X) will succeed and cause the term to be printed on the current output stream. So, for example, the items in a list, L, would be printed one after another by expose(L)

with the following definition

---

expose([ ]).
expose([X | Y]) :- write(X), expose(Y).

In connection with this, there is another useful built-in predicate

nl

which means "new line" and has the effect that all succeeding output is printed on the next line.

Another built-in predicate is

tab(N)

which, when N is instantiated to a natural number, causes the cursor to move to the right by N spaces.

7.9.2 read(X)

The predicate

read(X)

will attempt to unify X with the next term that is input on the current input stream. The term must be followed by a full stop and a non-printing character, such as a space or a return.

7.9.3 Debugging and tracing

You can get a full running report of what Prolog is doing with the instruction

trace.

When this occurs as a goal the tracing facility is turned on. The result of this is that Prolog will write every goal which it attempts to satisfy, including subgoals, failures and backtracking. The trace can be turned off with

notrace.

The problem with trace is that such a large amount of information is reported. You may only wish to see what Prolog is doing in regard to certain goals. Suppose we are interested in a predicate

p(X,Y,Z)

with arity 3. We could ask for a report of attempts to satisfy goals involving this predicate with the instruction

spy(p/3)

and this can be turned off with

nospy(p/3).

In general the correct syntax for the spy argument is

predicate-name/arity.

So, for example, if we wanted to follow what Prolog was doing with append(X,Y,Z), we could use

spy(append/3).

7.9.4 *Assertions and retractions*

Suppose that in the middle of running Prolog we decide that we would like to add a new fact, say

   p(a,b).

to our program. We could of course stop, add the new fact and rerun Prolog. However it is also possible to add the fact immediately, as follows

   asserta(p(a,b)).

In general if X is a clause, we can add X to the beginning of the program with

   asserta(X).

A clause X can be added to the end of the program with

   assertz(X).

A clause X can be removed from the program with

   retract(X).

You can see what clauses are currently in the program with the query

   clause(Head,Tail).

7.10 Arithmetic in Prolog

Prolog has built-in all the usual binary predicates for inequality between integers:

   $X < Y$, $X =< Y$, $X > Y$, $X >= Y$.

Prolog also has built-in function symbols for some arithmetic operations:

   $X + Y$, $X - Y$, $X * Y$, X / Y, X mod Y.

There is also an assignment command in Prolog which sets a variable X to the value of an expression, E, which can be evaluated to give an integer or a real number. This is written

   X is E.

Thus

   X is $(1+2)*3$.

succeeds with X=9. Similarly

   $(2+3) < 4*5$.

succeeds, first evaluating $2+3$ and then evaluating $4*5$ and then comparing.

   Notice, however, that we need another version of equality, since, for example

   $4 = 2+2$.

will fail, since the response of Prolog to this will be to try to unify 4 and $2+2$, which is not possible. What we need is a binary predicate which evaluates two arithmetic expressions and then checks to see if the results are the same. This is written

   $X =:= Y$.

Example 7.3 *Suppose we want to define a predicate sum(X,Y) meaning that X is a natural number and Y is the sum of the natural numbers from 0 to X inclusive. This could be done as follows.*

```
sum(X,0):- X = < 0.
sum(X,Y) :- Z is X − 1, sum(Z,W),Y is W + X.
```

If we give this the query
sum(999,S).
we will get the answer S=999500. The program, given X, will find Y so that sum(X,Y) is true. However it will not work in reverse. So the program, given S=999500, will not find X so that sum(X,S). This is because when the program gets to line 2, it will try to evaluate X − 1 and fail since X is uninstantiated.

Example 7.4 *The following program finds the greatest common divisor K of two integers I and J.*

```
gcd(I,0,I).
gcd(I,J,K) :- R is I mod J, gcd(J,R,K).
```

As above this only works when I and J are instantiated.

Prolog has a built-in predicate
integer(X)
which succeeds if X is a whole number. If X is an expression, it is not evaluated inside this predicate. So integer(9) will succeed but integer (7+2) will fail. Also, if X is uninstantiated, integer(X) will fail. In particular the goal
integer(X).
will not result in Prolog's choosing an integer.

Suppose we wanted a predicate which would list the natural numbers. We could write this as follows.

```
natural(0).
natural(X):- X is Y+1, natural(Y).
```

7.11 Using terms for structures

We have said that complex terms can be built up by application of function names to lists of simpler terms.

For example, suppose we decide to use f as a binary function name and s as a unary function name. We can then write the term
f(s(X),f(Y,s(s(X))))
Such a term has a parse tree.

We may if we wish think of the term as a name for the corresponding parse tree. With this convention we can use terms to represent finite trees.

Consider, for example, the living things tree shown in figure 2.1. We could represent this in Prolog as a term

animals(protozoa, multicellular(porifera,
    neural(invertebrates, vertebrates)))

The labels on the arrows were ignored, and one of the nodes which did not have a name had to be given one.

We can still think of the function names as names of operators, but the operators act to combine together trees to produce other trees. In the above case

animals

is the name of a binary operator which combines

protozoa

and

multicellular(porifera, neural(invertebrates, vertebrates))

to produce

animals(protozoa, multicellular(porifera,
    neural(invertebrates, vertebrates)))

Problem 7.25 *It is said that the Martians have been using Prolog for as long as there have been Martians. Instead of basing computing on mathematics, and basing mathematics on logic and set theory, the Martians use Prolog as the foundation of mathematics. The key text in the foundation of Martian mathematics is the following program:*

```
whole(start).
whole(next(X)):- whole(X).
heap(X,start,X).
heap(X,next(Y),next(Z)):- heap(X,Y,Z).
cross(X,start,start).
cross(X,next(Y),Z):-cross(X,Y,W), heap(X,W,Z).
```

The Martians insist that all mathematics is contained in this short text.
  Can you explain what the program does and how it is related to human mathematics?

7.12 Declaring operators

Any atom in Prolog can be used as a function or operator symbol. If we don't say anything more about it, we can use it in prefix form. Suppose, for example, that we want to represent statement forms as terms in Prolog with the logical operators indicated by the function names. So, for example, we could use a term

and(p,q)

instead of the list [p,and,q] which we had before. In this way, we could write $(p \wedge (q \vee r))$ as and(p,or(q,r))

This prefix notation has some good features, but it is not what we are accustomed to. Therefore Prolog has a set of conventions for defining functions symbols with various formats.

A remarkably complex collection of understandings surrounds the use of operator symbols in ordinary language and mathematics. Consider, for example a symbol such as

$+$

A number of different arities may be associated with this symbol. It may have one argument, two arguments, or more than two arguments. Let's look at the two argument case. The usual convention is to write this function symbol in infix form, i.e. between its arguments.

There is still more to say about this symbol. It has relations of precedence with other function symbols. These relations of precedence allow us to write compound terms without all of the brackets which would otherwise be needed. When the lack of brackets gives us a choice we evaluate lower precedence operators before higher ones. For example, we would understand

$X + Y * Z$

to mean

$(X + (Y * Z))$

and we could express this by saying that $*$ comes before $+$ in the precedence ordering.

So far we have decided that a function symbol has associated with it a name, a format, and a precedence. We can specify function symbols with the built-in Prolog predicate,

op(Prec,Spec, Name)

The usual $+$ symbol has a built-in specification. This standard specification could be expressed using the op predicate as follows:

op(31,yfx,+)

On the other hand, multiplication could be specified by

op(21,yfx,*)

The precedence number of multiplication is less than the precedence number of addition to indicate that multiplication should be done before addition when possible.

The yfx specification says that the operator is written infix, and associates to the left. So, for example

$(X + Y + Z)$

is understood as

$((X + Y) + Z).$

We can now define statement forms as fairly natural looking terms. For example, we could decide that

and

should be a binary operator, to be written infix, and declare this by:

op(31,yfx,and)

Having said this, Prolog should understand

A and B and C

as ((A and B) and C).

Problem 7.26 * *Determine precedence for the logical operators: and, or, not, implies, iff. Declare them in Prolog.*
The unary operator, not, should be declared
op(Prec,fy,not)

We have not yet explained how the format specification works. We have seen several examples:

xfy for the infix binary operators +, *, and

fy for the prefix unary operator not.

The general rule is that a specification for a function symbol of arity n is a string of length $n + 1$, with one

f

in it to show the position of the operator name, and n other symbols, either x or y, to show the positions of the arguments. An x is used if the argument must have a strictly lower precedence class than the operator, and a y is used if the argument is allowed to have the same precedence class as the operator. So

not

is declared using

fy

since we want

not not a

to be acceptable syntax.

7.13 Another way of looking at lists

The only property of the cons operator [X | Y] which we have used is that

[X | Y] = [Z | W]

only if X = Z and Y = W.

This is not an uncommon property. In fact if we knew nothing about a function f except that it had two arguments, we could never prove f(X,Y) = f(Z,W) unless we knew X = Z and Y = W.

So if we did not have the list notation, we could just pick a function symbol at random and use it as the name of the cons operation. We could then define a membership predicate as before

```
memb(X,f(X,Y)).
memb(X,f(Z,W)) :- memb(X,W).
```

We could then represent a list [a,b,c] as f(a,f(b,f(c,[ ]))).

Everything which we can do with the ordinary list notation we can also do with this one.

7.14 Interpreters

Suppose you are dissatisfied with Prolog as it is and wish to modify it in some way. One way to do this is as follows.

It is possible to write a Prolog program, called an interpreter, which imitates what Prolog does. That is, the interpreter will consider a Prolog program as a piece of data, and then do to it whatever Prolog normally does. Once you have this working, you can try whatever modifications you wish. In this way you can get your own version of Prolog working inside the standard Prolog.

Some built-in Prolog predicates may be helpful here. There is a built-in Prolog predicate

```
clause(X,Y).
```

When this predicate is a goal, Prolog matches X and Y with left and right hand sides of existing clauses in the program.

There is also a built-in Prolog predicate

```
true
```

which always succeeds.

Interpreters are usually constructed by starting with the following:

```
solve(true):- !.
solve((Goal1,Goal2)):- !, solve(Goal1), solve(Goal2).
solve(Goal):-clause(Goal, Subgoals), solve(Subgoals).
```

The second line in the above uses the built-in Prolog comma

,

for conjunction. It says that to solve a conjunction of goals, you solve the first one and then continue with the others. The third line says that, to solve a goal, you try to match the goal with the left hand side of a clause in the program, and then you continue with the new goals given on the right hand side. If X matches a fact in the program, clause(X,Y) will succeed with Y=true. That is, facts are here considered to be rules with

```
true
```

on the right hand side.

You can construct alternative versions of logic programming by modification of the solve predicate defined above.

Problem 7.27 * *One of the problems we have with Prolog is that it ties itself into infinite loops by considering goals which are subgoals of themselves. In order to try to prevent this happening, we could keep a list of goals which have been considered so far, as follows.*

```
solve(true,History):- !.
solve((Goal1,Goal2)),History):- !, solve(Goal1,History),
                   solve(Goal2,History).
solve(Goal,History):-clause(Goal,Subgoals),
                   solve(Subgoals,[Goal | History]).
```

Modify the solve predicate so that it will stop trying to satisfy a goal which is already (without any unification) in its History list. It should happen that if you put

p:- p.

at the end of your program, and ask

solve(p,[ ]).

you should get the answer

no,

demonstrating that you have fixed part of one of Prolog's problems.

7.15 Typed Prolog

There are several logic programming languages which have attempted to improve on Prolog. A particularly interesting one is the Gödel system. See Hill and Lloyd (1994) in the references in chapter 13.

Prolog is a language with only one type. A variable in Prolog stands for some unspecified object, and the objects are understood to belong to one big domain in the Herbrand universe.

The Gödel language, on the other hand, has a multiplicity of types. There are constructors, such as, for example, lists, which produce new types from old ones. So if we had a type, integers, we might also have lists of integers, lists of lists of integers, lists of lists of lists of integers, lists of integers and lists of integers, and so on. In fact, as long as there is one constructor and one type to begin with, an infinite number of distinct types are generated. As in ML, such a typing system is both useful and also potentially cumbersome.

Another difference between the Gödel language and Prolog is that the former has abandoned the cut, but uses a related construction called *commit*. A virtue of the commit operation is that programs written with it have a meaning which is not entirely destroyed by changing the order of the statements in the program.

Gödel allows definitions with quantifiers. This implies that a full implementation of the language cannot be specified.

Gödel also continues to follow the extreme form of the declarative ideal, which is that the procedural part of a program should be automatically and unobtrusively derived from the declarative part. My opinion is that this is a serious mistake.

7.16 Summary of chapter 7

Lists in Prolog may be written as a sequence of terms, separated by commas and enclosed in square brackets.

[X | Y],

read as X cons Y is the list with head X and tail Y.

Predicates on lists are usually defined by recursion. An important example is append(X,Y,Z) which is defined by two rules

append([ ], X, X).
append([X | Y], Z, [X | W]) :- append(Y,Z,W).

Terms in Prolog include constants and variables and the set of terms is closed under formation of lists and application of function symbols.

Two terms A and B are unified by a substitution α if $A_\alpha = B_\alpha$.

A substitution α is a most general unifier of two terms A and B if

- α unifies A and B
- if β is any other unifier of A and B, there is a substitution δ so that $\alpha \circ \delta = \beta$.

We have an algorithm to find a most general unifier of any two terms. When Prolog matches a goal with a fact or the head of a rule, it does so by finding a most general unifier.

Using lists and recursion, we can write short programs in Prolog with very powerful computational behaviour. As an example of this, the semantic tableau algorithm is implemented in Prolog. We can also easily write recognisers for context free languages in Prolog.

On the other hand, there are many short programs in Prolog which look right at first but are badly flawed. There are also programs which may be correct but for which correctness is hard to prove.

It is pointed out that it is unscientific to claim that a program is somehow validated by reported correctness on some examples invented by the writer of the program.

Prolog programs using recursion and cuts should be viewed with especially sharp scepticism.

Chapter 8

Predicate calculus semantics

The predicate calculus is the study of the logical operators $\wedge$, $\vee$, $\neg$, $\rightarrow$, $\leftrightarrow$, $\forall$, $\exists$. The first five of these, $\wedge$, $\vee$, $\neg$, $\rightarrow$, $\leftrightarrow$ are called propositional operators, and the other two, $\forall$ and $\exists$, are called quantifiers.

Using the quantifiers we can continue the process which we started earlier of analysing the logical structure of texts in English.

The quantifiers, together with the propositional operators, give us a great deal of linguistic freedom. It seems that we can now say what we mean -- or at least we can get much closer than before.

We have learned how to define complex predicates in terms of simpler ones in Prolog. The results of this seem to me unsatisfactory and unnecessarily indirect and complicated. My opinion is that one of the difficulties with Prolog is that it has tried to do logic without using the full power of the quantifiers.

8.1 Predicates and quantifiers

Example 8.1 *Consider*

If wishes were horses then beggars would ride.

The best we could do with this previously, with the propositional operators only, was $(w \rightarrow r)$, *where w means that wishes are horses and r means that beggars will ride.*

If we now take apart "wishes are horses" looking for predicates, we see $wish(X)$ *and* $horse(X)$. *At this point there seems to be an ambiguity in the English. Does it mean that all wishes are horses, or only some wishes are horses? The* $\forall$ *symbol means "for all" so*

all wishes are horses

would be translated as

$(\forall X)(wish(X) \rightarrow horse(X))$

The $\exists$ *symbol means "there exists" so*

some wishes are horses

would translate as

$(\exists X)(wish(X) \wedge horse(X)).$

Similarly "beggars will ride" is ambiguous. It could be either

$(\forall X)(beggar(X) \rightarrow rides(X))$

or

$(\exists X)(beggar(X) \wedge rides(X)).$

Once we resolve the ambiguities in the English we get a result such as

$((\forall X)(wish(X) \rightarrow horse(X)) \rightarrow (\exists X)(beggar(X) \wedge rides(X)))$

which seems perfectly reasonable. Note that the meaning of this is not changed and the style is improved if we change one of the names of the quantified variables. For example

$((\forall X)(wish(X) \rightarrow horse(X)) \rightarrow (\exists Y)(beggar(Y) \wedge rides(Y)))$

Remark The forms used in the above example

$(\forall X)(A(X) \rightarrow B(X))$

and

$(\exists X)(A(X) \wedge B(X))$

occur very often in mathematics. By contrast,

$(\forall X)(A(X) \wedge B(X))$

is usually broken up into two independent statements, and

$(\exists X)(A(X) \rightarrow B(X))$

is something that hardly anyone ever wants to say.

Example 8.2 *Consider the following argument: "Esmerelda is a duck. Ducks like ponds. Therefore Esmerelda likes ponds." To start analysis of this we have to decide what the basic predicates are. We seem to have*

$duck(X), pond(Y), likes(X,Y)$

So we could translate "Esmerelda is a duck" as

$duck(Esmerelda)$

and "Ducks like ponds" as

$(\forall X)(\forall Y)((duck(X) \wedge pond(Y)) \rightarrow likes(X, Y))$

and "Esmerelda likes ponds " as

$(\forall Y)(pond(Y) \rightarrow likes(Esmeralda, Y))$

Note that we could also translate the second statement as

$(\neg(\exists Y)(pond(Y) \wedge (\neg likes(Esmeralda, Y))))$

Example 8.3 *Suppose we try: "There is only one bicycle in the village." We see that we have predicates bicycle(X), in-the-village(Y); but how do we say that there is only one of something? This is a situation which occurs very often in mathematics. We want to state existence and uniqueness of X such that bicycle(X) $\wedge$ in-the-village(X). Existence is easy since we have an existential quantifier*

$(\exists X)(bicycle(X) \wedge in\text{-}the\text{-}village(X))$

but how do we express uniqueness? This does not seem to be possible without introducing the equality predicate; or at least the usual solution of this problem in mathematics uses the equality predicate. We say, in effect, that any two objects which pass the test for being bicycles and also pass the test for being in the village must actually be the same:

$(\forall X)(\forall Y)((bicycle(X) \wedge in\text{-}the\text{-}village(X) \wedge$
$bicycle(Y) \wedge in\text{-}the\text{-}village(Y)) \rightarrow (X = Y))$

Problem 8.1 *This is along the lines of the previous example, but harder. Try to translate "All happy families are essentially the same, but each unhappy family is unhappy in its own particular way."*

Example 8.4 *Consider the following.*

"If α and β are morphisms and the codomain of α is the same as the domain of β there is a morphism $\gamma = \alpha \circ \beta$ so that the domain of γ is the same as the domain of α and the codomain of γ is the same as the codomain of β."

We first observe a predicate morphism(X). We seem also to have a function on morphisms, domain(X), and another function codomain(X). In addition to this, there is a function $\circ$ between morphisms. Having made these decisions, we get

$$(\forall X)(\forall Y)((morphism(X) \wedge morphism(Y) \wedge codomain(X)$$
$$= domain(Y)) \rightarrow ((morphism(X \circ Y) \wedge domain(X \circ Y)$$
$$= domain(X) \wedge codomain(X \circ Y) = codomain(Y)))$$

Example 8.5 *The variables in a Prolog program are always understood as being universally quantified. So, for example, in the program*

```
parent(a,b).
parent(c,b).
male(c).
father(X,Y):- parent(X,Y), male(X).
mother(X,Y) :- parent(X,Y), female(X).
```

---

the meaning of the two rules is

$$(\forall X)(\forall Y)((parent(X, Y) \wedge male(X)) \rightarrow father(X, Y))$$

and

$$(\forall X)(\forall Y)((parent(X, Y) \wedge female(X)) \rightarrow mother(X, Y))$$

On the other hand, queries to a Prolog program are understood as being existentially quantified. So, for example, the query

```
father(X,c).
```

should be understood as

$$(\exists X)father(X, c)$$

8.2 First order single sorted languages

As can be seen in the previous section, when we analyse the logical structure of a text in English, we decide what predicate symbols, function symbols and constants are needed to express the text. We then write the text using the logical operators in a language which has the predicate symbols, function symbols and constants we have chosen.

A first order single sorted language, L, is a language of the type described above, determined by a set of predicate symbols, a set of function symbols and a set of constants. The *terms* of such a language are all the expressions which can be obtained from variables and constants by repeated application of the function symbols. Terms are expressions which represent functions. The atomic formulae of such a language are expressions representing predicates which are obtained by one application of a predicate symbol to a list of terms. The formulae of such a language, L, are all expressions, representing predicates, obtained by combining atomic formulae with the logical operators $\neg, \rightarrow, \vee, \wedge, \leftrightarrow, \forall, \exists$.

A more detailed description of first order single sorted languages will be given below, after some examples.

The languages L_N, for first order single sorted arithmetic, and L_{ZF} for Zermelo-Fraenkel set theory, are typical first order single sorted languages. These languages were defined earlier.

Example 8.6 *$L_\leq$ is the first order single sorted language of partially ordered sets. The variables of this language are the same as in L_N and L_{ZF}. The terms are the same as the variables.* Atomic formulae *of this language are defined by:*

AtomicFormula := (**term** = **term**) | (**term** $\leq$ **term**)

and the formulae *are defined in terms of the* atomic formulae *as in L_N or L_{ZF}. So a typical formula of this first order language is*

$(\exists Z)((Z \leq X) \wedge (Z \leq Y))$

which is meant to say that X and Y have a lower bound.

■

Problem 8.2 *Try to say in $L_\leq$ that Z is the least upper bound of X and Y.*

■

Example 8.7 *L_G, the first order single sorted language of group theory, is defined as follows. The* formulae *of L_G are defined in the standard way from the atomic formulae. The* atomic formulae *are defined by*

Atomicformula := (**term** = **term**)

and the terms *are defined by*

term := (**term** $\circ$ **term**) | **term**$^{-1}$ | ι | variable

The term

ι

is a constant which is intended to represent the identity element in a group.

We have two function symbols in L_G,

$\circ$*, with arity 2, written in infix format, i.e. in between its arguments, (intended to stand for a group operation) and*

$^{-1}$*, with arity 1, written as a superscript in postfix format, i.e. after its argument (intended to stand for a group inverse).*

■

Problem 8.3 *If you know the axioms of group theory, try to write them in* L_G. ■

First order single sorted languages are so called because they have variables of just one type. For example, in L_N we only have variables for natural numbers, and we do not have variables for arbitrary sets of natural numbers. Languages with variables of several types are important, but we will not study them in this book.

We always use the same set of expressions for the *variables*, and we always define the *formulae* in the standard way from the *atomic formulae*. An *atomic formula* is a predicate symbol applied to a list of *terms* according to the format associated with the predicate symbol. A *term* is an arbitrarily complex expression which is built up from the function symbols, variables and constants of the language, using the formats which are associated with the function symbols.

Hopefully the patient reader will now be able to see that a *first order single sorted language* is something determined from a list of predicate symbols, a list of function symbols and a list of constants. We make a definition to note this.

Definition 8.1 *A signature,* Σ, *of a first order single sorted language is a list of lists of predicate symbols, a list of lists of function symbols, and a list of constants:*

$$\Sigma = \begin{cases} Predicate symbols : P_1, P_2, ... \\ Function symbols : F_1, F_2, ... \\ Constants : c_1, c_2, ... \end{cases}$$

In the list of predicate symbols, P_1 *is a list of predicate symbols of arity* 1, P_2 *is a list of predicate symbols of arity* 2, *and, in general, the* i^{th} *list consists of predicate symbols of arity* i.

In the list of function symbols, the first list, F_1, *is the list of function symbols of arity* 1, *the second list,* F_2, *is the list of function symbols of arity* 2, *and so on.*

Example 8.8 *The signature of* L_N *is*

$$\Sigma_N, = \begin{cases} Predicate symbols : [\,], [=] \\ Function symbols : ['], [+, *] \\ Constants : 0 \end{cases}$$

We assume the conventional formats for the equality predicate symbol, and for addition, multiplication and the successor. Note that we include the list of predicates of arity one, even though it is empty.

In general, if there is a common convention for the format of a predicate or function symbol, we will follow that convention. Otherwise we will use prefix format, that is, we will write the function or predicate name first and then the list of arguments enclosed in round brackets.

(If we find we want to define other formats, we can use the Prolog conventions which were discussed earlier.)

Because of the variety of formats, there is a slight difficulty with the notation in the following. Suppose F is a function symbol which has arity n and $t_1, ..., t_n$ are terms. We want some way of writing the new term which is obtained by applying F to this list of terms. If F used prefix format, we could write

$$F(t_1, ..., t_n)$$

but many commonly used function symbols do not have this format. The same minor difficulty occurs with predicate symbols, such as $=$.

We solve this, awkwardly, as follows. We assume that if we know a function symbol, F, we also know the correct format for writing it. If F has arity n, we will write

$$apply(F, t_1, ..., t_n)$$

to denote the correctly formatted way of writing the application of F to the list of arguments $t_1, ..., t_n$.

Suppose, now, that we are given a signature Σ.

$$\Sigma = \left\{ \begin{array}{l} Predicate symbols : P_1, P_2, ... \\ Function symbols : F_1, F_2, ... \\ Constants : c_1, c_2, ... \end{array} \right.$$

We will use L_Σ to denote the first order single sorted language with signature Σ.

1) The variables of L_Σ are the same as the variables of L_N.

2) The *terms* of L_Σ are defined by the following grammar

Term $:=$ *variable*

Term $:= c_j$, where c_j is a constant of Σ

termlist $:=$ **Term** | **Term**, **termlist**

Term $:= apply(f_j, \textbf{termlist})$, where f_j is a function symbol of Σ and the arity of f_j agrees with the length of **termlist**.

3) The *atomic formulae* of L_Σ are defined by

Atomic formula $:= apply(p_j, \textbf{termlist})$, where p_j is a predicate symbol of Σ, and the arity of p_j agrees with the length of **termlist**.

4) The *formulae* of L_Σ are defined in the standard way from the atomic formulae.

8.3 Free and bound variables

It often happens that a description of a predicate of arity n, with arguments $X_1, ..., X_n$ will use some other auxiliary variables, also called bound variables, which are not arguments of the final predicate. For example, we might say

For all Y and Z, if X divides $(Y * Z)$, then either X divides Y or X divides Z.

There are three variables in this statement. But it is really just a property of X which is being defined. The predicate described has arity one. Assuming that the domain we are talking about is the integers, we would say that the statement is true when $X = 2$. (We don't need to give values to Y and Z. In fact if you substitute constants for Y and Z in the statement above, it stops making sense.)

We will say that X is a free variable in the statement above, and that Y and Z are bound variables.

The distinction between free and bound variables in a statement is like the distinction between arguments and local variables in a function in a programming language, such as C.

Confusion between free and bound variables creates many problems, both in mathematics and in computing.

If you think about it, you will see that we really have to talk about a free or bound occurrence of a variable in a statement, rather than a free or bound variable. This is because the same variable may be used in two different ways in one statement. For example

$$Y = X + \int_0^T X^2 dX$$

is a predicate of arity three, with arguments Y, X, T. The first occurrence of X is free and the second two occurrences are bound. Most mathematicians would say that this statement is grammatically correct, but confusing, and that it ought to be rewritten in some way. We might change the bound variable name to S to avoid the appearance of conflict.

$$Y = X + \int_0^T S^2 dS$$

The meaning of this is the same, but the style is better.

In order to sharpen our wits about free and bound variables, we can give a precise definition in the context of first order single sorted languages, such as L_n and L_{ZF}.

Definition 8.2 *In an expression of the form* $(\forall \mathbf{X})$**wff** *or* $(\exists \mathbf{X})$**wff**, *the subexpression* **wff** *is called the* scope *of the quantifier.*

Definition 8.3 *An occurrence of a variable,* $\mathbf{X}$ *in a formula* **wff** *is* bound *if it occurs in* $(\forall \mathbf{X})$ *or* $(\exists \mathbf{X})$, *or in the scope of a quantifier* $(\forall \mathbf{X})$ *or* $(\exists X)$ *in* **wff**.

Definition 8.4 *An occurrence of a variable is* free *if it is not bound.*

Example $(\forall Z)((\exists W)((W + Z) = X) \rightarrow (\exists W1)((W1 + Z) = Y))$. In this formula, all occurrences of X and Y are free, and all other occurrences of other variables are bound. So this formula may express a predicate of arity two.

Definition 8.5 *A* sentence *is a formula with no free variables.*

Definition 8.6 *If* $F(\mathbf{X}_1, ..., \mathbf{X}_n)$ *is a formula with free variables* $\mathbf{X}_1, ..., \mathbf{X}_n$, *a* universal closure *of* $F(\mathbf{X}_1, ..., \mathbf{X}_n)$ *is* $(\forall \mathbf{X}_1)...(\forall \mathbf{X}_n)F(\mathbf{X}_1, ..., \mathbf{X}_n)$. *An* existential closure *of* $F(\mathbf{X}_1, ..., \mathbf{X}_n)$ *is* $(\exists \mathbf{X}_1)...(\exists \mathbf{X}_n)F(\mathbf{X}_1, ..., \mathbf{X}_n)$.

8.3.1 Translation of predicates

A lot of mathematics consists of translating between formal and informal representations of ideas. We can practice this technique with formal languages, such as L_N and L_{ZF}.

Example 8.9 *Consider:* $Z = X \cup Y$. *This is a predicate of arity three, and the domain is meant to be sets. To translate this into* L_{ZF}, *we have to think what this means in terms of set membership.*

$$(\forall W)((W \in Z) \leftrightarrow ((W \in X) \vee (W \in Y)))$$

Important: *When defining or translating a predicate of arity n, the defining statement must have n free variables. All other variables must be bound.*

It should be admitted that many people do not follow this excellent rule. Mathematicians often explain their ideas without telling their audience which are the free variables and which are the bound ones; they hope this is understood. Also some people like to leave off quantifiers from explanations, hoping that this will make the explanations look more friendly. Prolog routinely leaves off quantifiers, and sometimes considers variables free and at other times considers them bound. Suppose, for example, you want to define sister(X,Y) in Prolog. You might say

sister(X,Y) :- mother(Z,X), mother(Z,Y), X \ = Y, female(X), female(Y).

This means

$(\forall X)(\forall Y)(\forall Z)((\text{mother}(Z,X) \wedge \text{mother}(Z,Y) \wedge (\neg(X = Y)) \wedge \text{female}(X) \wedge \text{female}(Y)) \rightarrow \text{sister}(X,Y))$

which is true in the intended interpretation. So this expresses part of the truth that we want. But it should not be called a *definition* in my opinion. If it were a definition we could take any occurrence of sister(X,Y) and replace it with the right hand side of the rule without changing meaning. But this can't be so because the arities are wrong. (The right hand side depends on Z, to mention one difficulty. Suppose Z is Harry Truman. Then Z is not anybody's mother, so what happens to X and Y?) If we want a satisfactory definition, according to me, we need quantifiers. A satisfactory definition would be

$\text{female}(X) \wedge \text{female}(Y) \wedge (\neg(X = Y)) \wedge (\exists Z)(\text{mother}(Z,X) \wedge \text{mother}(Z,Y))$

Of course we cannot expect perfect correctness from Prolog, since it is trying to do without quantifiers in their full generality.

But now we have moved to the wider context of first order languages, and we do expect perfect correctness in this context.

Example 8.10 *"X is a square" is not correctly translated by:*
$((Y * Y) = X)$
since the arity of the first statement is one, and the arity of the second statement is two.

Example 8.11 *Let prime(X) mean that X is a prime natural number, i.e. X cannot be factored into two other natural numbers, unless one of them is 1. As a first attempt to translate this into L_N:*
$((Z * Y) = X) \rightarrow (Z = 0') \vee (Y = 0')$
This is semantically incorrect, since the arities are not the same. We have to quantify Z and Y. So we could try
$(\forall Z)(\forall Y)((Z * Y) = X) \rightarrow (Z = 0') \vee (Y = 0')$
Now at least the arities check. The intended meaning is probably correct. But the statement is syntactically wrong. It is not in fact part of L_N. The statement is also ambiguous. More brackets are needed to disambiguate it, and to make it syntactically correct.
$(\forall Z)(\forall Y)(((Z * Y) = X) \rightarrow ((Z = 0') \vee (Y = 0')))$
Note that there are many other ways of translating prime(X) into L_N. For example,
$(\neg(\exists Z)(\exists Y)(((Z * Y) = X) \wedge ((\neg(Z = 0')) \wedge (\neg(Y = 0')))))$
This is syntactically quite different, but more or less the same semantically. But we could have had:

$$(\forall Y)(\forall Z)(\forall W)(((W * X) = (Z * Y)) \rightarrow (\exists Q)(((Q * X) = Z(\vee(Q * X) = Y)))$$

That also means prime(X).

Try some of the problems now.

8.4 Interpretations

An interpretation of a first order single sorted language, L, is given by a set D called the domain of the interpretation, together with a list of lists of predicates over D interpreting the predicates of L, a list of lists of totally defined functions of several variables over D with values in D interpreting the function symbols of L, and a list of elements of D to interpret the constants of L. We will write

$$I = (D; \mathbf{P}_1, \mathbf{P}_2, ...; \mathbf{F}_1, \mathbf{F}_2, ...; \mathbf{c}_1, \mathbf{c}_2, ...)$$

to denote an interpretation, I, of a language with a signature

$$\Sigma = \begin{cases} \textit{Predicatesymbols} : P_1, P_2, ... \\ \textit{Functionsymbols} : F_1, F_2, ... \\ \textit{Constants} : c_1, c_2, ... \end{cases}$$

Note that the interpretations are supposed to be mathematical objects, whereas the signatures and languages are supposed to be syntactic objects.

In the above we are using bold typeface to denote objects in the interpretation and ordinary typeface to denote symbols in the signature. So, for example, c_1 is supposed to be the first constant symbol in the signature. Corresponding to this is an element of the domain of the interpretation, $\mathbf{c}_1$. Similarly, P_2 is a list of predicate symbols of arity 2. Interpreting this is a list $\mathbf{P}_2$ of predicates of arity 2 in the interpretation.

An interpretation I is also called a *structure*. Using the notation above, we would say that the structure I has domain D, predicates $\mathbf{P}_1, \mathbf{P}_2,...$ defined over D, functions $\mathbf{F}_1, \mathbf{F}_2, ...$ defined over D, and *distinguished individuals* $\mathbf{c}_1, \mathbf{c}_2, ...$ in D.

We said earlier that a *type* is a domain together with an associated list of functions. The predicates in a structure are, of course, functions with codomain the truth values. The distinguished individuals may also be regarded as functions of arity zero. So an interpretation of a first order language is a special case of a type. The concept of type is, however, much broader than this. Any set, together with any list of functions may be regarded as a type.

Example 8.12 *The intended interpretation of L_N is the natural numbers with the usual equality, the usual addition, multiplication and successor, and the usual zero:*

$$\mathcal{N} = (\mathbf{N}; [\ ], [\mathbf{equality}]; [\mathbf{successor}], [\mathbf{addition}, \mathbf{multiplication}]; \mathbf{zero})$$

where **successor** *means the function, defined on the natural numbers, which takes x to $x + 1$, and* **addition** *and* **multiplication** *are the usual functions from N^2 to N, and* zero *is the usual 0.*

This is also called the standard interpretation *of L_N.*

Example 8.13 *In the previous example, if we changed the domain to $\mathbf{Z}$, the integers, and kept the other predicates and functions as usual, we would get another interpretation of L_N. Another possibility would be interpret $+$ as the usual multiplication, and $*$ as the usual addition, keep equality as usual, and interpret 0 as the usual 1.*

Example 8.14 *Another non-standard interpretation of L_N would be*

$$Z_p = (Z/pZ; [\ ], [=]; [addone(X)], [\oplus, \otimes]; 0)$$

where $Z/_pZ$ means the integers modulo p, and p is some prime number, and $\oplus$ and $\otimes$ mean addition and multiplication modulo p, and $addone(X)$ is the operation of adding one modulo p, and 0 is the usual zero.

It should be clear from the above that an interpretation I of a first order single sorted language L need not be the same as the structure we imagined when we invented the language L. In order to be acceptable as an interpretation of a first order single sorted language a structure only needs to have some domain, a list of predicates defined on that domain with arities which match the signature of L, a list of functions somehow defined on the domain with arities which match the signature of L, and a list of distinguished individuals in the domain, and the three different lists in the structure and the signature have to be of the same length. Nothing else is assumed about an interpretation.

Even very well known predicate symbols, such as $=$, are not assumed to have their usual meanings in an interpretation. We do not want to impose any conditions on an interpretation, except those which are immediately implied by the form of the signature.

If we have some insistent ideas about how $=$ works, we intend to force ourselves to write these ideas out explicitly. Therefore we allow any structure of the right form to be considered as an interpretation of a first order single sorted language. Even if we believe we know what the language is *really supposed to mean*, we choose to ignore this for the time being. We hope in this way eventually to clarify our ideas.

Example 8.15 *Form a structure as follows.*

$$(\mathbf{N}[\eta]; [\ ], [=]; ['], [+, *]; 0)$$

The domain, $\mathbf{N}[\eta]$, consists of polynomials in variable η with natural number coefficients, i.e.

$$a_k\eta^k + a_{k-1}\eta^{k-1} + \dots + a_0$$

with k some natural number, and $a_0, \dots, a_k$ natural numbers.

Equality is defined to be the usual equality of polynomials, and addition, multiplication and successor are defined as usual.

This interpretation will be called $\mathbf{N}[\eta]$.

Problem 8.4 *Write a formula of L_N which means X is less than Y in the standard interpretation. What does this mean in $\mathbf{N}[\eta]$? What does it mean in Z_p?*

Example 8.16 *Let L_R be a first order single sorted language with one binary predicate symbol R, no constants and no function symbols. A typical sentence of L_R is:*

$$(\forall X)(\forall Y)(\exists Z)(R(X, Z) \wedge R(Y, Z))$$

In order to give an interpretation of this language we need to specify a domain, and to define a predicate $\mathbf{R}(X, Y)$ to interpret the predicate symbol R. The domain can be any finite or infinite set. If the domain is finite, we can specify the interpretation of the predicate symbol by a table.

We could for example take the domain $D = \{a, b, c\}$. The predicate $\mathbf{R}(X, Y)$ could be defined by the following table.

First argument	Second argument	Truth value
a	a	T
a	b	T
a	c	T
b	a	T
b	b	F
b	c	F
c	a	F
c	b	T
c	c	T

Then $I = (D; [\,], [\mathbf{R}]; ;)$ is an interpretation of L_R.

At this point, please look carefully at the sentence displayed above, which was said to be a typical sentence of L_R. On an intuitive level, we would expect that a sentence such as this would be either true or false in an interpretation, such as I. The sentence says something definite about I. In this case the interpretation I happens to be finite and we have displayed a table, which seems entirely to specify I. If we claim to understand the logical operators, we should be able to decide whether or not a sentence such as the one above is true in I. Try to do this. That is, look at the sentence and look at the table, and try to decide whether or not the sentence is true in this interpretation.

Let's assume you have done this. The question now is: how did you do it? If we say that a truth value is determined for a sentence by an interpretation, exactly how is this done?

We reject two possible answers immediately:
a) it is obvious;
b) it is an arcane process, which is unknowable and indescribable.

The problem of how truth values are determined in an interpretation is discussed in the next section.

Remark *We can extend L_R to $L_{R,=}$ by adding binary predicate symbol $=$ to the signature for L_R. If we interpret $=$ as genuine equality, we can extend our interpretation I of L_R to an interpretation $I*$ of the larger language $L_{R,=}$.*

$I* = (D; [\,], [\mathbf{R}, \mathbf{equality}]; ;)$

Note that $I*$ is also an interpretation of L_{ZF}, although the intended interpretation of L_{ZF} is nothing like this.

Example 8.17 *Let Σ be a finite alphabet of symbols, and let $\Sigma*$ be the set of finite strings of symbols from Σ. Let ι be the empty string. If X is a string, let X^{-1} be X written backwards. If X and Y are strings, let $X \circ Y$ be X followed by Y. Then*

$(\Sigma^*; [\,], [equality]; [X^{-1}], [\circ]; \iota)$

is an interpretation of L_G, the first order single sorted language of group theory.

8.5 Satisfaction, truth, logical validity

Let L be a first order single sorted language with signature

$$\Sigma = \left\{ \begin{array}{l} Predicate symbols : P_1, P_2, ... \\ Function symbols : F_1, F_2, ... \\ Constants : c_1, c_2, ... \end{array} \right.$$

and let

$$I = (D; \mathbf{P}_1, \mathbf{P}_2, ...; \mathbf{F}_1, \mathbf{F}_2, ...; \mathbf{c}_1, \mathbf{c}_2, ...)$$

be an interpretation of L.

Suppose we have a formula A of L, and we consider it according to interpretation I. That is, we interpret the function symbols in A as in I, and likewise the constants; and we interpret the predicate symbols according to the given predicates in I. Intuitively then, if A does not have any free variables it should turn out to be either true or false in this interpretation. If A does have some free variables the truth value of A should depend on what values in the domain these variables take.

This intuitive notion of truth is obviously fundamental in mathematics. Suppose we try to write down exactly what this means. This is done below. That is, we end up *defining* truth. This sounds more interesting than it is. The long definition below is somewhat irritating, as it does not seem to add anything to our understanding. (But this definition is not supposed to add anything. It is just supposed to express what we already know.)

Definition 8.7 *A valuation from interpretation I is a function which assigns a value in the domain D of I to some subset of the variables in our language.*

$$\sigma : Vset \rightarrow D$$

where $Vset \subseteq$ variables.

A valuation gives a value to some of the variables. We will say that a term is *covered* by a valuation if the domain of the valuation includes all the variables which occur in the term.

An interpretation tells us the meaning of the function symbols and the constants. This information allows us to evaluate any term of the language, given a valuation which covers the term.

Definition 8.8 *The value given to a term t in the interpretation by valuation σ which covers t will be written $eval(t, \sigma)$. This is defined recursively as follows.*

Basis: Suppose t is a constant c_j. We already have a value for this in the interpretation, $\mathbf{c}_j$. So we let $eval(c_j, \sigma) = \mathbf{c}_j$. The other simple case occurs when t is a variable, say $\mathbf{X}$. In this case we have a value defined from the valuation σ. We let $eval(\mathbf{X}, \sigma) = \sigma(\mathbf{X})$.

Recursive step: $eval(f_j(t_1, ..., t_n), \sigma) = \mathbf{f}_j(eval(t_1, \sigma), ..., eval(t_n, \sigma))$, for any function symbol f_j in the signature.

Of course, if t is a term which is not covered by valuation σ, we cannot expect to evaluate t using just this information and the interpretation. So $eval(t, \sigma)$ is undefined if σ does not cover t.

The predicate $Sat(A, I, \sigma)$, defined recursively below, is intended to say that formula A is true in interpretation I when the free variables of A are given values according to valuation σ.

For the sake of this definition define the complexity of a formula to be the number of logical operators which occur in it.

Definition 8.9 *Sat*(A, I, σ) *is a predicate defined when A is a formula of L, I is an interpretation of L, and σ is a valuation from I which covers all the free variables of A. Sat*(A, I, σ) *will be defined by recursion on the complexity of A.*

Basis: *This is the simplest case. Suppose A is an atomic formula. Then A is* $p_j(t_1, ..., t_n)$ *for some predicate symbol p_j in the signature, and some list of terms $t_1, ..., t_n$. The length n of the term list is the same as the arity of p_j. In the interpretation we have a predicate* $\mathbf{p_j}$ *to interpret this predicate symbol. Also we know how to evaluate the terms, using the values in σ and the functions given to us in the interpretation. We let* Sat$(p_j(t_1, ..., t_n), I, \sigma) = \mathbf{p_j}(eval(t_1, \sigma), ..., eval(t_n, \sigma))$.

Recursive step: *Here we wish to define the satisfaction predicate Sat*(A, I, σ) *for a complex formula A in terms of the satisfaction predicate for simpler formulae. We can suppose that A has some number, say k, of logical operators, and that we have already defined the satisfaction predicate for all formulae with less than k logical operators.*

There are two sections to this, the propositional section and the quantifier section.

Propositional section

In this section we use the truth table definitions of the propositional operators.

First suppose that our formula A is $(\neg B)$. *So B is simpler than A. We suppose we know what the satisfaction predicate does with B. So how do we define Sat*(A, I, σ)? *When is Sat*(A, I, σ) *true?*

We will say

Sat$((\neg B), I, \sigma) = T$ *if and only if* Sat$(B, I, \sigma) = F$.

That is,

$$Sat((\neg B), I, \sigma) = (\neg Sat(B, I, \sigma))$$

This makes sense because we have studied the semantics of the propositional calculus, and we can suppose now that we have agreed on and understand how the negation operator works.

We can continue in this way with the other propositional operators.

$$Sat((B \wedge C), I, \sigma) = (Sat(B, I, \sigma) \wedge Sat(C, I, \sigma))$$

In fact if op is any one of $\wedge, \vee, \rightarrow, \leftrightarrow$, we define

$$Sat((B op C), I, \sigma) = Sat(B, I, \sigma) op Sat C, I, \sigma).$$

Quantifier section

We assume at this point that we have a formula sitting in front of us which is in the form of a quantifier applied to a simpler formula. We suppose that we have defined, and understand, the satisfaction predicate as it applies to the simpler formula.

Let X be a variable. Here we need to define Sat$((\forall X)A, I, \sigma)$ *in terms of Sat*(A, I, σ_1) *for certain valuations σ_1. Suppose the free variables of $(\forall X)A$ are $Y_1, ... Y_k$. We suppose that σ covers these free variables. If σ_1 is another valuation, we will say that σ_1 agrees with σ on $Y_1, ..., Y_k$ if $\sigma(Y_1) = \sigma_1(Y_1)$ and ... and $\sigma(Y_k) = \sigma_1(Y_k)$.*

Sat$((\forall X)A, I, \sigma) = T$ *if and only if for all valuations σ_1 which cover the free variables of A and which agree with σ on the free variables $Y_1, ..., Y_k$ we have Sat*(A, I, σ_1).

$Sat(\exists \mathbf{X})A, I, \sigma) = T$ *if and only if there exists a valuation σ_1 which covers the free variables of A and which agrees with σ on the free variables $\mathbf{Y}_1, ..., \mathbf{Y}_k$ and is such that $Sat(A, I, \sigma_1)$.*

8.5.1 Central definitions of the predicate calculus

We are assuming that I is an interpretation of some first order single sorted language L, and that A is a formula of L and that v is a valuation from I which covers the free variables of A.

Note that $Sat(A, I, v)$ may depend on v if A has some free variables.

Definition 8.10 *if $Sat(A, I, v) = T$, we will say that formula A is true in interpretation I for valuation v. If this happens for all valuations which cover the free variables of A, i.e. if $Sat(A, I, v) = T$ for all valuations v which cover the free variables of A, we will say that A is true in interpretation I, and write*

$I \models A$

Definition 8.11 *If formula A is true for all interpretations, I, we will say that A is logically valid, and write*

$\models A$.

The notion of logical validity in the predicate calculus generalises the notion of tautology for the propositional calculus.

Definition 8.12 *Formulae A and B are logically equivalent if*

$\models (A \leftrightarrow B)$

If two formulae are logically equivalent, they *mean* the same. To show that two formulae are not logically equivalent, we must give an interpretation and a valuation which results in them having different truth values.

For example $(\forall X)(\exists Y)p(X, Y)$ is not logically equivalent to $(\exists Y)(\forall X)\,p(X, Y)$. To show this, interpret $p(X, Y)$ as equality in the natural numbers. Under this interpretation, one of the statements is true and the other is false. Usually if one formula is obtained from another by changing the order of the quantifiers, the two formulae are not logically equivalent.

Definition 8.13 *If Γ is a set of formulae and we can find an interpretation and a valuation which make all of Γ true we will say that Γ is satisfiable.*

Definition 8.14 *An interpretation M so that $M \models A$ for all formulae A in a set Γ will be said to be a* model *of Γ.*

Definition 8.15 *If Γ is a set of formulae, and A is a formula, we will say that A is a* logical consequence *of Γ if*

$M \models A$

for all models M of Γ.

We will write $\Gamma \models A$ to mean that A is a logical consequence of Γ.

For example mortal(Socrates) is a logical consequence of

human(Socrates)

and

$(\forall X)(\text{human}(X) \rightarrow \text{mortal}(X))$.

To give a less obvious example:

$(X = X)$

is a logical consequence of

$\Gamma = \{((X = Y) \rightarrow (Y = X)),$
$\qquad (((X = Y) \wedge (Y = Z)) \rightarrow (X = Z)),$
$\qquad (\exists Y)(X = Y)\}$

(You may have to think about this second example for a while to see that it is true. Recall that a model of Γ has to satisfy the universal closure of Γ.)

8.5.2 Aardvarks and spiders example

Let *afs*(*X*) mean

$\qquad$ *X* is an aardvark who is afraid of spiders

In order to show how *afs*(*X*) is built up from simple predicates using logical operators we need $a(X)$, *X* is an aardvark; $s(X)$, *X* is a spider; and $f(X, Y)$, *X* is afraid of *Y*. We now have a signature for a first order single sorted language.

$$\Sigma = \begin{cases} \textit{Predicate symbols} : [a(X), s(X)], [f(X, Y)] \\ \textit{Function symbols} : \\ \textit{Constants} : \end{cases}$$

That is, we have two predicate symbols of arity one and one predicate symbol of arity two. A first order single sorted language L_Σ is now determined. We can write a formula of this language which expresses *afs*(*X*):

$(a(X) \wedge (\forall Y)(s(Y) \rightarrow f(X, Y)))$

Problem 8.5 *Find another logically equivalent expression for afs*(*X*) *in this language.*

An interpretation *I* of this language consists of a domain, *D*, together with two predicates of arity one and one predicate of arity two.

$I = (D; [\mathbf{a(X)}, \mathbf{s(X)}], [\mathbf{f(X, Y)}]; ;)$

Note that although signatures and interpretations have somewhat similar notations they are quite different things. At this stage we have given a signature, but not given an interpretation. The signature tells us the form that an interpretation has to have.

We will sometimes speak of the signature of a structure to mean the signature of a language which has that structure as an interpretation.

We now give one of the many possible interpretations of L_Σ. See figure 8.1. The elements of the domain are indicated by nodes. The binary fear relation is indicated by an arrow. $X \rightarrow Y$ means that *X* is afraid of *Y*. For convenience of reference we also name the individuals in the domain, although this is not part of the interpretation since the language does not have any constants.

The information in this data structure can also be written out in lists and tables.

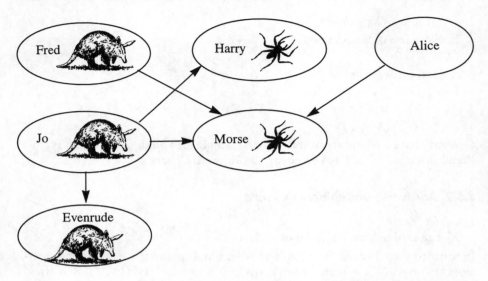

Figure 8.1 Spiders are morse and harry; aardvarks are evenrude, fred and jo. Jo is afraid of morse and harry; fred is afraid of morse

---

Problem 8.6 *What is the domain of the above interpretation? Give tables to show who are the aardvarks, who are the spiders and who is afraid of whom.*

Clearly the truth value of $afs(X)$ depends on the value given to X. From the picture, $afs(X)$ should be true if X is jo, but false if X is alice. (Alice is not even an aardvark.)

A valuation, σ, from this interpretation gives a value in the domain to some of the variables. $Sat(afs(X), I, \sigma)$ will only depend on the value $\sigma(X)$.

Suppose $\sigma(X) =$ fred, and $\sigma(Y) =$ evenrude. Then $Sat((s(Y) \rightarrow f(X, Y)), I, \sigma)$ = True since evenrude is not a spider. $Sat((f(X, Y), I, \sigma) =$ False, since fred is not afraid of evenrude.

What about

$$Sat((\forall Y)(s(Y) \rightarrow f(X, Y)), I, \sigma)?$$

According to our definition, this should be true if and only if, for all valuations τ with $\sigma(X) = \tau(X)$ we have $Sat((s(Y) \rightarrow f(X, Y)), I, \tau)$. So the question now is: can we find valuation τ so that $\sigma(X) = \tau(X)$ but

$$Sat((s(Y) \rightarrow f(X, Y), I, \tau) = \text{False}?$$

To find τ we need only extend σ to consider Y. Looking back at the interpretation, we see that fred is not afraid of harry, although harry is a spider. So we define τ by $\tau(Y) =$ harry, and $\tau(X) = \sigma(X)$.

Problem 8.7 *Check* $Sat((s(Y) \rightarrow f(X,Y)), I, \tau) = False$

Thus $Sat((\forall Y)(s(Y) \rightarrow f(X,Y)), I, \sigma) = $ False as we expected.

Problem 8.8 *Show* $afs(X)$ *is not logically equivalent to*

$(a(X) \wedge (s(Y) \rightarrow f(X,Y)))$

Problem 8.9 *How would you express* $afs(X)$ *in Prolog? Hint: invent a hypothetical least frightening spider, and a rule which says that if you are afraid of this least frightening spider you are afraid of any spider.*

Problem 8.10 *A better solution to the above problem might be to postulate, for each* X, *a spider which is least frightening to* X, *say favourite-spider* (X). *In this case favourite-spider* (X) *is a new function symbol. The extra complexity is justified if you wish to avoid the assumption that everyone has the same favourite spider. Try to write a formula* $A(X,Y)$ *of* L_Σ *defining* $Y = $ *favourite-spider* (X).

8.6 Prenex normal form

A formula of a first order single sorted language is in *prenex normal form* if all its quantifiers are at the front, i.e. if it is in the form

$(Q_1 \mathbf{V}_1)....(Q_n \mathbf{V_n})M$

where M is quantifier free, and $\mathbf{V}_1, ..., \mathbf{V_n}$ are variables and each Q_i is an element of $\{\forall, \exists\}$. It is required that M be in the scope of all the quantifiers.

The remark about the scope needs some explanation. We would say

$(\forall W)(p(W) \rightarrow q(Z))$

is in prenex normal form, provided that $p(W)$ and $q(Z)$ were quantifier free, but

$((\forall W)p(W) \rightarrow q(Z))$

is not in prenex normal form. This is because the $q(Z)$ is not in the scope of the quantifier. The outermost operator in the above formula is the implication. We have to be careful about the brackets here. Allowing ourselves to drop brackets, we would have

$(\forall W)p(W) \rightarrow q(Z)$

which is not in prenex normal form, since the scope of the quantifier is intended to be just $p(W)$.

Theorem *Any formula is logically equivalent to one in prenex normal form.*

Instead of proving this theorem we will describe a method for finding a prenex normal form for a formula.

Suppose we are given formula X.

1. We first get rid of all $\leftrightarrow$ operators in X by rewriting each subformula $A \leftrightarrow B$ as $(A \rightarrow B) \wedge (B \rightarrow A)$. After doing this as many times as possible we get a formula Y which is logically equivalent to X but does not use $\leftrightarrow$.

2. We next get rid of all uses of $\rightarrow$ in Y. We do this by replacing each subformula of the form $(A \rightarrow B)$ by the logically equivalent formula $((\neg A) \vee B)$. After doing this as many times as possible we get a formula Z, which is logically equivalent to the original formula X but which does not use implication or double implication.

3. Rename bound variables if necessary so that no variable occurs both bound and free in any subformula, and also so that no two different quantifiers use the same bound variable. For example, if we have $(A(X) \wedge (\exists X)B(X))$ replace this with $(A(X) \wedge (\exists Xnew)B(Xnew))$, where $Xnew$ is a new variable which does not occur anywhere else in the formula. On the other hand, if we had $((\exists X)A(X) \wedge (\forall X)B(X))$, we could replace this with $((\exists X)A(X) \wedge (\forall Xnew)B(Xnew))$, where $Xnew$ was a new variable.

4. Move quantifiers outside of negation. We rewrite

   $(\neg(\exists V)A)$ as $(\forall V)(\neg A)$.

   We also rewrite

   $(\neg(\forall V)A)$ as $(\exists V)(\neg A)$.

5. Move quantifiers outside of conjunction and disjunction. So, for example, $(A \wedge (\exists X)B(X))$ can be rewritten as

   $(\exists X)(A \wedge B(X))$

   If, after doing this as many times as possible, we do not yet have prenex normal form, go back to step 4).

The validity of step 5) above depends on previously having done step 3). For example $(A(X) \wedge (\exists X)B(X))$ is not logically equivalent to $(\exists X)(A(X) \wedge B(X))$ since the truth value of the first formula depends on free variable X. Applying step 3), however, we first rename X as some other variable, W say

   $A(X) \wedge (\exists W)B(W)$

and then get

   $(\exists W)(A(X) \wedge B(W))$

which is logically equivalent with the original formula.

Example 8.18 *Suppose we want prenex normal form for*

   $(\neg(\exists X)A(X) \vee (\forall X)B(X)) \wedge (\exists X)C(X)$

We could first change the names of two of the bound variables, using names which do not occur elsewhere in the formula.

   $(\neg(\exists X)A(X) \vee (\forall Y)B(Y)) \wedge (\exists Z)C(Z)$

We next put the negation inside the existential quantifier.

   $((\forall X)(\neg A(X)) \vee (\forall Y)B(Y)) \wedge (\exists Z)C(Z)$

The rules now allow us to move the quantifiers outside of conjunction and disjunction in any order. So we might, for example, obtain

   $(\forall X)(\forall Y)(\exists Z)((\neg A(X) \vee B(Y)) \wedge C(Z))$

But we could, with equal correctness, have obtained

   $(\exists Z)(\forall Y)(\forall X)((\neg A(X) \vee B(Y)) \wedge C(Z))$

All the formulae obtained in this way are logically equivalent with each other and with the original formula. This should not lead you to draw the conclusion that the order of quantification does not matter. In general, it does matter. You can see the reason why it does not matter in this case. Look back at the original formula. The three quantifications of X are independent.

■

Problem 8.11 *Find prenex normal form for*

$$((\exists X)A(X) \rightarrow B(X))$$

The result is slightly surprising.

■

8.7 Skolem form

A formula is in Skolem normal form if it is in prenex normal form and all the quantifiers are universal. For any formula A we can find a formula $SK(A)$ in Skolem form which is weakly equivalent to it in the sense that: A is satisfiable iff $SK(A)$ is satisfiable; also there is a model of A iff there is a model of $SK(A)$. However $SK(A)$ and A are not logically equivalent. Skolem form is found by introducing new function symbols and constants to eliminate existential quantifiers.

Suppose we are given a formula A. Here is a method for finding a Skolem form of A.

1. First put A in prenex normal form.

2. Then repeat the following process until a Skolem form is obtained: if the formula we have is not in Skolem form, then it has the form

$$(\forall \mathbf{X}_1)...(\forall \mathbf{X}_k)(\exists \mathbf{Y}_1)M(\mathbf{V}_1, ..., \mathbf{V}_n, \mathbf{X}_1, ..., \mathbf{X}_k, \mathbf{Y}_1)$$

where $\mathbf{V}_1, ..., \mathbf{V}_n$ are the free variables of the formula. Here k and n are some natural numbers, which may be zero. If $k + n > 0$, we invent a new function symbol, with arity $k + n$,

$$f(\mathbf{V}_1, ..., \mathbf{V}_n, \mathbf{X}_1, ..., \mathbf{X}_k)$$

and use this to replace the existential quantifier. We obtain a new formula

$$(\forall \mathbf{X}_1)...(\forall \mathbf{X}_k)$$
$$M(\mathbf{V}_1, ..., \mathbf{V}_n, \mathbf{X}_1, ..., \mathbf{X}_k, f(\mathbf{V}_1, ..., \mathbf{V}_n, \mathbf{X}_1, ..., \mathbf{X}_k))$$

On the other hand, if $k + n = 0$, we have a closed formula

$$(\exists \mathbf{Y}_1)M(\mathbf{Y}_1)$$

so we invent a new constant c, and use this to replace the existential quantifier. We obtain

$$M(c).$$

Definition 8.16 *Formulae A and B are* weakly equivalent *if the existence of a model for A implies the existence of a model for B and vice versa.*

A formula is weakly equivalent to its Skolem form. In fact a model of A can be extended to a model of a Skolem form of A just by appropriate definition of the Skolem functions and constants.

Example 8.19 *A Skolem form for*

$$(\forall X)(\exists Y)(\forall W)(\exists Z)p(X, Y, W, Z)$$

would be found as follows. Suppose this is true. The value of Y depends only on X. So introduce Skolem function $f(X)$. We rewrite our formula as

$$(\forall X)(\forall W)(\exists Z)p(X, f(X), W, Z)$$

Suppose this is true. We are in an interpretation in which an appropriate value of Z can be found depending on values of X and W. We invent a Skolem function, which records some choice of Z. So $Z = g(X, W)$. Then we obtain Skolem form

$$(\forall X)(\forall W)p(X, f(X), W, g(X, W))$$

If we are in an interpretation in which the original formula is true, then the functions $f(X)$ and $g(X, W)$ can be defined so that the Skolem form is true.

8.8 Clausal form

A *clause* is a quantifier free formula of the form

$$(((\neg A_1) \vee (\neg A_2) \vee ... \vee (\neg A_n)) \vee (B_1 \vee B_2 \vee ... \vee B_m))$$

where $A_1, ..., A_n, B_1, ..., B_m$ are all atomic formulae.

In logic programming, it is usual to write such a clause as

$$((A_1 \wedge A_2 \wedge ...A_n) \rightarrow (B_1 \vee B_2 \vee ... \vee B_m))$$

or even

$$B_1, ..., B_m : -A_1, ..., A_n$$

meaning that the disjunction of the B's is true if the conjunction of the A's is true. (Note, however, that we allow either n or m to be 0. If $m = 0$ the meaning is that the conjunction of the A's is false, and if $n = 0$ the meaning is that the disjunction of the B's is true.)

If A is a formula, a clausal form of A is a finite set Γ of clauses so that any model of A can be extended to a model of Γ and any model of Γ is a model of A.

A clausal form of a formula A is found as follows.

1. First find a Skolem form, $SK(A)$, for A.
2. Delete the universal quantifiers from the Skolem form.
3. Put the resulting quantifier free formula into conjunctive normal form. Break this up into a set of clauses, Γ. This is a clausal form of A.

Example 8.20 *For example, a clausal form of $(\forall X)(\forall Y)(\exists W)(\forall Z)\,((Z \in X \wedge Z \in Y) \leftrightarrow Z \in W)$ is*

$$Z \in X \wedge Z \in Y \rightarrow Z \in f(X, Y)$$
$$Z \in f(X, Y) \rightarrow Z \in X$$
$$Z \in f(X, Y) \rightarrow Z \in Y$$

where $f(X, Y)$ is the Skolem function we have chosen. (This Skolem function is usually written as $x \cap y$.)

A clausal form is relatively easy to understand, since it is just a set of quantifier free clauses. On the other hand, any model of the original formula can be extended to a model of the clausal form by appropriately defining the Skolem functions. So, in a sense, the clausal form makes the same demands on reality that the original formula does.

Sometimes mathematical statements in clausal form are *much* easier to understand than the original.

Example 8.21 *Consider*

$g(X, Y) \leftrightarrow (m(X) \wedge (\exists Z)(p(X, Z) \wedge p(Z, Y)))$

Suppose we want to put this in clausal form. We first put it into Skolem form.

$(\neg g(X, Y) \vee (\exists Z)(m(X) \wedge p(X, Z) \wedge p(Z, Y)))$
    $\wedge (g(X, Y) \vee (\forall W)(\neg m(X) \vee \neg p(X, Z) \vee \neg p(Z, Y)))$

$(\exists Z)(\forall W)(\neg g(X, Y) \vee (m(X) \wedge p(X, Z) \wedge p(Z, Y))$
    $\wedge (g(X, Y) \vee \neg m(X) \vee \neg p(X, W) \vee \neg p(W, Y)))$

$(\forall W)(\neg g(X, Y) \vee (m(X) \wedge p(X, f(X, Y)) \wedge p(f(X, Y), Y))$
    $\wedge (g(X, Y) \vee \neg m(X) \vee \neg p(X, W) \vee \neg p(W, Y)))$

Now we have Skolem form. To get clausal form, delete the quantifier, put the result on the false side of a semantic tableau, run it to completion, treating all the variables as constants, and read the CNF off by negating all the open branches. The result is

$g(X, Y) \rightarrow m(X)$
$g(X, Y) \rightarrow p(X, f(X, Y))$
$g(X, Y) \rightarrow p(f(X, Y), Y)$
$(m(X) \wedge p(X, W) \wedge p(W, Y)) \rightarrow g(X, Y)$

If we interpret $g(X, Y)$ as saying that X is the grandfather of Y, $m(X)$ as saying that X is male, and $p(X, Y)$ as saying that X is a parent of Y, the result seems reasonable. The Skolem function $f(X, Y)$ which was produced by mechanical application of the clausal form method means a person who is a child of X and a parent of Y, when X is a grandfather of Y. There is no word for such a person in English, or in any other language, as far as I know, but it seems a natural idea, given our definition of grandfather.

Problem 8.12 *Consider formula*

$(\exists Y)(\forall X)(X \circ Y = X \wedge Y \circ X = X \wedge (\forall Z)(\exists W)(X \circ W = Y))$

Find several different prenex normal forms for this. Pick the one that seems best, and find Skolem form and clausal form. The result should be familiar.

There is no uniform method for finding the best way of expressing a mathematical idea. But clausal form is the nearest approximation we have to such a thing. Whether or not it clarifies any particular case seems to depend on how "natural" the Skolem functions turn out to be.

■

Problem 8.13 *Express*

$sin(X)/X$ *tends to limit 1 as X tends to 0*

using the ϵ--δ definition of limit. Then put this idea into clausal form.

We define a *headed Horn clause* to be one of the form

$$(\neg A_1) \vee (\neg A_2) \vee ... \vee (\neg A_n) \vee B$$

The Prolog programs which we considered earlier were essentially lists of headed Horn clauses.

Any list of headed Horn clauses may be regarded as a logic program. As we know, however, Prolog cannot be guaranteed to work properly on an arbitrary list of headed Horn clauses.

8.9 Is $((\forall X)A(X) \rightarrow A(t))$ **valid?**

This section is in the form of a conversation between a,b,c,d.

a: Yes.

b: Do you mean that it is always valid, no matter what formula $A(X)$ is, in any language, and no matter what term t is?

a: Of course.

b: Proof?

a: OK.

TRUE	FALSE
	1) $((\forall X)A(X) \rightarrow A(t))$
2) $(\forall X)A(X)$, from 1)	3) $A(t)$, from 1) $\qquad \otimes$
4) $A(t)$ from 3)	

b: But you can't have any free variables in a semantic tableau.

a: Well, suppose the free variables are $Y_1, ..., Y_n$. Put $(\forall Y_1)(\forall Y_2)...(\forall Y_n)((\forall X) A(X) \rightarrow A(t))$ at the top of the false side of the tableau. Replace all the Y variables by new constants, using, say $\alpha = \{(Y_1, c_1), ..., (Y_n, c_n)\}$. Then the whole thing works as before, with substitution α.

b: Can the term t have variables in it?

a: Yes.

b: So you say that when you substitute t_α for X in $A(X)_\alpha$ you should get ...

a: $A(t)_\alpha$. The order in which you do substitutions does not matter.

b: I want a proof of this.

a: Use induction. If it were false, there would be a smallest formula $A(X)$ for which it were false. Now look at the cases. For example, $A(X)$ could be $(B(X) \lor C(X))$. We know my claim is true for $B(X)$ and for $C(X)$ since we said $A(X)$ was the *smallest* counterexample. So it works.

b: What if $A(X)$ is $(\forall Y)B(X, Y)$?

a: It still works.

b: What if Y appears in the term t? So t is $t(Y)$.

a: But then ... well. Hmmm.

c: What about this. Let $A(X)$ be

$$(\exists Y)(X + 1 = Y)$$

With the usual interpretation, this is true over the natural numbers, isn't it?

a: Evidently.

c: So if t is any term, according to you, $A(t)$ is true also in the usual model?

a: Yes. I'm beginning to have doubts.

c: Let t be Y. So $A(t)$ is ...

$$(\exists Y)(Y + 1 = Y)$$

which is false, unless $1 = 0$.

a: I give up. However I still think it is usually true.

d: It is valid when t is a constant term.

a: We know that. There must be some other general cases when it is valid.

d: Also, I think the statement that substitution order does not matter needs clarifying.

Problem 8.14 ** *Under what conditions can we be sure that*

$$((\forall X)A(X) \rightarrow A(t))$$

is logically valid? You don't need to prove that the condition you state is correct.

A condition solving the above problem is "t is free for X in $A(X)$", a definition of which can be found in Mendelson [1964], if you can't think of it yourself.

Problem 8.15 *** **Hard.** *Let $A(X)$ be a formula with no bound variables. Try to prove that $((\forall X)A(X) \rightarrow A(t))$ is logically valid for any term t.*

8.10 The Herbrand universe of a Prolog program

Let **P** be a Prolog program. Suppose **P** has function symbols $f_1, ..., f_j$ of arities $n_1, ..., n_j$, respectively, and predicate symbols $p_1, ..., p_k$ of arities $m_1, ..., m_k$, respectively. We will say a query q for this program is *appropriate* if it uses only these function and predicate symbols. We will allow appropriate queries to use extra constants which do not occur in the program. Let $c_1, ..., c_i$ be the constants either in **P** or in q.

With this collection of predicate symbols, function symbols and constants, we can form a first order language $L(P, q)$. Define the *ground terms* of this language to be the terms with no variables in them. The ground terms contain the constants and are closed under application of the function symbols.

For example, if the program has function symbols $s(X)$ and $f(X, Y)$ and the query uses constants cat and dog, then the ground terms would include

   s(s(cat))

and

   f(s(dog),f(cat,dog))

We do not want to jump to any conclusions about the meaning of the ground terms. A neutral way to proceed is to suppose that the meaning of a ground term is the parse tree associated with it. So, for example,

   f(dog,f(cat,cat))

is a name for a tree.

Even if the function symbols have a conventional meaning, we refrain from evaluating them in this world of the ground terms. For example, in this world, $((2 + 2) * 3)$ is not 12. $((2 + 2) * 3)$ is a parse tree.

To see that Prolog takes this idea seriously, try the following query:

   ((2+2)*3) = 12

on your Prolog. You should get the answer

   no

since the left and right hand sides are not the same. There is of course an operation of evaluation which acts on these ground terms, and this operation produces the same result. But the ground terms themselves are not the same.

In this case what do the function symbols mean in the world of the ground terms? The answer is stunningly simple.

If a function symbol has arity n it acts on n ground terms to produce another ground term.

In other words, the functions combine lists of parse trees into single parse trees. In the world of the ground terms, this makes perfect sense.

So for example, the function

   f

acts on dog and s(cat) to produce f(dog,s(cat)).

So far we have described the set of ground terms and interpreted the function symbols as functions acting on these ground terms. The result is called the *ground term algebra* associated with the original program and query.

The ground term algebra is part of the Herbrand universe associated with the program and the query. The Herbrand universe is an interpretation of the language $L(P, q)$. In order to complete the definition, we have to interpret the predicate symbols as predicates defined over the ground terms. This means that for each predicate symbol p_i with arity m_i and each list of ground terms of the right length, $t_1, ..., t_{m_i}$, we have to determine the truth value of

$$p_i(t_1, ..., t_{m_i})$$

To do this we first translate our program **P** into a list of statements, Γ in our language $L(P, q)$. We do this just by rewriting the rules

$$b : -a_1, ..., a_r$$

as $(\forall X_1)...(\forall X_k)((a_1 \wedge ... \wedge a_r) \rightarrow b)$ where $X_1, ..., X_k$ are the variables used.

We now define $p_i(t_1, ..., t_{m_i})$ to be true in the Herbrand universe if and only if

$$\Gamma \models p_i(t_1, ..., t_{m_i})$$

The Herbrand universe is now an interpretation of the appropriate language.

Problem 8.16 * *Show that the Herbrand universe is a model of Γ.*
Hint: you must use the fact that the original program consists of Horn clauses.

We can now state soundness and completeness properties for program **P** in Prolog. Suppose the query is $q(X_1, ..., X_n)$, with variables $X_1, ..., X_n$. Let H be the Herbrand universe.

Level 1 soundness If Prolog is given program **P** and query $q(X_1, ..., X_n)$ and Prolog eventually stops and says yes, with variables $X_1, ..., X_n$ instantiated as ground terms $t_1, ..., t_n$ then

$$H \models q(t_1, ..., t_n)$$

Level 2 soundness If Prolog is given program **P** and query $q(X_1, ..., X_n)$, and Prolog eventually stops and says no, then

$$H \models (\neg(\exists X_1)...(\exists X_n)q(X_1, ..., X_n))$$

Level 1 completeness If Prolog is given program **P** and query $q(X_1, ..., X_n)$ then Prolog eventually terminates.

Level 2 completeness If Prolog is given program **P** and query $q(X_1, ..., X_n)$, and after termination an unending sequence of

;

Prolog will eventually list all solutions in the Herbrand universe, i.e.

$$\{(t_1, ..., t_n) \mid H \models q(t_1, ..., t_n)\}$$

These are certainly desirable properties. However, not many programs will satisfy these properties. Level 1 completeness is quite rare for appropriate queries to Prolog programs. Even if we have level 1 completeness, level 2 completeness usually fails.

Also, unfortunately, level 2 soundness often fails for appropriate queries to Prolog programs. We did not succeed in writing any program for finding the way out of a labyrinth which was both level 1 complete and level 2 sound.

This should not be taken as a reason for rejecting the whole logic programming project. However it does bring out some shortcomings of Prolog.

Remark After thinking a while about the labyrinth problem, I am inclined to believe that the naive translation of the equivalence relations axioms was correct. Prolog *should have been able* to deal with

```
r(X,X).
r(X,Y) :- r(Y,X).
r(X,Z) :- r(X,Y), r(Y,Z).
```

8.11 Problems

Problem 8.17 *Translate the following statements into some first order single sorted language.*

a) Not all birds can fly.

b) If some human being is in prison than all human beings are in prison.

c) Some people hate everyone.

d) Gorillas are hairier than billiard balls.

e) $f(X)$ *is continuous at a. (Use* ϵ*--*δ *definition.)*

f) There is a town in Spain in which there is a barber who shaves everyone in the town who does not shave themselves.

g) Everyone is happy except for Jane.

h) There is only one bicycle in the village, and it has a flat tyre.

Problem 8.18 *a) Repeat the previous problem without using any existential quantifier.*

b) Repeat without using any universal quantifier.

Problem 8.19 *Put all the statements above into clausal form.*

Problem 8.20 L_N, *the language of arithmetic, is a typical first order single sorted language. What are the variables, constants, terms, atomic formulae and formulae of this language? Give a grammar for each, and an example of each.*

Problem 8.21 *Write a formula of* L_N *which, under the standard interpretation, says that* X *is the sum of the squares of two prime numbers. Indicate the free and bound occurrences of variables in your formula. Indicate the terms which occur in your formula; and also the atomic formulae which occur.*

Problem 8.22 *Give an interpretation in which*

$$((\forall X)(\exists Y)(R(X,Y) \to S(X)) \to (\exists Y)(\forall X)(R(X,Y) \to S(X)))$$

is true; and another interpretation in which it is false.

Problem 8.23 *a) Write the axioms of group theory in a first order single sorted language which has one constant for the identity, and a binary function symbol* $\circ$ *for the group operation, but has no function symbol for inverse.*

b) Repeat the above in a language with a binary function symbol, and no other function symbols or constants.

c) Repeat the above in a language with no function symbols or constants.

Problem 8.24 *Assume the standard interpretation of* L_N. *Find, if possible, valuations which satisfy and do not satisfy the following:*

a) $(((X + 0'') = Y) \wedge (\exists Z)((0'' * Z) = Y))$
b) $((X = (Y * Z)) \vee (\forall W)(\neg(W'' = X)))$.

Problem 8.25 *A partially ordered set is a set* D *with a binary relation* $\leq$ *so that the following three statements are true:*

$(X \leq X)$
$((X \leq Y) \wedge (Y \leq Z)) \rightarrow (X \leq Z)$
$((X \leq Y) \wedge (Y \leq X)) \rightarrow (X = Y)$

where $=$ *denotes the usual equality.*
In such a partially ordered set, we will say $(X < Y)$ *if* $((X \leq Y) \wedge (\neg (X = Y)))$

a) *Find a partially ordered set and a valuation so that*

$(\neg((X < Y) \vee (Y < X) \vee (X = Y))$

is satisfied.

b) *Define the constants, terms, atomic formulae and formulae of the language of partially ordered sets.*

c) *A rooted tree is a type of partially ordered set. One of its properties is that any two elements in the tree have a least upper bound. Extend your partially ordered set language by adding a binary function symbol* $lub(X, Y)$. *What are the terms in the new language?*

d) *Another property of a tree is that any element which is not the root has a parent, i.e. an element immediately above it. Invent a first order single sorted language appropriate for trees, and write axioms characterising a rooted tree in this language. (You might want a constant for the root? A parent*(X) *function? child*(X)? *a frontier predicate?)*

Problem 8.26 *Find prenex normal form for*

a) $((\forall X)(\exists Y)A(X, Y) \rightarrow (\forall U)S(U))$
b) $f(X)$ *is continuous at* a. *(Translate this into the usual* ϵ--δ *statement.)*
c) $((A(0) \wedge (\forall X)(A(X) \rightarrow A(X + 1))) \rightarrow (\forall X)A(X))$

Problem 8.27 *Put the previous statements into Skolem normal form.*

Problem 8.28 *Put the previous statements into clausal form.*

Problem 8.29 *Translate and put into clausal form.*

If some birds have no feathers then there is a bicycle with three wheels.

Problem 8.30 *Translate into some first order single sorted language:*

Substitution α *is a most general unifier of terms A and B.*

Problem 8.31 *Find out what the Chinese remainder theorem is and translate it into some first order single sorted language.*

8.12 Summary of chapter 8

This chapter defines and discusses first order single sorted languages. Such a language is specified by a signature, Σ, which is a list of lists of predicate symbols, a list of lists of function symbols and a list of constants.

Terms, atomic formulae and formulae are defined for a first order single sorted language L_Σ with signature Σ.

An interpretation I of a first order single sorted language is given by a domain D, together with interpretations in D for each function symbol, predicate symbol and constant in the signature of the language.

A valuation from an interpretation is a map from a subset of the variables into the domain of the interpretation.

We define

$$I \models A$$

to mean that formula A is true in interpretation I for all valuations from I which cover the free variables of A.

We define

$$\models A$$

to mean that formula A is true for all interpretations of the language. $\models A$ should be read to say: A is logically valid.

From the notion of logical validity, we define logical equivalence and logical consequence.

We give methods to compute prenex normal form, Skolem form, and clausal form for a formula.

We also define the Herbrand universe for a Prolog program, and claim that this is the intended interpretation. With this idea we are able to define clear notions of completeness and correctness for Prolog programs. It becomes unpleasantly clear that hardly any Prolog programs are complete and correct.

Chapter 9

A formal system for the predicate calculus

The *logical validity problem* for first order single sorted languages is the following.

Given formula A of some first order single sorted language L, decide whether or not $\models A$.

This problem is extremely hard.

Almost any problem in computing and mathematics can be represented in this form. So if we could solve this problem we could solve almost all other problems. For example, suppose we wanted to know whether or not a sentence Th in L_G is true in all groups. Th is true in all groups if and only if Th is a logical consequence of Γ, where Γ is the universal closure of the axioms of group theory; and this is so if and only if $(\Gamma \rightarrow Th)$ is logically valid. Therefore it does not seem reasonable to expect a complete solution to the logical validity problem.

Let's try, however, to say what a complete solution would be.

A complete solution to the logical validity problem would be an algorithm Ω which would accept as input any formula A of any first order single sorted language, and which in all cases would terminate after finitely many steps with the answer "yes" or "no", depending on whether or not $\models A$.

Not only do we not currently possess such an algorithm, it is currently believed that such an algorithm is impossible. (Not only do we not know Ω, but there is no such thing.)

Naturally, if we can't do something, we would like almost to do it. The semantic tableau algorithm which is given below is quite close to the allegedly impossible Ω. The difference is that it is non deterministic and it does not always terminate. If the given formula A is logically valid, then there is some way of choosing the operations allowed by the algorithm which will show in finitely many steps that A is logically valid. However if A is not logically valid, we may not be able to detect this after finitely many steps.

9.1 How to prove logical validity of first order single sorted statements

We extend the semantic tableau construction, for first order single sorted languages. We need four new rules to account for quantifiers. Suppose our first order single sorted language is L. For reasons which will become clear, we add countably many new constants to L to obtain a new language L^+. So L^+ has infinitely many constants $c_1, c_2, c_3, \ldots$.

Define the *ground terms* of L^+ to be all those terms which do not have any variables in them. So the ground terms include the constants, and also all expressions which can be obtained from the constants by application of the function symbols.

If t is a ground term and $A(X)$ is a formula with free variable X, we will use $A(t)$ to denote the formula which is obtained by replacing every free occurrence of X in $A(X)$ by t.

A closed formula of L^+ is one with no free variables. As before, define the universal closure of a formula A to be the closed formula which is obtained by prefixing A by a string of universal quantifiers, one for each free variable of A. Define the existential closure of a formula A to be the closed formula which is obtained by prefixing A by a string of existential quantifiers, one for each free variable of A.

■

Problem 9.1 *Show that a formula A is logically valid if its universal closure is logically valid.*

■

Closed formulae are also called sentences. The result of the problem above immediately reduces the logical validity problem for formulae to the logical validity problem for sentences.

We will insist that all formulae that appear in our tableaux are sentences. This is not really an essential restriction but it makes the exposition somewhat easier.

New semantic tableau rules

As before the purpose of the construction is systematically to attempt to find a counterexample to a formula S. If the construction becomes blocked by contradictions, there is no counterexample, and S is proved to be logically valid. In this case we write $\vdash S$.

Given a formula S of L, form the universal closure of S and put this sentence at the top of the false side of the tableau.

Apply all the previous rules as before. There are also four new rules. These are divided into two groups.

In the first group we simply give a name, a Skolem constant, for an object which is asserted to exist in the domain. The first group contains existential formulae on the true side and universal formulae on the false side.

Exists true case

Suppose we have $(\exists V)A(V)$ on the true side of an open branch α, and alive on α. Find a constant c which has not occurred so far in α and add $A(c)$ to the true side of α. (We recruit c to stand for that element which makes $A(V)$ true.) Put a reference back to $(\exists V)A(V)$ so that it is no longer alive on α.

For all false case

Suppose we have $(\forall V)A(V)$ on the false side of an open branch α, and alive on α. Pick, or invent, a constant c which has not yet occurred in α, and add $A(c)$ to the false side of α. Put a reference back to $(\forall V)A(V)$ so that it is no longer alive on α.

In both cases, the new constant is just introduced as a name for an object which must exist, according to this part of the tableau. It is of course essential that the constant which is introduced not occur previously in α, since we have no reason to believe that the object being named is one which is known in some other way. Other than that, we can use any name we please. The rules in the first group will be called Skolem rules.

The second group is much more problematic. The second group also contains two cases. One case is existential formulae on the false side and the other is universal formulae on the true side. The rules in the second group will be called substitution rules.

Exists false case

Suppose we have $(\exists V)A(V)$ on the false side of an open branch α. Pick a ground term t, and add $A(t)$ to the false side of α.

Add a reference back to $(\exists V)A(V)$, so we can see where $A(t)$ came from. However $(\exists V)A(V)$ remains alive on α.

The justification for this is that if $(\exists V)A(V)$ really is false then $A(t)$ must also be false, since, after all, t represents a fixed element of the domain.

For all true case

Suppose we have $(\forall V)A(V)$ on the true side of an open branch α. Pick a ground term t and add $A(t)$ to the true side of α.

Add a reference back to $(\forall V)A(V)$, so we can see where $A(t)$ came from. However $(\forall V)A(V)$ remains alive on α.

The justification is that if $(\forall V)A(V)$ really is true, then $A(t)$ must also be true.

For the substitution rules, any ground term whatever may be picked.

As you may anticipate, we will have problems deciding which ground terms to substitute.

As before, if a path contains a contradiction, it is closed. If all paths are closed, the tableau is closed, and this constitutes a proof of S.

The propositional rules and the Skolem constant rules need only be applied once to any formula on any branch. However the substitution rules may be applied over and over again. This is the most important thing to understand about this construction.

The fact that the substitution rules can be applied several times is reflected in the definition of the live part of a branch α. The point is: *We can't ever kill off a universal statement on the true side, or an existential statement on the false side; there is always the possibility that more information can be extracted from such a statement by making another substitution.* The new definition is:

Definition 9.1 *Let α be a branch in a semantic tableau, and S, a statement on α. Suppose S has label n. Then S is alive on α if S is of the form $(\forall X)A$, and S was found* *on the true side of α, or if S is of the form $(\exists \mathbf{X})A$ and S was found on the false side of α; or if S has some other form and there is no justification, from n, referring to S on α.*

The information which was contained in $(P \to Q)$ on the false side of a tableau is the same as the information contained in P on the true side and Q on the false side of a tableau; therefore $(P \to Q)$ can be, in effect, forgotten on a particular branch, once it has been considered on that branch. The same idea applies to $(\exists X)A(X)$ on the true side of a tableau. If this is true, we use a new constant c to name the object which makes it true. We add $A(c)$ to the true side of the tableau. We do not need $(\exists X)A(X)$ again.

However if we have $(\forall X)A(X)$ on the true side, the information contained in this can never be contained in any finite number of statements $A(t)$, where t is a ground term. The same remarks apply to $(\exists X)A(X)$ on the false side.

If the semantic tableau construction terminates with a closed tree, then we will call this tree a proof of the original formula S.

If a branch terminates with a counterexample to S, then, of course, S was not logically valid. A third possibility is that the construction does not terminate. The situation is complicated here by the fact that we may have a choice of terms t to substitute. Whether or not the construction terminates may depend on how the terms are chosen. It is sometimes necessary to make several different substitutions before a contradiction is obtained. Furthermore we don't know in advance how many substitutions may be necessary.

Example 9.1 *Suppose we want to test logical validity of $((\forall X)(A(X) \to B(X)) \to ((\forall X)A(X) \to (\forall X)B(X)))$. We put it on the false side of our semantic tableau. See figure 9.1.*

We end up with a closed tree, and so the original formula is logically valid.

On the other hand, suppose we test the converse of the above sentence, $((\forall X)(A(X) \to (\forall X)B(X)) \to (\forall X)(A(X) \to B(X)))$. In this case the method produces a small counterexample. Try it...

Warning We have allowed ourselves some latitude in the use of brackets in formulae, in the belief that we know what we are doing. So, for example, we have been writing such expressions as

$(\forall X)A(X) \to (\exists X)B(X)$

as an abbreviation for the correct expression

$((\forall X)A(X) \to (\exists X)B(X))$

This can cause difficulties when using the semantic tableau process. It is crucial to realise that the form of the expression just exhibited is

$(C \to D)$

rather than $(\forall X)E$. You have to use enough brackets so that you can determine the parse tree for the expression you are working on. It would be quite wrong to put

$((\forall X)A(X) \to (\exists X)B(X))$

on the false side of a semantic tableau, and then see this as a formula of the form $(\forall X)S(X)$, and then invent a new Skolem constant, c, and add

$A(c) \to (\exists X)B(X)$

to the false side of the tableau. You should always work on the logical operator which occurs on the top of the parse tree; and you should use enough brackets so that you are always sure you know which operator this is.

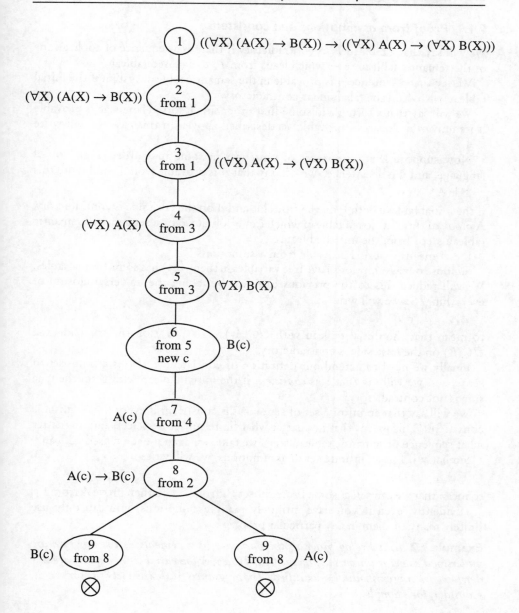

Figure 9.1 The Skolem constant c is introduced to stand for the object which makes $(\forall X)B(X)$ false. Subsequently, c is substituted into 2) and 4)

9.1.1 Proof from assumptions and consistency

We will say that a tableau T_x is contradictory if there is a sequence of applications of the semantic tableau rules which leads from T_x to a closed tableau.

We say that a sentence A is provable in the semantic tableau system if the initial tableau with A on the false side is contradictory.

We will say that a formula in some first order single sorted language is provable if its universal closure is provable, as described above. In this case we will write $\vdash A$.

Now suppose Γ is a finite set of sentences in some first order single sorted language, and A is a sentence. We will say that A is provable from Γ, and write this

$$\Gamma \vdash A$$

if the initial tableau with Γ on the true side and A on the false side is contradictory. A *proof* of this is a closed tableau which can be obtained by a sequence of semantic tableau steps from the initial tableau.

$\Gamma \vdash A$ means that A is provable from assumptions Γ.

Suppose our assumptions have free variables in them, or A has some free variables. We will reduce this to the previous case just by taking the universal closure of everything. So we will write

$$A_1, ..., A_n \vdash B$$

to mean that the initial tableau with $UC(A_1), ..., UC(A_n)$ on the true side and $UC(B)$ on the false side is contradictory.

Finally we need to extend our definition of consistency. If Γ is a finite set of sentences, we will say that Γ is *consistent* if the initial tableau with Γ on the true side is not contradictory.

We will say that an infinite set of sentences is consistent if every finite subset is consistent. This means that no matter what finite subset we select, and no matter what sequence of semantic tableau steps we take, we cannot get a closed tableau.

Similarly, if Γ is an infinite set of assumptions, we will write

$$\Gamma \vdash A$$

to mean that we can select some finite subset Γ_1 from Γ, and then prove A from Γ_1.

(Evidently, even if you have infinitely many assumptions, you can only use finitely many of them in any particular proof.)

Example 9.2 *In a Prolog program the variables in statements in the program are understood as being universally quantified. However the variables in a query are understood as being existentially quantified. The program is treated as a set of assumptions. Consider, for example,*

```
m(a).
m(b).
c(a,b).
c(b,x).
a(X,Z):-b(X,Y),c(Y,Z).
b(X,Y):-c(X,Y),m(X).
```

---

with query

c(Y,X).

To do this in our semantic tableau system we put assumptions

$$\Gamma = \{(\forall X)(\forall Y)(\forall Z)((b(X,Y) \wedge c(Y,Z))$$
$$\to a(X,Z)), (\forall X)(\forall Y)((c(X,Y) \wedge m(X))$$
$$\to b(X,Y)), m(a), m(b), c(a,b), c(b,x)\}$$

on the true side of a semantic tableau, and our query

$$(\exists Y)a(Y,x)$$

on the false side. We then have to choose substitutions of ground terms for variables to give us a closed tableau. Try to do this. Hint: imitate Prolog.

9.1.2 A conversation

a: $(((\forall X)(\exists Y)A(X,Y) \to B) \to ((\exists X)(\forall Y)(A(X,Y) \to B)))$ and therefore ...
b: Stop. Why?
a: I should have said that B does not have any free variables. So can I go on?
b: No.
a: Why not?
b: It does not look correct to me. Is this because $A(X,Y)$ means that ....
a: No, the thing I said is logically valid. It does not matter what $A(X,Y)$ means.
b: So prove it.
a: Well, suppose not.

See figure 9.2.

9.2 Soundness theorem for semantic tableau predicate calculus

Let L be any first order single sorted language. Extend L to L^+ by adding an infinite list of new constants to its signature: $c_1, c_2, c_3, \ldots$. These new constants will be used in the semantic tableaux.

The ground terms of L^+ are the terms without variables.

Example 9.3 *If L is L_N, L^+ would have constants $0, c_1, c_2, c_3, \ldots$. The ground terms of this new language would include $(c_1'' + c_2)$, $(c_4 * (0 + 0))$, etc.*

Let Γ be a set of formulae of L^+. An L^+ interpretation I is a model *of Γ if every formula of Γ is true in interpretation I.*

Example 9.4 *A model of the axioms of group theory is a group.*

Γ *is* satisfiable *if there is an interpretation I and a valuation σ from I so that $Sat(A, \sigma, I)$ for every A in Γ.*

Definition 9.2 *A semantic tableau T is* satisfiable *if there is a branch α of T, and an L^+ interpretation I so that, for every formula A, if A is on the true side of α then $I \models A$, and if A is on the false side of α then $I \models (\neg A)$.*

Note that all the formulae in a semantic tableau are sentences. So their truth or falsity depends only on the interpretation, not on a valuation.

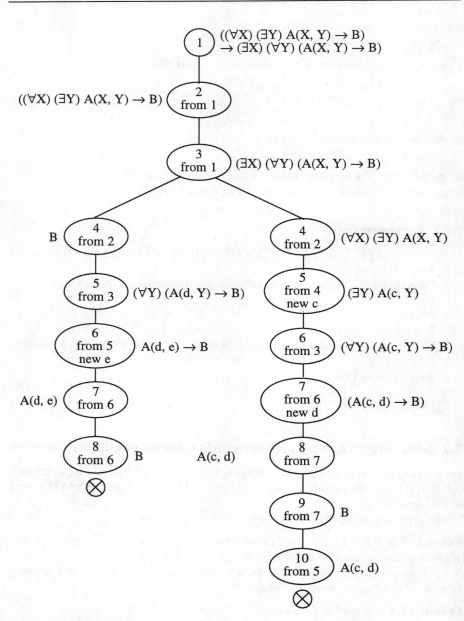

Figure 9.2 It must be assumed here that *B* is a sentence

Predicate calculus semantic tableau invariance lemma *Let T_x and $T_{x'}$ be semantic tableaux, and suppose $T_{x'}$ is obtained from T_x by one step of the semantic tableau process. Then T_x is satisfiable iff $T_{x'}$ is satisfiable.*

Proof The proof is by cases, depending on which rule is used to change T_x to $T_{x'}$.

The propositional cases are all the same as in the proof of the invariance lemma for the propositional calculus.

We have four quantifier rules to consider.

1) $(\exists X)A(X)$ **on true side.** We suppose $(\exists X)A(X)$ is alive on the true side of T_x on open branch α, and $T_{x'}$ is obtained from T_x by finding a new constant c_i, which does not occur anywhere in α and adding $A(c_i)$ to α, with a justifying reference back to $(\exists X)A(X)$. (We are saying that if there is such an X we will call it c_i.) Now suppose T_x is satisfiable in interpretation I. This means that I satisfies some open branch of T_x. If this open branch happens not to be α, then the identical open branch occurs in $T_{x'}$, and I satisfies $T_{x'}$, which is what we wanted to prove. But suppose I satisfies open branch α in T_x. This means that $I \models (\exists X)A(X)$. Thus there exists an element , say d, in the domain of I so that if $\sigma(X) = d$ then $Sat(A(X), I, \sigma) =$ True. Of course I will also have an interpretation for our new constant c_i, and this is unlikely to be d unless we are extremely lucky. So we change the interpretation I in this one detail. We define a new interpretation $I*$ which is just like I except that in $I*$ the constant c_i will be given value d. Since this constant did not occur in T_x, we still have that $I*$ satisfies T_x. But we also have $I* \models A(c_i)$, since $eval(c_i) = d$. Thus $I*$ satisfies $T_{x'}$. So $T_{x'}$ is satisfiable.

The other direction is easy. Suppose $T_{x'}$ is satisfiable. T_x is contained in $T_{x'}$. Thus T_x is satisfiable.

2) $(\exists X)A(X)$ **on false side.** Suppose this is on open branch α of T_x. Here $T_{x'}$ is obtained from T_x by selecting a ground term t and adding $A(t)$ to the false side of α.

■

Problem 9.2 *Suppose interpretation I satisfies α in T_x. Show that I also satisfies α in $T_{x'}$. This case is easier than the preceding since we do not have to change interpretation.*

3) $(\forall X)A(X)$ **on true side.** (Like case 2)).
4) $(\forall X)A(X)$ **on false side.** (Like case 1)).

Problem 9.3 *Do cases 3) and 4).*

□
■

Predicate calculus semantic tableau invariance theorem *Let T_{x_0} and T_{x_n} be semantic tableaux, and suppose T_{x_n} is obtained from T_{x_0} by n steps of the semantic tableau process. Then T_{x_0} is satisfiable iff T_{x_n} is satisfiable.*

Proof Induction on n, using the previous lemma.

□

Soundness theorem for predicate calculus *Let A be a formula of a first order single sorted language. If* ⊢ *A then A is logically valid.*

Proof (This is the same as the proof of the soundness theorem for the propositional calculus, replacing the references to the propositional invariance theorem by references to the predicate calculus invariance theorem. Try to write the proof yourself.)

9.3 Gödel completeness theorem

Completeness theorem for predicate calculus *Let A be a formula of a first order single sorted language. If A is logically valid, then* ⊢ *A.*

Proof We prove the contrapositive. That is,

not ⊢ $A \Rightarrow$ not $\models A$

So suppose that formula A is not a theorem. Let $UC(A)$ be the universal closure of A. $UC(A)$ is not a theorem. Let T_{x_0} be an initial tableau with $UC(A)$ on the false side. Since $UC(A)$ is not a theorem, *no matter what* choices we make in the semantic tableau process we never get a closed tableau from T_{x_0}.

Suppose that we insist on making the choices in an especially systematic manner, by putting a priority on each possible operation and always applying each rule in order of priority on each branch. To begin with we give all the propositional rules highest priority. So if a propositional operation is possible we do it before any quantifier operation. Next in priority we take the easy quantifier cases, $(\exists \mathbf{X})S(\mathbf{X})$ on the true side, or $(\forall \mathbf{X})S(\mathbf{X})$ on the false side. Lowest in priority we take the rules which require substitution, $(\forall \mathbf{X})S(\mathbf{X})$ on the true side, of $(\exists \mathbf{X})S(\mathbf{X})$ on the false side. For these rules we still have infinitely many choices, since we can choose to substitute any ground term. Therefore, we make a list $t_1, t_2, t_3, \ldots$ of all possible ground terms in L^+ and always do the substitutions in order according to this list, that is, in every case we first try t_1, then t_2, etc.

If we were trying to find a proof, this systematic search would probably not be very efficient. We are assuming, however, that there is no proof. What we want to ensure, by this systematic search, is that no possible rule application or substitution has been ignored. We want to be sure that everything that could be done is eventually done.

The assumption that the operations are considered in this systematic way will be called *fairness*.

It may be that a counterexample to $UC(A)$ is produced after finitely many steps. In this case $UC(A)$ is evidently not logically valid.

Suppose, however, that the construction never terminates. In this case at least one infinite open branch must be produced, by König's lemma. Let α be such an infinite open branch. Because of our systematic method of applying the rules, we can suppose that any operation which is ever possible on α is eventually done. That is, nothing which could be done, no substitution or propositional operation, is delayed indefinitely. The claim now is that this infinite open branch, α, defines a counterexample to $UC(A)$.

We use α to define an interpretation I_α. This interpretation is very similar to the Herbrand universe which was discussed earlier. The domain of this interpretation will be the ground terms of L^+. Under this interpretation, we let the constants stand for themselves. We now have to interpret the functions. Let f_j be a function symbol of arity n, and let $t_1, ..., t_n$ be elements of the domain. So $t_1, ..., t_n$ are ground terms. We define our function $\mathbf{f_j}$ as follows.

$$\mathbf{f_j}(t_1, ..., t_n) = \mathrm{apply}(f_j, t_1, ..., t_n)$$

Note that the functions map ground terms to ground terms.

So far we have a domain, and we have interpreted constants and function symbols. From a mathematical point of view, the thing we have is just the same as the thing we previously called the ground term algebra. (It does not matter whether the ground terms are regarded as names for themselves, or as names for their parse trees; the two algebras are the same.)

Next we have to specify the meaning of the predicate symbols. Suppose p_j is a predicate symbol of arity n in L^+. Let $t_1, ..., t_n$ be elements of the domain. How are we going to determine whether or not $\mathbf{p_j}$ would be true of $(t_1, ..., t_n)$? Assuming that we have our hands on α, an infinite open branch, the answer is staring us in the face. We define $\mathbf{p_j}(t_1, ..., t_n)$ to be true if and only if it actually occurs on the true side of α.

Note that this part of the interpretation is not quite the same as the Herbrand universe of a Prolog program. For example, if we had started with a disjunction $(A \vee B)$ on the true side, our branch α must choose to make one of $\{A, B\}$ true, even if neither is a logical consequence of the other statements on the branch.

One of the agreeable features of the Herbrand universe of a Prolog program is that there is only one of them. A Prolog program (given an appropriate query) really does have a single intended interpretation. In our construction however this is not the case. The semantic tableau tree may have many infinite open branches. We have just picked one of them.

We now have an interpretation, I_α.

Lemma I_α *satisfies* α.

Proof There are two parts to this. We need to show that if S is on the true side of α then $I_\alpha \models S$; and also that if S is on the false side of α then $I_\alpha \models (\neg S)$. We use proof by contradiction. Suppose the statement were false. Then, by the well ordering principle for Σ^*, there would be a minimal length counterexample, S. S must be either on the true side of α or on the false side.

1) Suppose S is an atomic formula. Then S is $p_j(t_1, ..., t_n)$ for some predicate symbol p_j. If S is on the true side of α we defined I_α in such a way as to make S true. If S is on the false side, it is not also on the true side, since α is open. Therefore in our definition of p_j we set $p_j(t_1, ..., t_n)$ to be False since we did not find it on the true side of α.

2) Suppose S is a propositional combination of simpler formulae. There are several subcases here.

a) S is of the form $(A \wedge B)$.

Suppose S was found on the true side of α. By the fairness assumption, both A

and B are found on the true side of α. But we suppose S was the minimal length counterexample. So $I_\alpha \models A$, and also $I_\alpha \models B$. It follows that $I_\alpha \models S$. $\bigotimes$.

On the other hand, suppose S was found on the false side of α. By the fairness assumption, the appropriate rule must have been applied at some point to S. This would result in a splitting of the branch constructed up to that point. So either A must be found on the false side of α, or B must be found on the false side of α. Assume A is found on the false side of α. We suppose S is the minimal counterexample to the lemma. So $I_\alpha \models (\neg A)$. But then $I_\alpha \models (\neg S)$. $\bigotimes$.

Problem 9.4 *Do the other cases, i.e.* $\vee, \neg, \rightarrow, \leftrightarrow$.

---

3) Suppose S is obtained by the application of a quantifier to a simpler formula. There are two subcases.

a) S is $(\exists \mathbf{X})R(\mathbf{X})$.

If S is found on the true side of α then by our fairness assumption, S is eventually operated on. So $R(c_i)$ must occur somewhere on the true side of α, for some constant c_i. Since S was a minimal counterexample, $I_\alpha \models R(c_i)$. Thus $I_\alpha \models S$. $\bigotimes$.

Suppose S is found on the false side of α. By our fairness assumption, $R(t)$ can be found somewhere on the false side of α, for every ground term t. Since S was the minimal counterexample, $I_\alpha \models (\neg R(t))$, for every t in the domain. Thus $I_\alpha \models (\neg S)$. $\bigotimes$.

b) S is $(\forall \mathbf{X})R(\mathbf{X})$.

Problem 9.5 *Do the case where S is* $(\forall \mathbf{X})R(\mathbf{X})$.

$\square$

By the lemma, we have $UC(A)$ is false in interpretation I_α. This means that $UC(A)$ is not logically valid. That implies that A is also not logically valid.

$\square$

In spite of the soundness and completeness theorems, there is no algorithm to decide whether or not a formula of a first order single sorted language is logically valid.

9.4 Other sound and complete deductive systems

There are a number of other deductive systems for first order single sorted predicate logic which are sound and complete. The computer language ML was originally designed to write a theorem prover for one of these systems, the sequent calculus, which is closely related to semantic tableaux.

A *sequent* is an expression of the form

$$\Gamma \vdash \Delta$$

where Γ and Δ are sets of formulae.

The meaning of a sequent such as the above is that the conjunction of the formulae in Γ implies the disjunction of the formulae in Δ. The sequent calculus is defined by a number of rules of inference for sequents. For example, one of the rules is

$$A, B, \Gamma \vdash \Delta$$
$$\overline{\qquad\qquad}$$
$$(A \wedge B), \Gamma \vdash \Delta$$

We may start with a basic sequent, which is obviously valid because the same formula appears on both sides, such as

$$A, \Gamma \vdash A, \Delta$$

and operate forwards with the rules of inference to produce new valid sequents. Or we may try to find a proof of a goal sequent by running the rules backwards. (In this case we get another version of semantic tableaux.)

In fact, we can produce an adequate set of sequent rules just by looking back at our semantic tableau rules and writing them down backwards. There will be two rules for each operator, one for each side. So, for example, we will get two sequent rules for negation:

$$\Gamma \vdash \Delta, A$$
$$\overline{\qquad\qquad}$$
$$(\neg A), \Gamma \vdash \Delta$$

and

$$A, \Gamma \vdash \Delta$$
$$\overline{\qquad\qquad}$$
$$\Gamma \vdash \Delta, (\neg A)$$

There are also two rules for implication:

$$A, \Gamma \vdash \Delta, B$$
$$\overline{\qquad\qquad}$$
$$\Gamma \vdash \Delta (A \to B)$$

and

$$\Gamma \vdash \Delta, A \qquad\qquad B, \Gamma \vdash \Delta$$
$$\overline{\qquad\qquad\qquad\qquad\qquad}$$
$$(A \to B), \Gamma \vdash \Delta$$

Problem 9.6 *Write down the two sequent rules for conjunction.*

The rules for the quantifiers can be found in a similar way, although they need to be stated carefully. For the universal quantifier we have the following:

$$A(t), (\forall X)A(X), \Gamma \vdash \Delta$$

___

$$(\forall X)A(X), \Gamma \vdash \Delta$$

for any *constant* term t; and also

$$\Gamma \vdash \Delta A(c)$$

___

$$\Gamma \vdash \Delta, (\forall X)A(X)$$

provided that c is a constant which does not occur in Γ or Δ.

A dazzling logical rabbit can now be pulled out of the hat: if you take a semantic tableau proof and turn it upside down, you get a proof in the sequent calculus. Notice that the semantic tableau proof is an indirect proof, a proof by contradiction; and the sequent calculus proof is direct. The proof by contradiction is a branching downwards tree, with each branch ending in an obvious contradiction since the same formula appears on both sides. The sequent proof starts with many branches and contracts to obtain the conclusion. Each branch begins with a basic sequent which is obviously true, since the same formula appears on both sides.

Problem 9.7 *Write a semantic tableau proof of your favourite tautology. Turn the proof upside down to get a direct sequent proof of the same tautology.*

As people read proofs, they tell themselves little stories, to justify the steps. It is an odd fact that the stories and justifications and running commentaries for the semantic tableau proofs and the sequent proofs are entirely different. On the other hand, the results are the same.

An ML theorem prover for a sequent calculus is given in Paulson (1992) in the references in chapter 13. The theorem prover does not decide whether or not a given formula is a theorem; however the claim is that in many interesting cases it does produce a proof.

(**Warning**: in the system given by Paulson, it should be noted that arbitrary terms can't be used in the quantifier rules.)

Problem 9.8 *Show that the following rule is not valid for arbitrary terms t. Let $\alpha = \{(X, t)\}$.*

$$A_\alpha, (\forall X)A(X), \Gamma \vdash \Delta$$

___

$$(\forall X)A(X) \vdash \Delta$$

Rules of inference like this have a history of confusing people.

9.5 How to finish quickly (continued)

Suppose we have a formula which we think is logically valid. We now know that if it is valid there is some way to get a proof of this using the semantic tableau algorithm. The problem is: how do we choose the order of operations in such a way as to get closure quickly? In general this is a hard problem. However it is possible to make some useful remarks about this subject.

Everything said previously about the propositional case still applies. That is, many branches seem undesirable. So it seems best to do non-splitting propositional operations before splitting ones.

We can divide our operations into four groups.

1) Non-splitting propositional operations.
2) Splitting propositional operations.
3) Quantifier operations which create new constants, i.e. $(\exists X)$ on the true side and $(\forall X)$ on the false side.
4) Quantifier operations which involve repeated substitution of ground terms, i.e. $(\forall X)$ on the true side and $(\exists X)$ on the false side.

Generally speaking, it seems advisable to do all possible operations in the first three groups before doing any of the substitution operations.

Let's suppose that this advice has been followed. Imagine we have a tableau in which only substitution operations are possible. We pick a ground term t and do a substitution. But the question is: how do we choose this ground term? In the proof of the Gödel completeness theorem, we just choose the next one in some ordering. This has the virtue of thoroughness, but hardly seems likely to produce closure quickly.

At the moment when we do the substitution, it appears difficult to look ahead in the proof to see what ground term we should use.

9.5.1 Metavariables and Skolem functions

The following technique then suggests itself. Suppose we introduce a new kind of variable, beginning with the Greek letter τ; we will call these metavariables. They are not part of the language L. They are purely for our convenience in our role as theorem provers. A metavariable, $\tau 1$ for example, is a symbol we can use for an unspecified ground term. If we substitute $\tau 1$ we are saying, in effect: this thing $\tau 1$ is a ground term, but I have not yet decided which one it is. Later on in the proof we can use a process of unification to decide what ground terms the metavariables ought to be.

This technique implies an important modification to the semantic tableau algorithm. We can no longer use Skolem constants to replace existential quantifiers on the true side or universal quantifiers on the false side. We must use Skolem functions instead, which depend upon all the metavariables which occur in the expression being considered.

See figures 9.3 and 9.4 for example.

Suppose, looking at figure 9.4, we try to unify $(A(\tau 1, c(\tau 1))$ and $A(d(\tau 2), \tau 2)$.

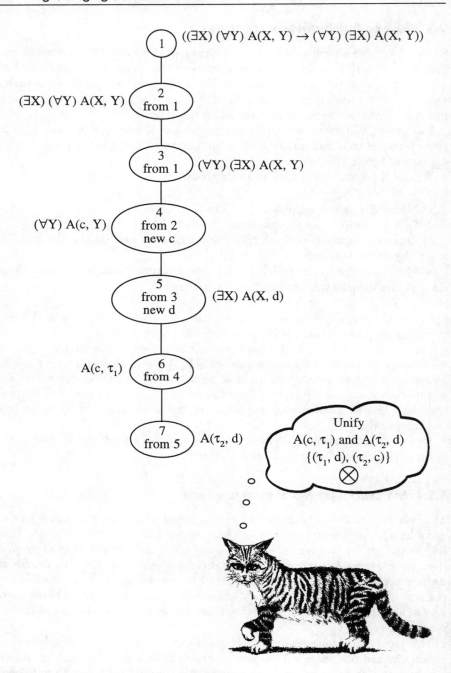

Figure 9.3 $((\exists X)(\forall Y)A(X, Y) \rightarrow (\forall Y)(\exists X)A(X, Y))$

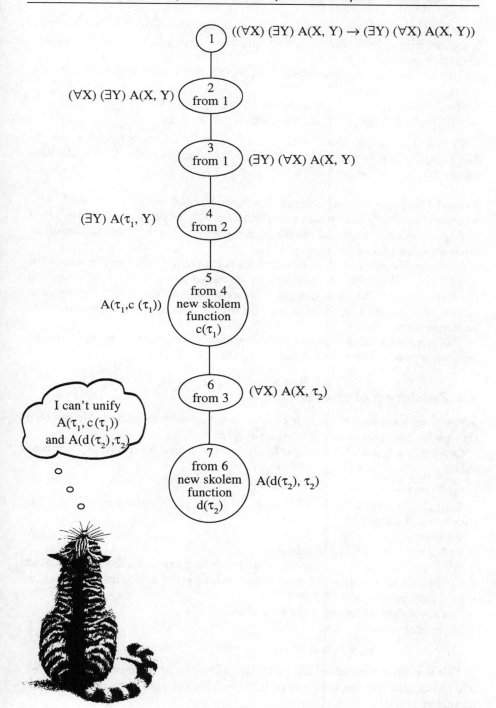

Figure 9.4 $((\forall X)(\exists Y)A(X, Y) \to (\exists Y)(\forall X)A(X, Y))$

Look back at the unification algorithm, if necessary. We see that $\tau 1$ must be $d(\tau 2)$. It follows that to get unification, we would have to have $\tau 2$ the same as $c(d(\tau 2))$. This is impossible.

On the other hand the unification succeeds in figure 9.3 and after unification the tableau becomes closed.

Here is another example. Suppose we are trying to prove

$$(\exists X)(\forall Y)(\exists Z)A(X, Y, Z) \rightarrow (\forall Y)(\exists X)(\exists Z)A(X, Y, Z)$$

We put this on the false side of an initial tableau. After a few steps we get $A(c, \tau 1, f(\tau 1))$ on the true side and $A(\tau 2, d, \tau 3)$ on the false side. After unification we get $A(c, d, f(d))$ on both sides.

Remark Many proofs in mathematics turn upon "magic" substitutions. Although it is often possible to follow each step of such a proof, the proof checker may be left feeling bewildered. How did the theorem prover ever think of this substitution? Now we know part of the answer to this.

Note that the metavariables are playing a role here which is like the role of the variables in Prolog. You may wonder why we bother to use Greek τ to distinguish the metavariables. Why not just use ordinary variables? The reason for this is to be sure that the metavariables are not the same as variables which are quantified inside the formulae.

This metavariable and Skolem function technique is related to the resolution and unification method described in the next section.

9.6 Resolution of clauses

Suppose we want to test whether or not a given sentence A is valid. We can turn this question around to ask: is $(\neg A)$ satisfiable?

One approach to this is to begin by finding the clausal form of $(\neg A)$. Suppose this is

$$\Gamma_1 = \{D_1, ..., D_n\}.$$

Each D_i is a clause. Let $\Gamma_u = \{UC(D_1), \dots, UC(D_n)\}$, where each $UC(D_i)$ is a universal closure of D_i

We have

$\models A$ if and only if Γ_u is inconsistent.

We know that Γ_u is inconsistent if and only if there is some substitution of ground terms for variables in Γ so that the resulting set of quantifier free sentences is inconstistent.

The resolution technique is the following.

Every clause has the form

$$A_1 \vee A_2 \vee \dots \vee A_i \vee \neg B_1 \vee \neg B_2 \vee \dots \vee \neg B_j$$

This is a disjunction of atomic formulae and negations of atomic formulae. We will call an atomic formula a positive literal, and the negation of an atomic formula a negative literal.

Since we know that disjunction is associative and commutative we may as well represent each clause as a set of alternative literals:

1. $\{\neg a, b)$
2. $\{\neg b, c\}$
3. $\{a, \neg c\}$
4. $\{a, b, c\}$
5. $\{\neg a, \neg b, \neg c\}$
6. resolve 1,3. $\{b, \neg c\}$
7. resolve 4,6. $\{a, b\}$
8. resolve 1,7. $\{b\}$
9. resolve 2,8. $\{c\}$
10. resolve 3,9. $\{a\}$
11. resolve 8,5. $\{\neg a, \neg c\}$
12. resolve 9,11. $\{\neg a\}$
13. resolve 10,12. $\{\ \}$

Figure 9.5   Repeated application of resolution

$$\{A_1, A_2, \ldots, A_i, \neg B_1, \neg B_2, \ldots, \neg B_j\}$$

Definition 9.3 *Suppose S_1, S_2, and S_3 are sets of literals. We will say that S_3 is a resolvant of S_1 and S_2 if there exists an atomic formula A so that A is in S_1 and $\neg A$ is in S_2, and $S_3 = (S_1 - \{A\}) \cup (S_2 - \{\neg A\})$*

Note that in particular the empty clause is a resolvant of $\{A\}$ and $\{\neg A\}$. The resolution rule of inference is

S_1, S_2

_____

S_3

where S_3 is a resolvant of S_1 and S_2. In terms of semantic tableaux, what is happening here is that S_1 and S_2 split around the common literal, one branch gets closed and the other two get absorbed into S_3.

For an example of repeated application of this rule, see figure 9.5.
The resolution procedure is the following.

_____

Suppose given a list Γ of clauses, each clause a set of literals.
Set LC $= \Gamma$
While the empty clause does not occur in LC

• Pick two clauses C and D in LC

• Pick a positive literal H in C and a negative literal $\neg G$ in D

• Try to unify H and G. If this succeeds, let α be the most general unifier. Add a resolvant of C_α and D_α to LC

_____

This procedure can only terminate if it generates an empty clause. If it does terminate then the original set of clauses Γ has inconsistent universal closure.

A problem with this method is that we may not see how to choose which pair of literals in which pair of clauses to unify at each step.

For more discussion of the resolution idea, see Schöning [1989].

Although the metavariable and Skolem function technique is related to the resolution technique they are not equivalent computationally. In some situations one technique will be faster and in other situations the other one will be faster. We can not in general distinguish between these situations in advance. However in those cases in which it is obvious to a human that a sentence is valid, the meta variable and Skolem function technique seems to finish more quickly. We could, for example, quickly show that $(\forall X)A(X) \rightarrow (\exists X)A(X)$ in this way. But if $A(X)$ is itself a complicated formula, the resolution technique may spend a long time finding clausal form of the negation, and then continue to spend a long time doing the unifications and resolutions necessary to get the empty clause.

The advantage of the resolution technique is that it avoids the branching of semantic tableaux. The disadvantage is that it resolves only on the lowest level, i.e. between atomic formulae and their negations.

9.7 Transitivity

Proofs in mathematics often have the following form. We have some set of assumptions, Γ, and we wish to prove some sentence S. Instead of proving S directly from Γ we may first prove various lemmas.

$\Gamma \vdash A_1$

$\Gamma \vdash A_2$

.

.

.

$\Gamma \vdash A_k.$

Having done this, we show

$\Gamma \cup \{A_1, ..., A_n\} \vdash S.$

Suppose we have such an indirect proof of $\Gamma \vdash S$. Since we have the completeness theorem we know that it must be possible to get a direct proof. So it is possible to start a semantic tableau with Γ on the true side and S on the false side and get closure after finitely many steps. However, it is a mysterious fact that such direct proofs sometimes seem to be, necessarily, much longer and harder to understand that the indirect proof.

In order to speed up and clarify our proofs, we may use the following:

Transitivity rule *If we have proved* $\Gamma \vdash A$, *then we may add* A *to the true side of a semantic tableau which has* Γ *on the true side.*

This is a powerful and sound rule.

Of course it is difficult to use. If we are trying to prove $\Gamma \vdash S$, how do we know which of the many statements we have previously proved from Γ might be useful to add? To make matters even worse, it is not necessary that we have *previously* proved the lemmas, which are used to prove *S*. Often in mathematics the lemmas needed are invented by the person who proves the theorem.

Another form of the above rule, possibly even more annoying, is the following:

Lateral thinking rule *For any sentence A, we may add* $(A \lor (\neg A))$ *to the true side of any semantic tableau branch.*

The idea here is that if we have assumptions Γ and wish to prove *S*, the quickest method may be to introduce some other sentence

$(A \lor (\neg A))$

and then to split into two branches, one having *A* true and one having *A* false, and then to prove $\Gamma \vdash A$, closing off one branch and then $\Gamma, A \vdash S$, closing off the other branch.

These ideas cannot currently be used as they stand by a computer. However they can be used to construct theorem proving systems in which human beings collaborate with computers. Usually the role of a human in such a system would include suggesting intermediate steps between the hypotheses and the conclusion.

■

9.8 Problems

Either show that the following statements are logically valid, or provide a counterexample.

Problem 9.9 *Esmerelda is a duck and all ducks like ponds so Esmerelda likes ponds.*

Problem 9.10 *If all burglars are barbers and all barbers are bakers then all burglars are bakers.*

Problem 9.11 *If all burglars are barbers and no bakers are not barbers then not all bakers are burglars.*

Problem 9.12 *If all burglars are barbers and all barbers are bakers and some baker is not a burglar then some barber is not a burglar.*

Problem 9.13 *If all burglars who live in Bristol are either barbers or bunglers and no bungler who lives in Bristol is a baker, then no burglar who lives in Bristol is both a barber and a baker.*

Problem 9.14 *Assume X does not occur free in B.*

a) $((\forall X)(A(X) \to B) \leftrightarrow ((\exists X)A(X) \to B))$
b) $((\forall X)(A(X) \to B) \leftrightarrow ((\forall X)A(X) \to B))$

Problem 9.15 $((\exists X)(A(X) \to B) \leftrightarrow ((\forall X)A(X) \to B))$ *where X does not occur free in B.*

Problem 9.16 *There isn't a town in Spain in which there is a barber who shaves everyone in the town who does not shave themselves, and only those in the town who do not shave themselves.*

Problem 9.17 *There isn't a town in Spain in which there is a barber who shaves every man in the town who does not shave himself, and only those men who do not shave themselves.*

Problem 9.18 *Let Γ be the axioms for a partially ordered set, as given in chapter 8. Either show that Γ logically implies the following or give a counterexample.*

a) For every X and Y there is a Z so that $X \leq Z$ and $Y \leq Z$.
b) For all X and Y and Z, if $Y \leq X$ and $Z \leq$ then $Z \leq X$.
c) Define $X < Y$ if $((X \leq Y) \land (\neg(X = Y)))$. Define $successor(X, Y)$ if $X < Y \land (\neg(\exists Z)(X < Z \land Z < Y))$. In this case we will say that Y is a successor of X.

Give a partially ordered set in which every element has a unique successor, but some elements are not successors of any other element.

Problem 9.19 *Let $P[X]$ be the set of polynomials in X with integral coefficients. Use this as the domain to define an interpretation of L_N. Give a sentence of L_N which is true under the standard interpretation, and not in this one, and vice versa.*

Problem 9.20 *Suppose that $(A \lor B)$ is a logical consequence of a set of assumptions Γ. Is it necessarily true that $\Gamma \models A$ or $\Gamma \models B$?*

Problem 9.21 *Show that if a set of sentences in a first order single sorted language is consistent, then it has a countable model.*

Problem 9.22 *Assume the result of the previous problem. Show that if the axioms for ZF set theory are consistent, there is a countable model of Zermelo-Fraenkel set theory. How do you explain the fact that within ZF set theory we can prove that the set of real numbers is uncountable?*

Problem 9.23 *See next chapter. Show that a statement in the first order single sorted language of group theory is a logical consequence of the axioms of group theory if and only if it is true in every group. (See Chapter 10.)*

Problem 9.24 *Show that a set of closed statements in a first order single sorted language is consistent if and only if it has a model.*

Problem 9.25 *Suppose you had an algorithm to decide logical validity of a formula in the first order single sorted language of group theory. Show that this would give you an algorithm to decide whether or not a statement in this language was true in all groups.* ∎

9.9 Summary of chapter 9

In this chapter a complete and sound semantic tableau style system is given for reasoning in first order single sorted languages.

The semantic tableau method systematically attempts to find a counterexample to whatever formula it is considering. Either the construction eventually succeeds, in which case the formula being considered is not valid, or some parts of the construction become blocked by contradictions, in which case we have a formal proof of the formula.

However the semantic tableau method, as given here, is non deterministic, offering the user many choices at each stage, and we do not know how to run it efficiently.

Chapter 10

The axiomatic method

10.1 A conversation about stacks

In some restaurant kitchens plates are kept in a pile in a sort of cylindrical container with a base supported by a spring. When you *push* a plate onto the pile it goes down, so all you see is the *top* plate. In general, you either can see the *top* plate, or you can see that the pile is *empty*. If you pop a plate off the top, then you see the *top* of the *rest of the pile*. That's an example of a *stack*. According to (... handwaving...) what I mean by a *stack*, you can (... more handwaving...) *push* any object onto the *top* of it. If the *stack* is not *empty*, you can pop off the object on the *top*. The last object that was *push*ed onto the stack is always the first object to get popped off. I hope you understand that we are not just talking about plates here.

$$(\forall X)(\forall Y)(stack(X) \rightarrow stack(push(Y,X)))$$
$$(\forall X)((stack(X) \land (\neg empty(X)))$$
$$\rightarrow (stack(rest(X)) \land push(top(X), rest(X)) = X))$$
$$(\forall X)(\forall Y)(stack(X) \rightarrow (top(push(Y,X)) = Y$$
$$\land rest(push(Y,X)) = X))$$

Can't you say the same thing more simply? Also, haven't you left something out? I'm not sure what ...

To avoid breaking plates and other things, we need to pay attention to both the modes of communication exemplified above, and also to all the traffic in between them.

10.2 History of the axiomatic idea

The source of the axiomatic idea is Classical and Alexandrian Greece. The Greeks believed that as any body of knowledge approaches the condition of a science it should take on an axiomatic form. This consists of definitions, axioms, proofs and theorems, as in Euclidean geometry. The guiding idea is clarity. Everything should be self evidently true. When you read or are told a definition, your reaction is supposed to be: yes, that is what I thought all along. If you understand what an axiom says, you will naturally agree with it without any doubt. In the same way the proofs begin with the axioms and each step of a proof is to be beyond question.

It should be said that the Greeks themselves did not in fact do what they said they were doing (any more than contemporary "computer scientists" necessarily do what they say they are doing.) Euclid's proofs are often muddled and incomplete and the definitions are preposterous. When this is presented uncritically as a model of clarity it can be extremely irritating. This has led many strong minded people, Buckminster Fuller for example, to reject the whole axiomatic project.

It is known that much creative mathematical thinking is extremely non systematic. It even seems that people often arrive at deep insights by persisting with confusion and contradiction. The most convincing example of this is the development of real analysis in seventeenth and eighteenth century Europe. In spite of its non-rigorous origin, real analysis remains the centre, and the best achievement of mathematics.

Religious ideas have been quite influential in mathematics. Isaac Newton spent the best energies of the last years of his life writing a mystical treatise. In the seventeenth century it was generally considered that mathematics was part of the mind of God. This was linked with extraordinary confidence in reason. Especially remarkable was the point of view of Leibnitz, who thought reasoning could, eventually, be mechanised. Around 1700, he envisioned symbolic methods "capable of increasing the power of reason more than any optical instrument has ever aided the power of vision." He hoped that all problems could be resolved by a Universal Calculator. So if (!!) a difference of opinion should arise, he imagined the two people could sit down in front of this Universal Calculator and settle the question by calculation.

In Victorian times and the early part of the twentieth century there was a great effort to clean up analysis. This meant giving formal or semi-formal versions of ideas which had previously been expressed informally, (for example the Weierstrass formalisation of the idea of a limit by the epsilon–delta definition) and combing through proofs to see what assumptions were really needed.

There was a strong belief in abstraction.

Emmy Noether, 1882–1935, the great algebraist, expressed this:

> "All relations between numbers, functions and operations first become perspicuous, capable of generalisation, and truly fruitful after being detached from specific examples, and traced back to general conceptual connections."

An important event in the development of abstraction was the publication of Van de Waerden's book *Modern Algebra*. Abstract structures such as groups and rings were separated out from the field of real numbers, and real geometry.

Hilbert, observing that when an axiom system becomes completely formalised, proofs can be reduced to syntactic transformations, took the formal idea to an extreme. He proposed the project of developing a formal system, F, which would be adequate for all of mathematics.

For such a system, F, the main task would be to prove:

a) F is consistent

b) F is complete. That is, for any meaningful statement S, either S or the negation of S must be a theorem of F.

Russell and Whitehead proposed a candidate for such a system in *Principia Mathematica*. Russell stated the view that mathematics is essentially an axiomatic game, which cannot have any meaning. Suppose we say that from axioms Γ we can prove theorem S. This must be so under all possible interpretations, in all possible worlds, with no appeal to the so-called "meaning" of the axioms. Therefore, according to this, mathematics consists of elaborate statements which, considered closely, are true just by their linguistic form, such as "A is A".

Kurt Gödel in 1931 showed that *Principia Mathematica* was incomplete. In fact he showed that any reasonable formal system for mathematics must be either wrong or incomplete. This is called Gödel's incompleteness theorem, and it showed that Hilbert's extreme formalist project was impossible.

It remains true that progress in mathematics and computing depends on dialogue between formal and informal representations of ideas.

10.3 Single and multi-sorted languages

We can classify languages according to the types of objects which may occur in the predicates. A language with only one type of object is called first order single sorted. This simplest case is the one we are concentrating on in this book. It should be clear, however, that the more complex cases are important and also need analysis.

A language with several different types of objects is called multi-sorted. Multi-sorted languages can be reduced to the single sorted case by adding predicates to distinguish the types. For example a statement such as

"For every real number X there is an integer I so that $X \leq I$"

may be understood as having two types of object, but can be expressed

$$(\forall A)(real(A) \rightarrow (\exists B)(integer(B) \wedge A \leq B))$$

Although this reduction to a single sorted case can always be done, it is not always desirable.

The notion of order is not quite so clear. Intuitively, the picture is that the objects in a higher order language are arranged in a hierarchy, with the higher order objects constructed from the lower order ones. For example, we might consider both natural numbers and sets of natural numbers in a higher order language. Or we might consider both natural numbers, and functions defined on the natural numbers.

Another possibility is that in a higher order language we could discuss the truth or syntax of a lower order one. One version of temporal logic, for example, studies reasoning about statements of the form

$$holds(p, t)$$

which can be interpreted as saying that predicate p is true at time t. The predicate p might be expressed in any first order single sorted language. We would say that the $holds(p, t)$ predicate is second order, since one of its arguments is a first order predicate.

Another important example is the study of random processes, in which the central concern is reasoning about

$$Prob(p, t)$$

which is the probability that predicate p is true at time t.

As above with multi-sorted languages, it is possible to embed higher order languages in first order single sorted languages. But this is not necessarily a good idea.

In many cases, for example in temporal logic and the study of random processes, it seems easier to reason about the subject in a higher order or multi-sorted language rather than in a first order language.

We focus on simple cases in the following and try to use first order single sorted languages.

10.4 First order single sorted theories

Definition 10.1 *A* first order single sorted theory *consists of a first order single sorted language, L, together with a set* Γ *of axioms written in L.*

A *model* of a first order single sorted theory is an interpretation of the language in which the axioms are true.

Note that if the axioms have free variables in them they are required to be universally true in a model.

Many branches of mathematics are naturally defined as the study of models of first order single sorted theories.

Many branches of mathematics and computing, however, seem to require variables of more than one type. Such situations can't be conveniently described by first order single sorted languages or first order single sorted theories. (However many of the techniques and results discussed in this book generalise to multi-sorted languages and theories. The definition of logical validity can be generalised. The semantic tableau algorithm can be generalised. The soundness and completeness theorems can be generalised, with no essential alteration in the proofs.)

How to deal with multiple types is a very difficult and important problem, which is only partly understood. One of the problems is that although it is convenient to have multiple types in a language, this can also make the language quite cumbersome; and it is often useful to say that such and such a thing of type A is "really", when looked at in another manner, also a thing of type B. Thus the type structure of language is potentially useful and it is also potentially useful to transgress this structure.

10.4.1 The predicate calculus with equality

Let L be a first order single sorted language, and suppose that $=$ is a predicate symbol of L. In this subsection we will develop a set of axioms for equality in L.

To begin with we should say that equality is reflexive, symmetric and transitive.

E1) $X = X$
E2 $(X = Y \rightarrow Y = X)$
E3) $((X = Y \wedge Y = Z) \rightarrow X = Z)$

In a model of these axioms, equality will be an equivalence relation. But we expect more of equality than this. We expect that objects which are equal in a model cannot be distinguished by the functions and predicates of the language. (A relation of this kind is called a *congruence*.) So we need

E4) $((X_1 = Y_1 \wedge X_2 = Y_2 \wedge ... X_n = Y_n) \rightarrow f(X_1, X_2, ..., X_n) = f(Y_1, Y_2, ... Y_n))$

for every function symbol f, of arity n, for every n, in the language L.

We also need the corresponding statement for predicates.

E5) $((X_1 = Y_1 \wedge X_2 = Y_2 \wedge ... X_n = Y_n) \rightarrow p(X_1, X_2, ..., X_n) \leftrightarrow p(Y_1, Y_2, ... Y_n))$

for every predicate symbol p in the language L, where p has arity n.

These axioms encapsulate what we know about equality in first order single sorted theories. Define a *canonical* interpretation of a first order single sorted language with $=$ to be one in which $=$ is interpreted as genuine equality.

Problem 10.1 *Suppose M is a model of the equality axioms in first order single sorted language L. Use the interpretation of equality to define an equivalence relation on the domain of M. Show that the equivalence classes form a canonical interpretation of L.*

It seems reasonable to say that a person who understands what equality means in mathematics will be compelled to agree with these axioms.

10.4.2 Partially ordered sets

The language $L_<$ for partially ordered sets was defined earlier. The axioms are

PO1) Equality axioms for $L_<$
PO2) $X \leq X$
PO3) $((X \leq Y \wedge Y \leq X) \rightarrow X = Y)$
PO4) $((X \leq Y \wedge Y \leq Z) \rightarrow X \leq Z)$

A canonical model of the above set of axioms is called a *partially ordered set*.

When we are talking about partially ordered sets, it is usual to use $X < Y$ as an abbreviation for $(X \leq Y) \wedge (\neg(X = Y))$; we will also use $X > Y$ to abbreviate $Y < X$.

Problem 10.2 *Give two different partially ordered sets so that the sentence*
$(\forall X)(\forall Y)(X \leq Y \vee Y \leq X)$
is true in one and false in the other.

There are many different examples of partially ordered sets. When we read the axioms we are supposed to think of a whole range of models. There is no such thing as a typical partially ordered set. The axioms are being used here to express a consensus about an idea. A partially ordered set is decreed to be a canonical interpretation which satisfies these axioms. From now on, if someone says "partially ordered set" we know exactly what they mean.

Problem 10.3 *Let* N *be the natural numbers, and let* D *be the collection of partially defined functions of one variable from* N *to* N. *Each function* f *in* D *will have a subset of* N *as domain. Let* ⊥ *be the completely undefined function. For two functions* f *and* g *in* D, *we will say*

$$f \preceq g$$

if the domain of f *is included in the domain of* g, *and if* $f(X) = g(X)$ *for all* X *in the domain of* f.

Of course we then have $\bot \preceq f$ *for all* f *in* D. *So* ⊥ *is the* bottom *of* D.

The structure (D, $\preceq$) *is an example of a* Scott domain. *These play an important role in certain theoretical aspects of computing.*

  a) *Do every two elements of* D *have a greatest lower bound? Do every two elements of* D *have an upper bound?*

  b) *Try to write a set of axioms for* (D, $\preceq$). *Include as much information as you can.*

  c) *We will say that a subset* S *of* D *is* directed *if any two elements of* S *have an upper bound in* S. *Is it true that if* S *is any directed subset of* D, *there exists an element* $f*$ *of* D *so that* $f*$ *is a least upper bound of* S? *Try either to prove this, or to give a counterexample.*

10.4.3 Well ordered sets

Let S be a subset of the domain of a partially ordered set. We will say that X is a *minimal element* of S if X is an element of S, and if there does not exist Y in S with $Y \leq X \wedge (\neg Y = X)$.

We will say that a partially ordered set M is *a well ordered set* if every non-empty subset of the domain has a minimal element.

Well ordered sets are very important in mathematics and computing. However there is no way to express the concept in a first order single sorted language such as $L_<$. The very idea of well ordering needs to consider two different types of entities, elements of the domain, and sets of elements of the domain.

Suppose a set A is contained in the domain of a partially ordered set. We will say that A is an *antichain* if there are no two elements X and Y in A so that $X < Y$

Problem 10.4* *Let* $(M, \leq)$ *be a partially ordered set. Interpret* $=$ *as genuine equality. Show that the following conditions are equivalent:*

a) $(M, \leq)$ is well ordered and has no infinite antichain.

b) If (X_i) is any infinite sequence from M, then for each i there exists j with $i < j$ so that $X_i \leq X_j$.

c) If (X_i) is any infinite sequence from M, it must have an infinite ascending subsequence.

d) If S is any non-empty subset of M there must exist a finite subset S_0 of S so that $(\forall X \in S)(\exists Y \in S_0)(Y \leq X)$.

A partially ordered set which satisfies any of the above properties will be called strongly well ordered.

Problem 10.5 Let Σ be any finite set. If A and B are finite strings in Σ^*, define $A \preceq B$ if $A = a_1a_2....a_n$ and there exist strings, possibly empty, $B_0, ..., B_n$ so that
$$B = B_0a_1B_1a_2....a_nB_n$$
Show that this is a well ordering.

Problem 10.6 Show that the above well ordering is also a strong well ordering.

10.4.4 Groups

The first order single sorted language of group theory, L_G, was defined earlier. The axioms for group theory in this language are:

G0) Equality axioms for L_G
G1) $X \circ (Y \circ Z) = (X \circ Y) \circ Z$
G2) $X \circ \iota = X$
G3) $X \circ X^{-1} = \iota \wedge X^{-1} \circ X = \iota$

A canonical model of this is called a group.

Problem 10.7 Use semantic tableaux to show that $\iota \circ X = X$ is a logical consequence of the axioms of group theory.

Group theory is an example of an equational theory. The axioms are the equality axioms together with a list of equations between terms.

There are many different groups. For example, the symmetries of a square form a group, as do invertible 3 by 3 matrices with rational entries. The axioms are being used to summarise a body of knowledge about a large collection of related structures.

We can say that this is a *good* first order single sorted theory. Other equivalent axiom systems can be given, but this appears to be a good choice. The axioms seem to occupy a logically central position in the theory. By contrast, the axiom system given earlier for H seems to be a travesty.

A formalisation of an idea is a design, and it can be criticised, in terms of good and bad, as any other design, according to how well it serves its purpose. A bad effect of the extreme formalist position is that it discouraged such criticism, since the meaning of a statement was seen as an unnecessary or possibly even undesirable associate of the syntax.

Problem 10.8 *Let f be a function whose domain and codomain is the x − y plane. Focus attention on some square in the plane. We will say that f is a symmetry of the square if f is distance preserving, i.e. the distance from a point p to a point q is always the same as the distance from f(p) to f(q); and if f leaves the square unchanged, i.e. a point p is in the square if and only if the image f(p) is in the square. We can compose symmetries as functions. So if f and g are symmetries, f ∘ g means the symmetry obtained by first applying g and then applying f. Suppose someone claims that there can be symmetries f, g, h so that f ∘ g = f ∘ h, but g ≠ h. Either show that this is impossible, or give a concrete example in which it happens.*

Problem 10.9 *List the symmetries of the square and give their multiplication table.*

10.4.5 The natural numbers

The Peano postulates and induction

Recall that we defined $\mathbf{N}$, the natural numbers, to be $\{0, 1, 2, 3, ...\}$, i.e. the non-negative integers.

Suppose we try to describe what we know about $\mathbf{N}$.

The natural numbers may be generated from 0 and the operation of adding 1. We represent $X + 1$ as X'. We read X' as "the successor of X".

P1) 0 is a natural number.
P2) If X is a natural number, so is X'.

This seems to be something like a grammar. Suppose we consider these two statements as postulates. From this point of view, these two statements are not yet a satisfactory description of the natural numbers. How do we know that $(\neg(X' = 0))$? For that matter, how do we know that $(\neg(0'' = 0'''))$? Intuitively, we think that if you start at 0 and go on adding 1 you never get back to 0, and also you never get the same thing twice. So we add two more postulates:

P3) $(\neg(X' = 0))$.
P4) $((X' = Y') \rightarrow (X = Y))$.

Postulate P3) prevents the iterated operation from ever looping back to 0, and P4) prevents any subsequent loop. (If 13 plus 1 were 11, then by P4) 12 plus 1 would be 10, and repeating this argument would get 2 plus 1 is 0, which contradicts P3).)

So far so good. But suppose that someone claims to accept these postulates, and also insists that 1/2 is a natural number. It seems that there is no way to argue with such a person. So we must have left out something.

We want to say that the natural numbers are the *smallest set* satisfying P1), P2), P3), P4). This is not a very complicated idea, apparently, but most of the difficulty in the foundation of mathematics raises its head at this point. We add another postulate:

P5) If S is any set of natural numbers which contains 0, and is such that X' is in S whenever X is in S, then S contains all the natural numbers.

Postulates P1), P2), P3), P4), P5) are called the Peano postulates for the natural numbers, after the mathematician G. Peano. Postulate P5) is called the induction postulate.

To the above five postulates, we usually add postulates which are intended to define addition and multiplication recursively in terms of the successor function.

P6) $((X + 0) = X)$.
P7) $((X + Y') = (X + Y)')$.
P8) $((X * 0) = 0)$.
P9) $((X * Y') = ((X * Y) + X))$.

Problem 10.10 *Show that if we leave P5) out, the rest of the axiom set consists of headed Horn clauses. Show that the Herbrand universe of P3), P4), P6), P7), P8), P9) is exactly the standard interpretation of L_N.*

10.4.6 *First order single sorted Peano arithmetic*

We will now develop a first order single sorted theory for the natural numbers. This is quite different from what we did previously for partially ordered sets and groups. In those first order single sorted systems we have an axiom set which summarises our knowledge about a large number of related structures. The axioms do not have any standard interpretation.

In the case of first order single sorted arithmetic we have our hands on a language, L_N, and we are really almost entirely interested in the standard interpretation. We are not quite sure what the axioms should be.

We will try to translate the Peano postulates into L_N. To begin with, P1) and P2) are unnecessary. Since we have a constant 0, it has to be interpreted in the domain, and the domain has to be closed under the operation of the ' function, which represents successor.

We can take P3), P4), P6), P7), P8), P9) as they stand.

Our problem is with the induction postulate P5), since we don't have variables for subsets of the domain. Consider: how can the induction postulate actually be used? Suppose we wanted to prove

$$(\forall X)A(X)$$

where $A(X)$ was some formula of L_N with free variable X. If we could prove

$$A(0)$$

and we could also prove

$$(\forall X)(A(X) \rightarrow A(X'))$$

we could use the induction postulate to convince ourselves that $(\forall X)A(X)$ was true.

Part of the meaning of the induction postulate is that if S is a subset of the natural numbers and S is defined by a formula $A(X)$ of L_N, and if 0 is in S and if X' is in S whenever X is in S, then S is all of the natural numbers. This part of the meaning of the induction postulate can be expressed by an axiom scheme in L_N.

P5*) $((A(0) \wedge (\forall X)(A(X) \rightarrow A(X'))) \rightarrow (\forall X)A(X))$

for every formula $A(X)$ of L_N with free variable X.

We define first order single sorted Peano arithmetic to be the first order single sorted system with language L_N and axioms P3), P4), P5*), P6), P7), P8), P9), and also the equality axioms for L_N. This is an infinite axiom system since there are infinitely many axioms in the scheme P5*).

If we wish to be critical we can say that this first order version of the Peano postulates seems both much more complicated than the original, and also may be less powerful, since there may be statements of L_N which are true in the natural model, but which cannot be proved in the first order theory, since the sets which would be needed cannot be defined in L_N.

However it is a fact that most of elementary number theory can be stated in L_N and proved in the first order theory.

10.4.7 The universe of sets

The original version of Peano postulates seems to be quite a good axiomatic description of the natural numbers. Unfortunately, however, it essentially uses the idea of "set", which is so far undefined. In a similar way, most of contemporary mathematics can be traced back to definitions involving sets. Therefore one of the main projects in the foundation of mathematics in the twentieth century has been to try to give an axiomatic treatment of set theory. We have a language, L_{ZF}. However, there has been some difficulty in deciding what the right set of axioms should be. This subject will not be discussed in any depth in this book. A few paragraphs are given below just to indicate what the difficulties are.

Suppose we take the point of view that every object in mathematics and computing should be represented as a set. Our axioms will tell us that the universe of sets is closed under certain operations, such as taking the union of two sets. So the axioms will permit us to construct new sets from old ones.

Can the universe of sets itself be a set? It seems that the answer to this question must be "no". Suppose, for the sake of a contradiction, that the universe of all possible sets was also a set, say U. Of course U would be an element of itself; also every subset of U would be an element of U. Define $V = \{X : X \in U \wedge (\neg(X \in$

$X))$}. This V is certainly a set since it is a subset of a known set U defined by a simple predicate. Consider the question: $(V \in V)$. If this is true, then V must satisfy the defining condition for V. So

$$V \in U \wedge (\neg(V \in V))$$

This clearly implies the negation of $V \in V$. So that is impossible. But suppose $(\neg(V \in V))$. In this case V does satisfy the defining condition for elements of V. So $V \in V$! Whatever we do here, we get a contradiction. This is a version of Russell's paradox.

It seems that we must conclude that the universe of sets is not a set, and thus not a mathematical object. How can this be understood? The simplest resolution of this difficulty is to suppose that the universe is, in some sense, unfinished; it is not a completed totality. We may have, at present, constructions which give us the sets we are interested in, but it is possible that in the future some other constructions will be invented.

So our ambition in the following is to think of some axioms which will allow us to construct a good part of the sets in the universe.

It is possible to write everything we want to say directly in L_{ZF}. For the sake of exposition, however, the axioms will be described in a larger language rather than written in L_{ZF}.

We start with

s0) The equality axioms for L_{ZF}.

Intuitively, a set is a collection of objects. These "objects" may also be sets. We will say that an object is an *atom* if it does not have any elements. So the predicate $atom(X)$ is defined by

s1) $(atom(X) \leftrightarrow (\neg(\exists Y)(Y \in X)))$.

Is there any hope of imitating the Peano postulates for set theory? We might start, for example, by announcing

s2) $\emptyset$, the empty set, is a set, and also an atom. Also $((\neg atom(X) \wedge (\forall Z)(Z \in X \leftrightarrow Z \in Y)) \rightarrow X = Y)$.

So there is at least one atom, which we refer to as the empty set, and if two sets which are not atoms have the same elements they are equal.

Problem 10.11 *Extend L_{ZF} by adding a predicate symbol for atom (X) and a constant for the empty set. Give the signature of the extended language.*

Presumably, we also have:

Singleton axiom s3) if X is a set, there is another set $\{X\}$, called singleton X, whose only element is X.

■

Problem 10.12 *Write the above axiom in pure L_{ZF}. Put the axiom in Skolem form, introducing a function symbol for singleton X. Extend the signature of L_{ZF} by adding this new function symbol. Now write the axiom again in the larger language.*

■

Simple union axiom s4) if X and Y are sets, there is another set $X \cup Y$, called the union of X and Y, which contains all the elements of either X or Y or both.

Suppose, in the interests of simplicity, we tried to stop at this point.

Before, we were able to claim that the natural numbers were the smallest collection of things which contained 0 and were closed under application of the successor function. It would not be equally reasonable to claim that the universe of sets is the smallest collection of things which contains the empty set and is closed under application of the singleton and union functions. There is such a smallest collection of things, but this collection also seems to be a set; we might call it the set of finite sets. So although the universe of sets satisfies s0), s1), s2), s3), and s4) it is not the smallest possible collection satisfying these postulates.

We might try starting from some other basis, rather than the empty set, and closing under some other operations. However, a little thought will show that the same difficulty will occur. It seems that if A is any initial set of objects, and if B is any set of operations defined on sets, it is reasonable to say that there exists a smallest set C so that A is contained in C and C is closed under all the operations in B. The current consensus among mathematicians (see discussion above) is that the universe of sets can't itself be a set, and therefore that it can't possibly be constructed by starting with some basis and closing under some operations. So we are left with an uneasy feeling that there is something vague about the concept of "set".

Although we can't see how to construct the universe of sets, it is possible to try to write a list of postulates which summarise our knowledge of sets.

We will write $(\forall X \in Y)A(X)$ to mean $(\forall X)(X \in Y \rightarrow A(X))$. We will also write $(\exists X \in Y)A(X)$ to mean $(\exists X)(X \in Y \wedge A(X))$. We will call these bounded quantifiers. The bounds can be any set, Y. A formula with bounded quantifiers is one in which every quantifier is bounded, although the bounds might be different for different quantifiers.

Since we don't have a very firm mental grip on the universe of all sets, it would seem that a predicate defined by quantification over this universe is not very clear. On the other hand, predicates defined with bounded quantifiers seem relatively clear.

Axiom of replacement s5) If *dom* is a set and $R(X, Y)$ is any formula of L_{ZF} with only bounded quantifiers, and with free variables including X and Y, and if for all X in *dom* there is a unique Y so that $R(X, Y)$, then there is a set *codom* so that

$$(\forall Y)((\exists X)(X \in dom \wedge R(X, Y)) \leftrightarrow (Y \in codom))$$

Intuitively, this says that if $R(X, Y)$ defines a function with domain *dom*, then the codomain of the function is also a set. Note that $R(X, Y)$ may be any one of infinitely many formulae; thus the axiom of replacement is an axiom scheme, which contains infinitely many axioms. This version of the axiom of replacement is unusually restrictive. The more usual version of the axiom does not require the quantifiers to be bounded. Even this version seems less than absolutely convincing to me. My opinion is that if anything is wrong with this axiomatic system, it is wrong at this point.

Power set axiom s6) For any set X there is another set Y, called the power set of X, whose elements are exactly the subsets of X

$$(\forall X)(\exists Y)(\forall W)(W \subseteq X \leftrightarrow W \in Y)$$

Union axiom s7) For any set X there is another set Y which is the union of all the elements of X.

$$(\forall X)(\exists Y)(\forall W)(W \in Y \leftrightarrow ((\exists U)(W \in U \wedge U \in X)))$$

Axiom of choice s8) Let T be any set whose elements are non-atoms and disjoint. There exists a set S so that if X is any element of T then $X \cap S$ is a singleton. This means that S picks out one element from each of the non-empty disjoint elements of T.

Axiom of infinity s9) This axiom asserts the existence of a set, $\mathcal{F}$, which contains $\vee$ and is closed under singleton and union operations

$$(\exists \mathcal{F})(\vee \in \mathcal{F} \wedge (\forall X)(\forall Y)(Y \in \mathcal{F} \wedge X \in \mathcal{F}) \rightarrow X \cup \{Y\} \in \mathcal{F}))$$

It is a remarkable fact that almost all mathematics can be stated in L_{ZF} and proved from this axiom set using semantic tableaux, or any of the other adequate deductive systems for first order single sorted logic.

How is mathematics translated into L_{ZF}? This is a long story. But, hopefully, from the work we have done with Prolog it should be clear that once finite lists have been defined, almost all other definitions can be constructed recursively using lists.

We will write $\{X_1, ..., X_n\}$ for the set which is the union of $\{X_1\},..., \{X_n\}$. The sets which we have been dealing with so far are unordered. For example $\{a, b\} = \{b, a\}$, since they have the same elements. For almost any application we need the concept of ordered sets, which, in the finite case, are the same as the lists discussed earlier in Prolog. How are we going to represent these lists in terms of sets? We saw before that we can build up lists from the empty list, [ ], and the cons operation $[X \mid Y]$.

Presumably the mysterious looking [ ] is some kind of atom.

There are various ways of embedding the cons operation into unordered sets, none of them entirely satisfactory. What we would like is that given $[X \mid Y]$, it should be possible to find both the head, X, and the tail, Y. One of the usual solutions is the following. We suppose that X and Y are already objects of some kind. We then represent $[X \mid Y]$ by

$$\{\{X\}, \{X, Y\}\}.$$

■

Problem 10.13 *Show from the axioms that for any X and Y there is a unique set* $\{X, Y\}$ *whose only elements are X and Y.*

Problem 10.14 *Show that the head, X, is uniquely determined from*

$$\{X, \{X, Y\}\}.$$

Problem 10.15 *Find Skolem forms of s6), s7), and s9). Give a signature for an extension of L_{ZF} which includes all the constants and function and predicate symbols needed for a succinct expression of the above axiom set.*

Problem 10.16 *Show that if d is any set and $p(X)$ is any formula with bounded quantifiers in L_{ZF} then $\{X : X \in d \wedge p(X)\}$ is a set. Hint: define a function whose domain is d and whose codomain is the set we want. Then use the axiom of replacement.*

Problem 10.17 *Show that if X is any set the intersection of all the elements of X is also a set.*

Problem 10.18 *Show from the axioms that there is a smallest set* **N** *so that* $\vee \in$ **N***, and* $(\forall X)(X \in \mathbf{N} \rightarrow (X \cup \{X\}) \in \mathbf{N})$*. Give a one to one correspondence between the natural numbers and this set. Is it reasonable to say that this set is the natural numbers?*

Problem 10.19 *Write the axiom of choice out explicitly in L_{ZF}.*

Problem 10.20 *It can be argued that a cleaner way to represent lists is just to postulate a* $cons(X, Y)$ *operation with the desired properties. State axioms for* $cons(X, Y)$*, to be added to the axiom set above. Also give axioms for* [ ].

Problem 10.21 **Russell's paradox.** *It seems natural to assume that if we write down any formula $p(X)$ of L_{ZF} with one free variable, X, this should define a set Y consisting of those sets X for which $p(X)$ is true. However, this leads to contradictions. Consider, for example, the formula $(\neg(X \in X))$. If we could define*

$$Y = \{X : (\neg(X \in X))\}$$

we would have

$$(\forall X)((X \in Y) \leftrightarrow (\neg(X \in X)))$$

Show that this is impossible by showing that both $Y \in Y$ and $(\neg(Y \in Y))$ lead to contradictions.

We met another version of Russell's paradox earlier, in the person of the barber who shaves everyone who does not shave himself or herself, and only shaves such persons. Even though the definition is grammatical, the idea is impossible to realise.

Russell's paradox shows that we cannot assume that if $p(X)$ is any formula of L_{ZF} then $\{X : p(X)\}$ is a set. This leads to contradictions. However, so far contradictions have not been derived from the axiom system given above. Is there any chance that the system given above might be inconsistent? The answer to this question must unfortunately be *yes*. (For example, if from the above axioms you could prove the existence of a universal set consisting of all the sets which could be proved to exist from the axioms, then Russell's paradox would raise its head in this setting. This does not seem impossible. In addition to this, there must be many other ways in which things can go wrong.)

Problem 10.22 *Consider the following argument:*

"*Suppose X is a set, and we know that none of its elements are atoms. So we know*

$$(\forall Y)(Y \in X \rightarrow (\exists W)(W \in Y))$$

If we put this in prenex normal form we get

$$(\forall Y)(\exists W)((Y \in X) \rightarrow (W \in Y))$$

Let $f(Y)$ be a Skolem function for W. So we have:

$$(\forall Y \in X)(f(Y) \in Y)$$

This proves the axiom of choice."

Comment. You either have to reject the argument, or reject the use of Skolem functions, or accept the axiom of choice.

■

10.4.8 Category theory

Category theory is a branch of mathematics in which it is not natural to use a first order single sorted language.

Category theory has two types, *objects* and *morphisms*. Each morphism is supposed to have a domain and a codomain, which are objects. So we will have a domain function and a codomain function from morphisms to objects. Also there is an operation of composition, written ∘, defined between two morphisms α and β, provided that $codomain(\alpha) = domain(\beta)$.

The axioms are:

1) If α is a morphism, then $domain(\alpha)$ and $codomain(\alpha)$ are objects.

2) If α and β are morphisms and $codomain(\alpha) = domain(\beta)$, then there is a morphism $\gamma = \alpha \circ \beta$ so that $domain(\gamma) = domain(\alpha)$ and $codomain(\gamma) = codomain(\beta)$.

3) The composition operation between morphisms is associative, wherever it is defined.

4) For each object, X, there is an identity morphism, id_X, so that if α is any morphism:

if $domain(\alpha) = X$, then $id_X \circ \alpha = \alpha$;

if $codomain(\alpha) = X$, then $\alpha \circ id_X = \alpha$.

Examples of categories

1) Sets and functions, the sets being the objects and the functions being the morphisms.

2) Nodes and paths in a data structure.

3) Statement forms and substitutions, the statement forms being the objects and the substitutions being the morphisms.

4) Groups and group homomorphisms. Similarly, the models of any first order theory can be formed into a category.

5) Languages and translations, the languages being the objects and the translations being the morphisms.

6) Formulae of a language are objects, and proofs that one formula implies another are morphisms between the objects.

7) For any physical system, let the states of the system be represented by objects; the possible transitions between states are morphisms.

8) A finite state machine has a finite set I of input symbols and a finite set S of internal states. The internal states change according to the inputs. This can be represented by a data structure whose nodes are labelled with the internal states and whose arrows are labelled with the input symbols. This data structure is called the transition graph of the finite state machine. This is also a category whose objects are the nodes and whose morphisms are sequences of transitions.

For more discussion of category theory, see *Categories and Computer Science*, by R. F. C. Walters (1991) in the references in chapter 13.

10.5 Problems

Problem 10.23 *What is a queue? Write an informal description and translate this into a formal system. State a theorem about queues which is, or ought to be, a logical consequence of your axioms.*

Problem 10.24 Comparison between statement forms and natural numbers
Viewed as combinatorial objects, there are interesting similarities between the statement forms and the natural numbers, because of the iterative way in which they are generated.

We will say that a set is closed *under an operation if whenever the operation is applied to elements of the set the result is another element of the set.*

We could describe the natural numbers as the smallest set of real numbers which contains 0 and is closed under the operation of addition by 1.

Similarly, we could describe the statement forms as the smallest set of strings which contains the proposition names *and is closed under the operations* $\neg, \vee, \wedge, \rightarrow, \leftrightarrow$ *applied to strings.*

Other statements about the natural numbers can be similarly transferred to statements about the statement forms.

For example, we could say that if Y is a natural number, then either $y = 0$ or Y is of the form $x + 1$ where X is a natural number.

If A is a statement form, then either A is a proposition name, or A has the form $(\neg B)$, where B is a statement form, or A has one of the forms $(B \vee C)$, $(B \wedge C)$, $(B \rightarrow C)$, $(B \leftrightarrow C)$, where both B and C are statement forms.

The induction principle for the natural numbers: Let P be a property which is either true or false for natural numbers. If P is true for 0, and P is true for $x + 1$ whenever P is true for x, it follows that P is true for all natural numbers.

Exercise *State a corresponding induction principle for the statement forms.*

It should be clear that transfers of the above type can be made for many other formal languages, not just for the statement forms.

Exercise *Review the definition of L_N given above. Define the terms of L_N as the smallest set of strings containing such and such and closed under so and so operations. Repeat this for the formulae of L_N.*

Since syntactic things, such as languages, can be discussed as mathematical objects, and since the natural numbers seem to be implicit in everything, there is great scope for confusion here. What is called syntax and what is called semantics seems to depend on point of view. It seems that the syntax of one language could be discussed in another language, and it can even happen that some of the syntax of a language can be discussed by the language itself, and part of the semantics of a language could be reflected in its syntax. The hall of mirrors aspect of this is brilliantly exploited by Gödel, as we shall see later.

10.6 Computational use of the axiomatic method

Logic programming is an attempt to make computational use of the axiomatic method.

The central idea is to represent a database by an axiom set Γ. Then, given a question Q, we try to decide whether or not Q is a logical consequence of Γ.

We have seen, using Prolog, that there are applications where this can be done.

On the other hand, since the logical validity problem is recursively unsolvable, it seems extremely unlikely that there could exist a satisfactory implementation of a general purpose formal reasoning system for first order single sorted languages.

To what extent, then, is it possible to make computational use of the axiomatic method?

There is a good example of what can be done in the case of computational group theory.

Suppose we take the language L_G of group theory and add finitely many constants, $c_1, ..., c_n$. A ground term in the extended language is called a *word*. Let Γ be the axioms of group theory, and let Γ_e be obtained by adding finitely many equations,

$$v_1 = u_1, v_2 = u_2, ..., v_k = u_k$$

between words.

Note that Γ_e is a finite set of headed Horn clauses. So Γ_e defines a Herbrand universe G_e. In group theory, this construction is well known. Γ_e is called a finite presentation of the group G_e, and G_e is called a finitely presented group. There are many finitely presented groups of practical importance.

Obviously each Γ_e is an axiom system for its group G_e. We expect that we can get some useful information about G_e from Γ_e.

The *word problem* for a finite presentation of a group Γ_e is to decide, given two words, w_1 and w_2, whether or not $w_1 = w_2$ in G_e. This is equivalent to deciding whether or not $\Gamma_e \vdash w_1 = w_2$.

We have, in a sense, quite a simple situation here. Γ_e is a set of headed Horn clauses, and our problem is just an equation between ground terms.

It has been shown, nevertheless, that this problem is in general recursively undecidable. That is: there is no algorithm which can solve the word problem. In fact, this problem, even though it has a simple form, is just as difficult as the logical validity problem.

In spite of this fact, there is a remarkable technique, called the Knuth-Bendix procedure, which can be applied to this problem and which, in many cases, gives a solution.

The object of the Knuth-Bendix procedure is to get an improved version of the axiom set Γ_e, i.e. another axiom set, say Γ_f, logically equivalent to Γ_e but with better computational properties with respect to the word problem. So the Knuth-Bendix procedure takes as input an axiom system such as Γ_e, and, if it terminates, produces a new axiom system Γ_f

$$\Gamma_e \Rightarrow \textbf{Knuth-Bendix} \Rightarrow \Gamma_f$$

It may happen that the Knuth-Bendix procedure does not terminate. However if it does terminate the axiom system Γ_f which is produced is guaranteed to solve the word problem for words in G_e.

Given a possible identity

$$w = \iota?$$

Γ_f can be used to produce a sequence of simplifications of w

$$w = w_1 = w_2 = w_3 = \ldots = w_k$$

which is guaranteed to terminate in a normal form. It is guaranteed that $G_e \models w = \iota$ if and only if the final word , w_k, in the sequence is, literally, ι.

Of course the reason why this fails to solve the word problem in general is that the Knuth-Bendix procedure does not always terminate. Nevertheless, the Knuth-Bendix procedure in many interesting cases produces an axiom system which can be used computationally.

The Knuth-Bendix procedure, as it stands, only applies to equational theories. However, the success in this area shows that it is possible to make progress with hard problems in computational axiomatics.

For more information about this subject, see the paper by Knuth and Bendix (1970), and also the related work on Gröbner bases in computer algebra (Davenport, Siret and Tournier, 1988) in the references in chapter 13.

10.7 Summary of chapter 10

The axiomatic method is a technique for compression of representation of knowledge.

Given a field of knowledge, the technique is to condense everything we know into a set of axioms. The whole field can then be deduced from the axioms.

This ancient and beautiful technique is most developed in mathematics.

Good examples are group theory and the theory of partially ordered sets, where we have a firm understanding of a wide variety of models; and first order arithmetic where we think we understand the standard model. The problem with set theory seems related to the fact that we find it hard to comprehend any of the models, if there are such.

Chapter 11

The Gödel incompleteness theorem

Dear Professor James,

I do not feel like doing philosophy this afternoon.

Gertrude Stein's successful answer to the final examination in philosophy set by William James.

A formal deductive system consists of a formal language together with a formal definition of proof for statements in that language. The most general version of the Gödel incompleteness theorem is that no correct formal system can prove all the true statements of mathematics. As a consequence of this: neither mathematics nor computing can be completely formalised.

The original version of Gödel's incompleteness theorem applied to *Principia Mathematica* of Russell and Whitehead: this was a formal deductive system which was intended to include all of mathematics. Gödel managed to construct a sentence of L_N which could be interpreted to say that its own self was not provable in *Principia Mathematica*. So (!) either it must be true and unprovable in *Principia Mathematica*; or *Principia Mathematica* has a false theorem.

11.1 Cantor's diagonal argument

We don't know how Gödel got his ideas. But a possible source for the incompleteness proof is Cantor's diagonal argument, showing that the set of real numbers is uncountable.

Definition 11.1 *We will say that a set is* countable *if it is finite or if there exists a bijection between the set and the natural numbers, i.e. if it can be listed.*

The integers and the rational numbers are countable.

Problem 11.1 *Show that if a set Σ is countable, so is Σ^*.*

A subset of a countable set is also countable.

The set of real numbers is not countable.

Proof (Cantor's diagonal argument) The proof is by contradiction. We suppose that the set of real numbers were countable. Imagine, then, that we have all the real numbers in a list, expressed in decimal form, with no infinite sequence of 9's:

$$[x_1, x_2, x_3, \ldots\ldots]$$

For example, the list might begin:

$x_1 = 0.0000456871233\ldots$

$x_2 = 13245555.33002761\ldots\ldots$

.

.

.

If x is a real number, expressed in decimal with no infinite sequence of 9's, let $x(i)$ be its ith digit to the right of the decimal point. So $x_i(i)$ may be visualised as the digit to be found on the ith diagonal position of the list.

Now define a real number α in $(0, 1)$:

$\alpha(i) = 0$ if $x_i(i) \neq 0$, and $\alpha(i) = 1$ if $x_i(i) = 0$.

The number α is not equal to any number in the list. But the list was supposed to include all the real numbers. $\otimes$.

Therefore the set of real numbers is not countable.

$\square$

11.2 The incompleteness theorem for Peano arithmetic: the formally proved impossibility of completely formalising mathematics or computing

First order single sorted Peano arithmetic was described in the previous chapter. We will say $\vdash_P S$ if S, a formula of L_N, is a theorem of this system. Let $\mathbf{N}$ be the standard model for first order single sorted arithmetic, i.e. the natural numbers with the usual addition, multiplication, successor, and equality. We can probably agree that the axioms for first order single sorted Peano arithmetic are true in $\mathbf{N}$. Since we believe in the soundness of our deductive system, we have

$$\vdash_P S \Rightarrow \mathbf{N} \models S$$

The Gödel incompleteness theorem shows that the converse is false. In other words, it shows that there exist sentences S of L_N which are true in the standard model, but are not theorems of our formal system.

A Gödel numbering of the formulae of L_N is a computable injection

$$g : \{formulae \ of \ L_N\} \rightarrow \mathbf{N}$$

i.e. a coding of formulae by the natural numbers. It does not have to be surjective. However, given a natural number, we do require that there is a way of deciding whether or not it is the code of a formula in L_N, and, if so, it is possible to invert the code to find the formula.

There are many different ways of constructing such a Gödel numbering. One method was described earlier in the problems in chapter 1.

Gödel's incompleteness theorem for first order arithmetic *There is a sentence A of L_N so that* $\mathbf{N} \models A$ *but it is not true that* $\vdash_P A$.

Sketch of proof Let g be a Gödel numbering of formulae of L_N. If A is a formula of L_N, then $g(A)$ is a natural number which is a code for A.

Define a predicate $p(X)$ as follows.

$p(n)$ is True if and only if n is the Gödel number of a formula $A(X)$ of L_N so that $A(X)$ has one free variable, X, and $\nvdash_P A(n)$.

This means that

$p(n)$ is False if and only if either n is not a Gödel number of a formula $A(X)$ with one free variable X, or $n = g(A(X))$, where $A(X)$ is such a formula and $\vdash_P A(n)$.

Claim: the predicate $p(X)$ can be translated into L_N. This means that we can find a formula $A(X)$ with one free variable, X, so that

$p(X)$ is True if and only if $\mathbf{N} \models A(X)$.

(We are not proving this claim. You can either accept that Gödel did this, or look up his original paper, or try to do it yourself.)

$A(X)$ is a definite formula of L_N. We know that via the Gödel numbering, it means the same thing as $p(X)$. But to someone who hadn't seen the origin of $A(X)$, it would look like a complicated statement about a natural number X. In fact, the "meaning" of $A(X)$ seems to depend on how you look at it. It obviously is, literally, a statement about a natural number X, built up from addition and multiplication, equality and the logical operators; it also is a translation of $p(X)$.

We can now define an interesting number

$n* = g(A(X))$

The number $n*$ is a perfectly ordinary natural number, albeit large. The predicate $p(n*)$ is either true or false.

Suppose first that $p(n*)$ were false. (Please look back at this point to the description of what happens when $p(X)$ if false.) Certainly $n*$ is the Gödel number of a formula $A(X)$ with one free variable X. It must be then that $\vdash_P A(n*)$. But $A(n*)$ is false in the natural model! We have already decided that our formal system is correct for the natural model, so this cannot happen.

We are left with the extraordinary conclusion that $p(n*)$ is true. (Please look back at this point at the description of what happens when $p(X)$ is true.) We know that $A(n*)$ is not a theorem of our system. However, $A(n*)$ is true in the natural model, since $A(n)$ translates $p(n)$.

So we have found $A(n*)$, a true sentence of L_N which is not a theorem of our system.

$\square$

You may think at this point that the situation can be repaired by just adding the new truth $A(n*)$ to the Peano axioms. However, the whole mechanism of the proof applies just as well to the new system as it did to the old one.

11.3 Applications to computing

The above incompleteness proof can be modified to apply to any general purpose computer language.

We have seen that a natural problem in Prolog is whether or not a given program with a given query will terminate. Call this the termination problem for Prolog.

Suppose someone claims to have solved this problem. That is, someone claims to have an algorithm which, given a Prolog program and a query, will tell us whether or not Prolog will terminate in this situation. Furthermore, let's say, the algorithm is guaranteed always to terminate. Is this possible?

We have already seen that a Prolog interpreter can be written inside Prolog. It seems reasonable then that we can expect that the hypothetical termination algorithm can be implemented in Prolog. Suppose this had been done.

Suppose then that we have in front of us a Prolog program, P_1, defining a predicate

stop(X).

The claim is: if we append any other program P_2 to P_1, and let X be any query, then the query about X

stop(X).

always terminates, and tells us whether or not P_2 given X will terminate.

To see that this is impossible, consider the following:

---

start:-stop(start),start.

start.

Let P_2 be this, followed by P_1, and let the query be

start.

Does this terminate? If it does, stop(start) succeeds, and thus it does not terminate, $\otimes$.

Suppose it does not terminate. In that case stop(start) fails. So

start

terminates and succeeds. $\otimes$.

This is obviously impossible. So our assumption that stop(X) solved the termination problem must be mistaken.

The termination problem is just the most obviously unsolvable of the natural problems in computing. Computing should be seen as a small region of simplicity in a huge landscape of unsolvable problems and unanswerable questions.

11.4 Summary of chapter 11

Gödel's wonderful incompleteness theorem shows that mathematics and computing can never be completely formalised.

Chapter 12

Collections of interacting processes

One of the most interesting current formalisation projects is the attempt to understand systems as collections of interacting processes or *agents*. We are certainly surrounded with such systems, and are always relating to them or reacting to them, or trying to imagine better ones. So we must know a lot about them. However the formalisation process for these ideas is definitely not finished; on the contrary, it is in the early, seething, proliferating stage. The reader is invited to look at the excellent books of Hoare (1985) and Milner (1989).

My opinion is that understanding such systems requires probability theory. Milner's ideas are introduced below with a probabilistic slant.

12.1 Agents and actions

Imagine a system. It might be a collection of water molecules, or a collection of people, or a network of communicating machines. We divide the system up into parts which are called *agents*. Each agent has a collection of possible states, and a collection of possible actions which perform transitions between the states. So we may imagine the states of an agent as being the nodes in a data structure, whose arrows are labelled with actions. We suppose also that the actions are occurring in continuous time, and that each action has two random variables associated with it, the waiting time for that action to begin and the duration of the action.

There are two types of actions: internal actions and external actions. Internal actions may be done by the agent autonomously. However, an external action, α, may only be done if an agent is part of a system, obtained by composition of agents, and another agent in the system does a complementary action. The waiting time until an action, α, may start, $w_{\text{start}\alpha}$, and the duration dt_α are both random variables. This means that there are functions

$p(t) = \text{Probability}(w_{\text{start}\alpha} \leq t)$

$q(t) = \text{Probability}(dt_\alpha \leq t)$

which give the distributions of the waiting times and the durations. We suppose these functions have continuous derivatives and that $p(0) = 0$. (Naturally we also suppose that $p(t)$ and $q(t)$ are never more than 1, and that their derivatives are non-negative.)

In the examples below, we will consider actions which occur at rate λ and happen

215

instantaneously. This means that the duration is always 0, and $p(t) = 1 - e^{-\lambda t}$. But of course other distributions are quite possible.

So how does an agent evolve in time?

From now on, an agent means an agent which is in a particular current state.

Suppose A is an agent, and its current state is s. We can say that A is located at s in its data structure. Imagine we start a clock at time 0 and observe A. A instantaneously considers the possible actions which may be initiated from state s. These are just the labels on arrows leading away from s. Each arrow has random variables for start times and durations associated with it. Using these random variables, which are supposed to be independent, the agent picks a start time $w_{\text{start}\alpha}$ and a duration dt_α for each action α which can be initiated from s.

The agent now has a set of start times and durations for its actions. *We assume that the random variables are such that with probability* 1 *the start times can be discretely ordered.*

The agent A then orders the actions in a list according to the start times. The list has the form:

$(\beta_1, w_{\text{start}\beta_1}, dt_{\beta_1}), (\beta_2, w_{\text{start}\beta_2}, dt_{\beta_2}), \ldots$

Nothing has yet happened. The agent just has a list of actions it would do if it could.

We will say that an action, β, in this list is offered at time t if $t_{\text{start}\beta} \leq t$. We will say β is *possible* at time t if it is offered at t and it is an internal action, or if it is offered at t and A belongs to a composite in which another agent offers the complementary action to β at time t.

The action which is performed by A is the first one in the list which becomes possible.

An agent in isolation just does internal actions, hopping from node to node in its data structure. Such an agent will offer various possibilities of external actions at various times but since the agent is in isolation none of these offers will be taken.

As soon as an agent begin to perform an action at time t, it continues to do so for the duration of the action. All other actions which were on offer by the agent before time t are withdrawn. When the action is completed a new list of possibilities is instantaneously formed. Thus internal and external actions can preempt each other.

To say that two agents interact is to say that they do complementary actions which begin at the same instant.

Milner attempts to give a short list of operations on actions and agents which will produce new agents. The hope is to see systems as compound agents which are obtained by combining together simpler ones using the operations. Here is the list.

1) Prefix. If α is an action and E is an agent, $\alpha.E$ is the agent which first performs action α and then becomes agent E.

2) Summation. Let S be a set of agents. ΣS is the agent which does nothing until one of the agents in S, say E, performs an external action. Then S becomes E. In this case we will say that E is the survivor of S. (It is supposed here that no two of the agents in S have complementary external actions.)

3) Composition. Let E_1 and E_2 be agents. The composition of E_1 and E_2 is written $E_1 \mid E_2$. This is an agent whose states are pairs of states from E_1 and

E_2. All previous internal and external independent actions are allowed. However there are some new internal actions. Whenever E_1 and E_2 have a complementary external action, say x and x', the composite $E_1 \mid E_2$ can do both actions, starting simultaneously. This synchronised action is considered as external from the point of view of E_1 or E_2, but is considered to be an internal action of the composite.

4) Restriction. If E is an agent and L is a set of external actions, $E \backslash L$ is the agent which is the same as E except that it has external actions L removed, i.e. all arrows with these actions are deleted.

5) Relabelling. If E is an agent and f is a function from actions to actions, $E[f]$ is the agent which is obtained by replacing each action x of E by its image, $f(x)$ under relabelling function f.

It is clear that everything becomes an agent in this way of describing the world. A system is just a composition of agents, and is itself an agent. An environment for an agent is just another agent. To say that we put an agent in an environment means that we form the composite.

The sum of two agents can be visualised as follows. We put the two data structures side by side and run the stochastic processes independently. This continues until one of them does an external action, and then the other one vanishes.

Example 12.1 *The Hoare vending machine has two buttons, one marked big and one marked little. You either put in 2p and press the big button and then collect your big chocolate bar or you put in 1p and press little and collect your little chocolate bar. This is described by the following equation.*

$$V = get2p_1.notebig_1.givebig_1.V + get1p_1.notelittle_1.givelittle_1.V$$

The subscripts on the actions mean that they are supposed to occur at rate 1.

Problem 12.1 *Draw the simplest possible representation of the Hoare vending machine.*

We can now decree that actions occur in complementary pairs
$(get2p, give2p)$,
$(get1p, give1p)$,
$(notebig, pressbig)$,
$(notelittle, presslittle)$,
$(givelittle, getlittle)$,
$(givebig, getbig)$.
So we can write a customer for the Hoare machine as
$$C = give2p_\lambda.pressbig_\lambda.getbig_\lambda.C$$
Another customer would be
$$D = give1p_\lambda.presslittle_\lambda.getlittle_\lambda.D$$
and of course $C + D$ would be still another customer.

Problem 12.2 *Describe the difference between C + D and E, described by*

$$E = give1p_\lambda.presslittle_\lambda.getlittle_\lambda.E + give2p_\lambda.pressbig_\lambda.getbig_\lambda.E$$

12.2 In praise of randomness

We can think of complex systems which evolve in time as being deterministic, non-deterministic, or random. In a deterministic model each part of the system changes at each instant according to its current state and the current state of its surroundings. In a non-deterministic model, there is some free choice in the behaviour of the parts of a system. In a random model, there is still free choice, but probabilities are associated with the choices, and what is actually done depends on making the choices randomly, depending on the probabilities associated with them.

The experience of statistical mechanics shows that the assumptions of local randomness can result in large systems which are stable, reliable and orderly. However the deterministic and the indeterministic models are relatively intractable.

Problem 12.3 *Decide whether or not the following should be true:*

a) $A \mid (B \mid C) = (A \mid B) \mid C$
b) $A + (B + C) = (A + B) + C$
c) $\alpha.(B + C) = \alpha.B + \alpha.C$
d) $\alpha.(B \mid C) = \alpha.B \mid \alpha.C$
e) $A + A = A$

12.2.1 Discussion

Io: The agents on the left and right hand sides of the equality sign in part d) above are the same. The reason is that anything one can do the other can do.

Calypso: No they are not the same because the data structure for the left hand side is not the same as the data structure for the right hand side.

Io: I don't care about the data structure, since you can't observe it. All you observe is the behaviour. The left hand side and the right hand side have the same behaviour, so they have to be the same.

Terpsichore: Let's agree that we are talking about some equivalence relation on agents and we are writing this as equality. We will call it observational equivalence, as Milner does.

Melpomene: I don't agree that the behaviours are the same, although I agree that any particular thing one can do the other can do and vice versa.

Io: What do you mean?

Melpomene: There are two different α's going on independently on the right hand side. Suppose α is sometimes quick and sometimes slow. Obviously $\alpha.B \mid \alpha.C$ is faster and better than $\alpha.(B \mid C)$. One of these agents has, so to speak, two chances to get it right, and the other has only one.

Calypso: It is the same α in all cases. Having two chances at the same thing does not help.

Melpomene: No the α's are not the same. They are distributed in the same way but they are independent. When you form the composite all the actions in the two agents are independent until synchronisation occurs.

Io: I don't think it makes any difference. We don't want to get involved in the details of the timing.

Melpomene: On the contrary, that is exactly what we need to think about.

Io: I hope at least you agree that $A + A = A$.

Melpomene: I am not even sure about that. $A + A$ starts faster than A.

Io: At least you would say that after the first action $A + A$ is the same as A.

Melpomene: No. What you get after $A + A$ is the winner of a race between two independent copies of A.

Calypso: In the definition it says that $A + B$ turns into either A or B depending on which one performs the first external action.

Melpomene: Sure, but the winner is in some internal state, which may be related to its being the winner.

Io: But this is just supposition.

Melpomene: No it is not. You really could give an example of an A so that $A + A$ could be distinguished experimentally from A.

Terpsichore: I notice that $A + A = A$ is an axiom in Milner. I challenge you to produce this example.

Problem 12.4 *Settle this part of the argument. That is, decide whether or not it is possible to distinguish observationally between $A + A$ and A. Suppose you have one agent in front of you which is either A or $A + A$. Can you give an experiment which will result in better than a random guess as to which one it is? If you think it is possible to do this, you can choose any A you wish.*

In a sense the correct way to settle the above argument is to read the definition of equivalence between agents given by Milner. However he calls the relation observational equivalence. We are entitled to complain if two agents which we can distinguish observationally are said to be observationally equivalent.

Problem 12.5 *We are given a specification for a system, using the above notation. This is transformed into a design using the following identities.*

1) $A \mid (B + C) = (A \mid B) + (A \mid C)$
2) $\alpha.(A \mid B) = \alpha.A \mid \alpha.B$

3) $A + (B \mid C) = (A + B) \mid (A + C)$

Can you be sure that the design meets the specification?

12.3 Dining philosophers

We suppose that there are five agents, which are called philosophers. These agents either think or go to the dining room, where they attempt to eat. For a philosopher to eat, two forks are required, since the only food given to these agents is spaghetti, and they can only manage this with two forks. However there are only five forks. So there are ten agents in this system, the philosophers and the forks:

System = philosophers | forks

The forks subsystem consists of a composite of five forks:

forks = *fork* | *fork* | *fork* | *fork* | *fork*

The philosophers subsystem consists of a composite of five philosophers

philosophers = *philosopher* | *philosopher* | *philosopher*
                 | *philosopher* | *philosopher*

Each fork can be picked up and put down.

fork = *picked-up*$_1$.*put-down*$_1$.*fork*

A philosopher may either think or eat.

philosopher = *thinking-philosopher* + *eating-philosopher*

The thinking behaviour of a philosopher is described by

thinking-philosopher = *thinking*$_1$.*philosopher*,

with the internal action of thinking.

The eating behaviour is more complicated, with external actions *take-fork* and *replace-fork*, complementary to *picked-up* and *put-down* respectively.

eating-philosopher = *take-fork*$_1$.*take-fork*$_1$.*eat*$_1$
                 .*replace-fork*$_1$.*replace.fork*$_1$.*philosopher*

An obvious difficulty in this situation is that if each philosopher takes one fork no one can do anything. This can be repaired just by allowing the philosophers occasionally to replace a fork, before they have eaten.

eating-philosopher = *take-fork*$_1$.(*take-fork*$_1$
                 .*eat*$_1$.*replace-fork*$_1$.*replace.fork*$_1$.*philosopher*
                 +*replace-fork*$_1$.*philosopher*)

We can now assert that any philosopher who takes a fork eventually eats with probability 1. We can also assert that the ratio of time spent eating tends to 1, almost surely, for any two philosophers. So, in a precise sense, the system is fair. (Also, this result does not depend on the number of forks, provided that there are at least two of them.)

We can even compute the expected waiting time for a hungry philosopher to eat.

It should be clear that many of the interesting features of the dining philosophers depend on the idea of probability, and cannot even be discussed in a non-deterministic or a deterministic setting.

12.4 Telephone exchanges

The system consists of N cities. Each pair of cities is linked by C telephone lines. Calls for city j arise at city i at rate v_{ij}. A call from city i to city j may either be sent directly from i to j if a line is free, or it may be rerouted via another city k. If a call cannot be sent directly or rerouted, it is lost.

There are two strategies for choosing a rerouting city k.

1) Pick k at random, each time a rerouting is needed.
2) Pick k at random at city i the first time a rerouting to city j is required. Subsequently stick to using k for rerouting calls for j from city i until such time as a call for city j is lost.

These two strategies have quite different results. It should be clear that analysis of this situation requires probability theory.

12.5 Conclusion

Computing is increasingly dominated by the problem of designing and predicting the behaviour of assemblies of interacting processes.

Small scale randomness in the natural world is a source of large scale order. It seems to me that gives an important clue for design and understanding interacting processes.

The point is that for the design or understanding of complex systems the deterministic and the non-deterministic models are equally useless, since they are far too complicated. However a model which takes account of randomness studies what usually happens, or what almost always eventually happens, and this can be much more manageable. For example a deterministic model of the microscopic behaviour of a glass of water is too complicated to deal with, and according to the entirely non-deterministic model there is a possibility that the water will spontaneously vaporise, or explode, or just jump out of the glass and fly around in a glob. It is only by taking probability into account that we get a manageable model.

Statistics is the correct generalisation of logic. What we need is to develop a statistical mechanics adapted to computing.

Chapter 13

Miscellaneous

"Logic, one current argument goes, is the creation of defensive male subjects who have lost touch with their lived experience and define all being in rigid oppositional categories modelled on a primal contrast between male and female. Or another: logic articulates oppressive thought structures that channel human behaviour into restrictive gender roles. Or: logic celebrates the unity of a pathological masculine self-identity that cannot listen and recognises only negation and not difference. These critical evaluations have been made by sociolinguists studying the asymmetries of male and female conversational styles, by post-structuralist feminist theorists struggling for an escape from the "prison-house" of sexist language, and by psychoanalysts exploring the darkness of Freud's pre-Oedipal material. But none of these theoretical deconstructions account for the fact that logic is an invention of men, that it is something that men do and say."

Andrea Nye, in Words of Power, a Feminist Reading of the History of Logic, Routledge 1990

You know, Sir, the great Design of this noble Science is to rescue our reasoning Powers from their unhappy Slavery and Darkness; and thus with all due Submission and deference it offers a humble Assistance to divine Revelation.

Logic: or the Right of Reason, Isaac Watts, 1726

Thesis of logic programming: A program is a first order theory and a computation is a deduction in that theory.

From a lecture, by Coates, at the Isaac Newton Institute on Fermat's last theorem:

"There is one part of the proof where the experts are not quite sure they understand what is going on; I will point this out carefully when we come to it. However, the experts are in no doubt that this will be cleared up and that this should be completed within two years."

Gertrude Stein's dying words:

Oh Alice, Alice, what is the answer? What is the answer?

(after a long pause...)

In that case, what is the question?

13.1 Solutions, partial solutions, hints and remarks

13.1.1 Chapter 1

According to Marxists, *reification* is the mistake of treating ideas as if they were physical objects. We are not doing this. We wish to consider ideas and processes as objects, but not necessarily as physical objects. So we would call a number an object.

13.1.2 Chapter 2

It is not reasonable in computing to regard a function as a set of ordered pairs. If this is not clear already, consider the ML function, which defines the identity operator.

    fun I x = x;

I is then a function, which, given any x, returns it unchanged. There is no use saying this thing does not exist. Also, it is *totally* defined. Can we regard I as a set of ordered pairs? I is an element of its own domain of course. So this contradicts the axiom of foundation. However, many people do not believe the axiom of foundation anyway. The problem is deeper than this. Suppose we discard the axiom of foundation. That is, we allow sets to be members of themselves, or members of members of themselves, etc. We still get into trouble if we try to regard I as a set of ordered pairs. We presumably have the projection operator in set theory, so the domain of I would have to be a set. Thus there would be a set of all sets. Call this universal set U. All sorts of things now go wrong. For example, the power set of U is a subset of U. If this line of thinking is followed, nothing remains of classical set theory. There is no way to insist that I is a set of ordered pairs and to preserve anything like the contemporary foundations of mathematics.

There is a polite academic solution to this which is to say that I is an *operator* and not really a function; and to add that we do not know just what operators are. It seems more constructive to me to say that I is a function, and to refuse to accept the classical definition.

Note that I is not an isolated example in ML. It is just simple.

Here is another less simple example, also in ML.

    fun twice f = fn x => f(f(x)) ;

Twice is a function which, given any object, applies it to itself, if possible.

We have said that a type is a set together with a list of functions which are associated with the set, $(D, f_1, ..., f_n)$. A *sort* is the name of a type. For example *Integer* might be a sort, standing for $(\mathbf{Z}, +, *)$.

13.1.3 Chapter 3

3.3)   The alphabet of symbols, Σ, is $\{n,',0\}$. The

n

is a grammatical symbol and the other two are terminal symbols. The strings in Σ^* which are terminal with respect to this grammar are those which do not have

n

in them, e.g. $000''0'0'000$, or $'''''''''0000000000$.

The language defined by the grammar consists of expressions which are terminal and also are derived from the initial symbol n, i.e. those of the form: $0, 0', 0'', 0''', \ldots$.

3.4)   To get another variable, and to represent division, we add rewrite rules:

F:= y

F:= (F/F)

3.5)

real:=sign integer decimal

sign:= + | - | λ

integer := digit | digit integer

digit := 0 | 1 | ... | 9

decimal := . | . integer | λ

3.10)   A derivation:

$S \Rightarrow (S \vee S) \Rightarrow (p \vee S) \Rightarrow (p \vee q)$

p and q are true if r is true = $(r \rightarrow (p \wedge q))$

p, q, r can't all be false unless p implies q. The A unless B operator tells us that falsity of B implies truth of A. There is some disagreement about the implication the other way. Lets say that it also means that truth of A implies falsity of B. In this case A unless B gets translated as $(A \leftrightarrow (\neg B))$. So for the original statement we would obtain

$((\neg((\neg p) \wedge ((\neg q) \wedge (\neg r)))) \leftrightarrow (\neg(p \rightarrow q))$

which presumably means the same as

$((\neg(p \vee (q \vee r))) \leftrightarrow (p \rightarrow q))$

or

$((p \vee (q \vee r)) \leftrightarrow (p \wedge (\neg q)))$

3.11)

$(\forall W)((W \in Z) \leftrightarrow ((W \in X) \wedge (W \in Y)))$

This says that Z is the intersection of X and Y.

3.12)   *prime*(X) can be translated as

$((\forall U)(\forall V)(((X = (U * V)) \rightarrow ((U = 0') \vee (V = 0'))) \wedge (\neg(X = 0')))$

3.13)   It is a fact that C is not a context free language. However it is a formal language, and a grammar for it is available.

3.14)   Define addition recursively from the successor function as follows

$$((X + 0) = X)$$
$$((X + Y') = (X + Y)')$$

Now define multiplication recursively in terms of addition and successor.

(There are a large number of other possible good answers to this question. You could, for example, give associative commutative and distributive laws for addition and multiplication, and state that 0 is the identity for addition and 0' is the identity for multiplication.)

3.17 a)

$$(\forall W)((W \in Z) \leftrightarrow ((W = X) \vee (W = Y)))$$

3.17c) f is a set of ordered pairs (a, b) where a is in X and b is in Y, and f is such that if (a, b_1) is in f and (a, b_2) is in f then $b_1 = b_2$.

For example the function $y = x^2$ on the domain $\{0, 1, 2\}$ would be represented by the set of ordered pairs $\{(0, 0), (1, 1), (2, 4)\}$. A function, f, with domain D would be represented by

$$\{(X, f(X)) : X \in D\}.$$

There is some disagreement among mathematicians as to whether the idea of a function should be reduced to set theory in this way or whether it should be considered as an independent fundamental.

13.1.4 Chapter 4

4.9) a) $((apa \wedge fs) \rightarrow jg)$
  e) $((\neg fs) \rightarrow (jg \rightarrow (\neg apa)))$

The main point here is to realise that "A only if B" is translated as $(A \rightarrow B)$. With this in mind, check 4.9 f).

4.12) $(p \rightarrow q)$ can also be written as $((\neg p) \vee q)$, or as $(\neg(p \wedge (\neg q)))$.

4.13) We can write $(p \vee q)$ as $((\neg p) \rightarrow q)$, and $(p \wedge q)$ as $(\neg(p \rightarrow (\neg q)))$.

So we can express everything just using $\neg$ and $\rightarrow$ if we wish. By CNF, DNF construction, we can also express everything in terms of (negation, and, or) if we wish. It is not possible to express everything in terms of (and, or) alone, since any statement form just using these two will be true when given the identically true interpretation. It is possible to invent a single binary logical operator, from which all the others can be expressed. (There are at least two solutions to this.)

Everything can be expressed in clausal form, which seems to use just (or, and, implication). However negation is sneaked in to clausal form, since we allow

$$(A \wedge B \wedge C) \rightarrow$$

which is a clause but is not a legal statement form and which means

$$\neg(A \wedge B \wedge C).$$

It is not possible to express everything by legal statement forms using only (and, or, implication). Maybe we should add constants T and F to the statement forms, and write a clause with no right hand side as

$(A \wedge B \wedge C) \to F$

which we could read as saying that A, B, C together imply a contradiction.

4.14)   You should be able at this point to give acceptable definitions of *logical equivalence* and *logical consequence*. Testing one of these then reduces to testing whether or not something is a tautology. Every question in the propositional calculus reduces to tautology testing.

4.15)   To show that a statement form is not a tautology, you must find an interpretation which makes it false. You can do this by constructing the whole truth table, or you can just give a counterexample directly if you can see one.

4.18 a)   We want CNF for $(((p \to q) \to r) \to s)$. We say to ourselves: when is this false? You can make a truth table to discover the false rows. Or you can think as follows. To begin with, s must be false, and $((p \to q) \to r)$ must be true. $((p \to q) \to r)$ is true if either $(p \to q)$ is false or if r is true. So the false rows are: (T,F,?,F), (?,?,T,F), where ? means that we don't care. So CNF is $(\neg p \vee q \vee s) \wedge (\neg r \vee s)$, and the corresponding clausal form is:

$p \to (q \vee s)$,
$r \to s$

Advice: learn some method of finding CNF.

4.22)   If $sat((A \to B), v) = T$, then either $sat(A, v) = F$ or $sat(B, v) = T$.

4.27)   A problem is that $prob((A \wedge B))$ is not in general determined from $prob(A)$ and $prob(B)$. Similar difficulties occur with $\vee, \to, \leftrightarrow$. Reasoning with probabilities requires the techniques of statistics.

4.28)   The argument is not valid. It would be expressed

$(ac \to (zl \to wop)), (\neg ac \to \neg wop), (zl \to ac)$

$(ac \leftrightarrow wop)$

One of the implications does follow from the premises and the other does not. You should be able to figure out which is which.

Questioning the basic assumptions

We are basing our development of the propositional calculus on the following two assumptions. 1) There are only two truth values T and F. 2) The truth value of a logical combination of propositions can be determined from the truth values of the propositions.

By making these assumptions we gain a certain clarity. However we also lose a great deal. So what happens when we question these assumptions?

We might start by questioning the first assumption but leaving the second one in place. So we might have three truth values, or five, or infinitely many. We need to make some assumptions about the domain of truth values; for example we should be able to find the minimum of any two truth values and the maximum of any two truth values. This gives us truth tables for conjunction and disjunction. There are now a bewildering number of possibilities for definitions of $\neg, \rightarrow, \leftrightarrow$. A great deal of work has been done in this area. There is a subject, called fuzzy logic, which is alleged to study this. A basic problem however, in all this work, is that we cannot seem to relate the expanded set of truth values to anything in experience.

If we question both assumptions simultaneously, there is an obvious real world possible meaning for what we are doing. The truth value of a proposition should be the probability that it is true. (Note that assumption 2) is definitely false in this case.) So the result of questioning the two assumptions, in my opinion, is that they both have to go; and we may be led to study statistics, which is the queen of science.

If we add the time dimension to logic, we get temporal logic, which studies propositions whose truth values depend on time. If we do the same thing to statistics, we get stochastic processes. (See Feller, 1975; Williams, 1991.)

There is also another interesting point of view, called intuitionism, which some people think is correct for the foundations of computing. (See Luo, 1994.) According to this point of view, mathematics and computing are about objects, whose construction may not be completed. We may have an object which is partially constructed, and we may have an algorithm which tells us how to attempt to continue the construction of the object, but we may never be able to complete the construction of the object. A proposition about such an object could be already known to be true, or already known to be false, as a consequence of the construction done so far; or the truth of a proposition about such an object might not yet be determined. So intuitionism rejects the principle of the excluded middle. Intuitionism also has an attractive way of understanding implication. To assert $A \rightarrow B$ intuitionistically means that we have a way to transform a proof of A into a proof of B. Like the probabilistic point of view, intuitionism rejects both of our main assumptions.

13.1.5 Chapter 5

5.13d) Put $((p \rightarrow q) \rightarrow ((\neg q) \rightarrow (\neg p)))$ on the false side of a semantic tableau. We then get figure 13.1

5.15) Put all the statements on the true side of a semantic tableau and run the process to termination.

5.17) You need to use the soundness theorem and the completeness theorem!

5.18) The "or" in the statement of the problem is the inclusive or. We suppose, to begin with, that Γ is consistent. Prove from this that Γ must be satisfiable. So take an interpretation which satisfies Γ. What does this do to A? What possibilities are there?

5.20) Suppose $\Gamma \cup \{A\}$ is inconsistent. This means that if we start an initial semantic tableau with Γ and A on the true side, we end up with a closed tableau.

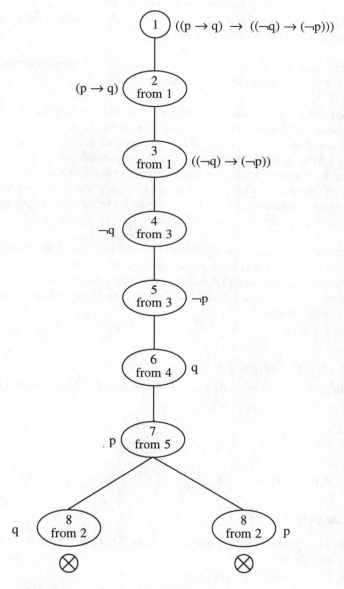

Figure 13.1 ⊢ $((p \to q) \to ((\neg q) \to (\neg p)))$

By our invariance theorem, no interpretation can satisfy $\Gamma \cup \{A\}$. Let σ be any interpretation which satisfies Γ and which covers A. σ must make A false. So σ satisfies $(\neg A)$. Thus $\Gamma \models (\neg A)$.

5.24) Hint: look at the terminal tableau. Suppose it has open branches $\alpha_1, ..., \alpha_n$. X is true iff at least one of these branches is satisfied.

5.27) Suppose we start with initial tableau T_{x0}, and this has complexity k: This means that there are k occurrences of logical operators in T_{x0}. Every time we extend the tree by one step of the semantic tableau process, we get one less logical operator on the live part of the new branches. So it is not possible to produce any branch longer than k. Since no node ever has more than two children, the whole tree is bounded. (If you do not wish to use König's lemma, you can directly find a bound on the number of nodes in a binary tree in which no branch has length greater than k. However, König's lemma is needed later.)

5.28) Put the statement form X on the false side of a semantic tableau. Run the process until termination. If there are no open branches, then X was a tautology. In this case its clausal form is empty. Suppose there are open branches $\alpha_1, ..., \alpha_j$. Suppose branch α_i has statement variables $a_{i,1}, ..., a_{i,n_i}$ on the true side and $b_{i,1}, ..., b_{i,m_i}$ on the false side. Then

   α_i is not satisfied

is equivalent to

   $\neg a_{i,1} \vee ... \vee \neg a_{i,n_i} \vee b_{i,1} \vee ... \vee b_{i,m_i}$

X is true iff $\alpha_1, ..., \alpha_j$ are not satisfied. So X is equivalent to the clausal form

   $a_{1,1} \wedge ... \wedge a_{i,n_1} \rightarrow b_{1,1} \vee ... \vee b_{i,m_1}$

   .

   .

   .

   $a_{j,1} \wedge ... \wedge a_{j,n_j} \rightarrow b_{j,1} \vee ... \vee b_{j,m_j}$

13.1.6 Chapter 6

6.5) There is a problem with aunts and uncles. There are two kinds of them. We might say, for example,

   aunt(X,Y) :- parent(Z,Y), sister(X,Y).

but what about aunts who are married to brothers of a parent of Y?

In order to talk about this second type of aunt, we seem to need the problematic concept of marriage. Marriage is symmetric.

   married(X,Y :- married(Y,X).

But we clearly cannot do this in Prolog. It is not possible correctly to define marriage in terms of parenthood.

We may think, then, that marriage should be a basic predicate, not defined in terms of anything else. In that case, how should we enter the data? We need both married(a,b) and married(b,a). Should we enter it twice? This is a possible solution.

Another equally unattractive idea is to invent a synonymous predicate

    wed(X,Y)

and to have rules

    married(X,Y) :- wed(X,Y).

    married(X,Y):- wed(Y,X).

married(X,Y) is then symmetric by definition. We can enter the data as

    wed(a,b).

or

    wed(b,a).

13.1.7 Chapter 7

7.1) Suppose T is a variable, and α and β are as in the statement of the theorem. If T is X_i, the T_α is S_i and $(T_\alpha)_\beta = (S_i)_\beta = T_\gamma$. If T is Y_i, then $T_\alpha = Y_i$ and $(T_\alpha)_\beta = A_i = T_\gamma$.

7.2) Hint. Suppose $T = f(T_1, \ldots, T_n)$. Then $(T_\alpha)_\beta = f(((T_1)_\alpha)_\beta, \ldots, ((T_n)_\alpha)_\beta)$, and $T_\gamma = f((T_1)_\gamma, \ldots, (T_n)_\gamma)$.

7.4) Substitutions are functions which transform terms into terms. To show $\alpha \circ (\beta \circ \gamma) = (\alpha \circ \beta) \circ \gamma$, we need to prove that for any term T

$$T_{\alpha \circ (\beta \circ \gamma)} = T_{(\alpha \circ \beta) \circ \gamma}$$

But $T_{\alpha \circ (\beta \circ \gamma)} = (T_\alpha)_{\beta \circ \gamma} = ((T_\alpha)_\beta)_\gamma$. You will get this result also if you try to evaluate the right hand side of the supposed equality above. Both sides just mean to first do α and then do β and then do γ.

In my opinion the best way to prove a version of correctness for the labyrinth exploring program is to define the depth first search algorithm in an abstract way. (This is done in most books about algorithms.) Once this is done, we can state a loop invariance property, which is that what the algorithm does is "just the same" as depth first search. This has to be stated more carefully of course. We can then prove this loop invariant, if the program has been correctly written. We have now reduced our particular problem to a well known one: is depth first search correct?

However, in a strict sense, none of these Prolog programs is sound, since

    path(a,b, Route, Avoid)

fails unless a and b are directly connected. It does not seem satisfactory to say that we *must* set the Avoid variable initially to a constant. A truly sound program would at least continue looking for a way to instantiate Route and Avoid variables to make the path predicate true.

There is another saying that there are three kinds of mathematicians: those who can count, and the other kind.

13.1.8 Chapter 8

8.11) $(\forall Y)(A(Y) \rightarrow B(X))$

8.13) We want to say that $\sin(X)/X$ tends to 1 as X tends to 0. The usual formalisation of this is

$$(\forall \epsilon > 0)(\exists \delta > 0)(((\neg X = 0) \wedge \mid X \mid < \delta) \rightarrow \mid 1 - \sin(X)/X \mid < \epsilon).$$

Our first difficulty is that we don't have a $(\forall \epsilon > 0)$ as an operator. This is meant to say "for all epsilon such that epsilon is greater than zero". So it is a quantifier with a condition which is meant to modify the range of the variable.

In general, if we have a predicate $p(X)$ and we want to say

(for all X such that $p(X))A(X)$

we can do this as

$$(\forall X)(p(X) \rightarrow A(X))$$

Also, if we want to say that there is an X satisfying $p(X)$ and $A(X)$ we can write this as

$$(\exists X)(p(X) \wedge A(X))$$

Note that the modified universal quantifier gets translated with an implication, but the modified existential quantifier gets translated with a conjunction.

In the present case we have

$$(\forall \epsilon)(\epsilon > 0 \rightarrow (\exists \delta)(\delta > 0 \wedge (((\neg X = 0) \wedge \mid X \mid < \delta) \rightarrow \mid 1 - \sin(X)/X \mid < \epsilon))).$$

This is the correct translation of the definition written above. That is, this means just what the original text meant. Unfortunately, it is clearly wrong. This is because it has a free variable X. However

$$\lim_{X \to 0}(\sin(X)/X) = 1$$

does not have any free variables in it. This limit statement does not depend on the value of X; it is either true or false. So there must be some mistake.

It appears that in the usual definition, the quantification of X is omitted, by convention. (Possibly this convention was adopted in order to make the definition look more friendly.) We now have to restore this missing quantifier. Before reading further, try to do this.

We get

$$(\forall \epsilon)(\epsilon > 0 \rightarrow (\exists \delta)(\delta > 0 \wedge (\forall X)(((\neg X = 0) \wedge \mid X \mid < \delta) \rightarrow \mid 1 - \sin(X)/X \mid < \epsilon).$$

The next step is to put this into prenex normal form.

$$(\forall \epsilon)(\exists \delta)(\forall X)(\epsilon > 0 \rightarrow (\delta > 0 \wedge (((\neg X = 0) \wedge \mid X \mid < \delta) \rightarrow \mid 1 - \sin(X)/X \mid < \epsilon))).$$

We then get Skolem form, by introducing a Skolem function $\delta(\epsilon)$.

$$(\forall \epsilon)(\forall X)(\epsilon > 0 \rightarrow (\delta(\epsilon) > 0 \wedge (((\neg X = 0) \wedge \mid X \mid < \delta(\epsilon)) \rightarrow \mid 1 - \sin(X)/X \mid < \epsilon))).$$

Deleting the quantifiers at the front, we get

$$(\epsilon > 0 \rightarrow (\delta(\epsilon) > 0 \wedge (((\neg X = 0) \wedge \mid X \mid < \delta(\epsilon)) \rightarrow \mid 1 - \sin(X)/X \mid < \epsilon))).$$

To get clausal form we need CNF of this. We put the formula on the false side of a semantic tableau, and treat the atomic formulae as proposition names. See figure 13.2.

The final result is

$$\epsilon > 0 \rightarrow \delta(\epsilon) > 0$$
$$\epsilon > 0 \wedge \mid X \mid < \delta(\epsilon) \rightarrow \mid 1 - \sin(X)/X \mid < \epsilon \vee X = 0$$

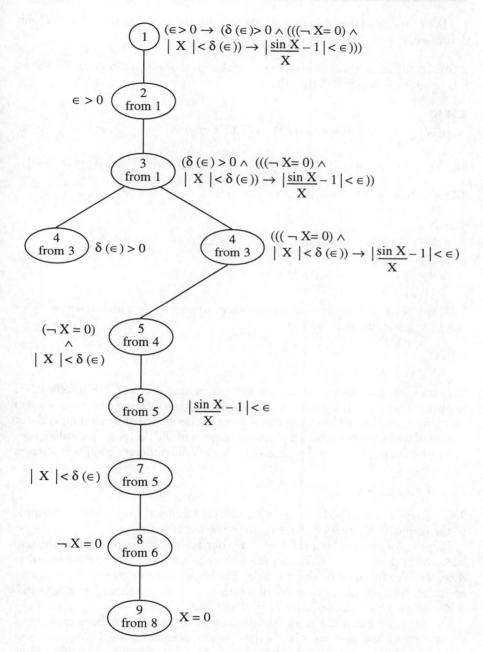

Figure 13.2   We get CNF $(\neg(\epsilon > 0) \vee \delta(\epsilon) > 0) \wedge (\neg)\epsilon > 0) \vee \neg(|X| < \delta(\epsilon) \vee X = 0 \vee |(\sin X / X) - 1| < \epsilon)$

I hope you agree that this analysis has revealed the logical structure of the limit definition.

8.14) A sufficient condition is that no variable in t is quantified in $A(X)$. However, it is possible to do a little better than this.

8.17 b)

$$((\exists X)(person(X) \wedge inprison(X)) \rightarrow (\forall X)(person(X) \rightarrow inprison(X)))$$

8.18 b) $((\exists X)(person(X) \wedge inprison(X)) \rightarrow (\neg(\exists X)(person(X) \wedge (\neg inprison(X)))))$

8.19 b) $(person(X) \wedge inprison(X) \wedge person(Y)) \rightarrow inprison(Y)$

8.23 a)

$$(\forall X)(\forall Y)(\forall Z)(((X \circ Y) \circ Z) = (X \circ (Y \circ Z)))$$
$$(\forall X)(X \circ \iota = X)$$
$$(\forall X)(\exists Y)(X \circ Y = \iota \wedge Y \circ X = \iota)$$

8.25) Consider subsets of the natural numbers ordered by the subset relation. Does this form a partially ordered set?

8.26 a)

$$(\exists X)(\forall Y)(\forall U)(A(X, Y) \rightarrow S(U))$$

Remark Various normal forms are defined in this book: CNF, DNF, PNF, Skolem. They have these names for historical reasons. They have been around for many years. Meanwhile computer science has developed quite clear ideas about canonical and normal forms. Unfortunately, none of the things we are calling normal forms are really normal forms in the sense of contemporary computer science.

13.1.9 Chapter 9

9.4) Suppose S has the form $(A \rightarrow B)$ and S is a minimal length counterexample to the lemma. S is either on the true side or on the false side of α.

Suppose S is on the true side of α. By our fairness assumption, S must have been considered at some point. So somewhere below S on α there must be either A on the false side or B on the true side. The lemma must be true of these shorter formulae. So if A is on the false side of α then $I_\alpha \models (\neg A)$ and thus $I_\alpha \models S$ Similarly, if B is on the true side of α, then $I_\alpha \models B$ and thus $I_\alpha \models S$.

On the other hand, if S is on the false side of α, S must have been considered at some point, and so A must be on the true side of α and B must be on the false side of α. Both A and B are shorter than S. So $I_\alpha \models A$ and $I_\alpha \models (\neg B)$. Thus $I_\alpha \models (\neg(A \rightarrow B))$.

9.11) See figure 13.3.

9.14 b) See figure 13.4.

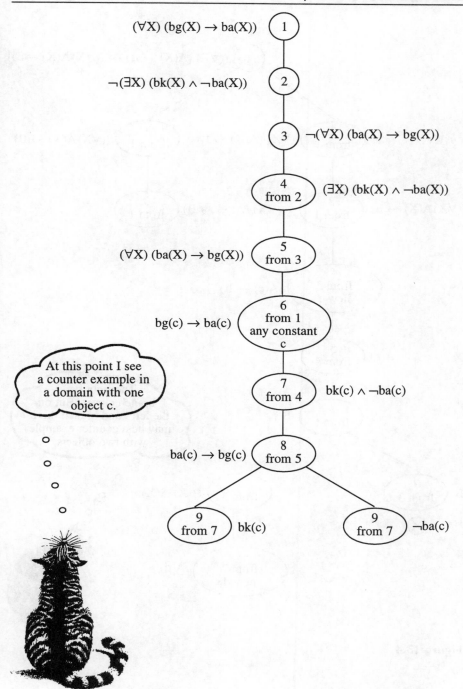

Figure 13.3

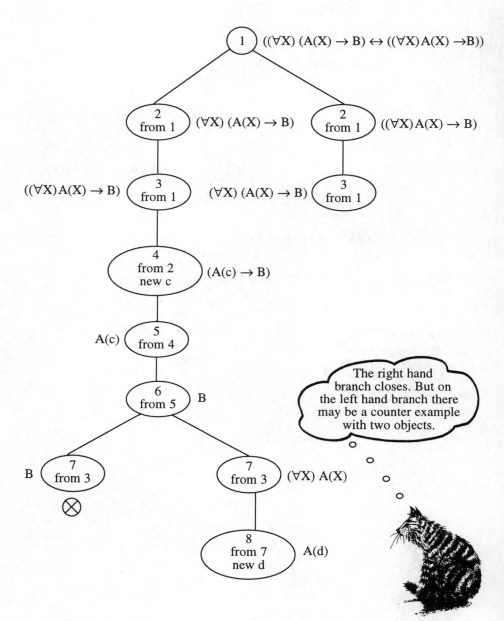

Figure 13.4

9.20) The answer to this is, unfortunately no. Let Γ be empty, and let B be $(\neg A)$. Then $\Gamma \models (A \vee B)$, but if neither A nor $(\neg A)$ is logically valid, it is not true that either

$\Gamma \models A$

or

$\Gamma \models B.$

If Γ is a set of headed Horn clauses, however, and A and B are sentences then $\Gamma \models (A \vee B)$ iff $(\Gamma \models A$ or $\Gamma \models B)$. This is because if Γ is a set of headed Horn clauses

$\Gamma \models S \Longleftrightarrow H \models S$

where H is the Herbrand universe of Γ.

Note that if A and B are not required to be sentences the statement is still not true, even if Γ is a set of headed Horn clauses. For example, A could be $X = Y$ and B could be the negation of this.

9.23) Let Γ be the universal closure of the axioms of group theory. Let S be a formula in the language of group theory.

$\Gamma \models S$

iff

$\Gamma \models UC(S)$

iff

$\models \bigwedge \Gamma \rightarrow UC(S)$ (since Γ is finite)

iff

$\vdash \bigwedge \Gamma \rightarrow UC(S)$ (by the soundness and completeness theorems)

iff

$\Gamma \vdash UC(S)$

Theorem *Let Γ be a set of sentences in some first order single sorted language. Then Γ is consistent if and only if Γ has a countable model.*

Proof By the soundness theorem, if Γ is inconsistent, it cannot have any model; and so it can't have a countable model. So if it has a countable model it must be consistent.

Now suppose Γ is consistent. Start the semantic tableau process with a finite subset of Γ on the true side. Continue as in the proof of the Gödel completeness theorem, but, from time to time add a new sentence from Γ to the true side of all open branches. We get, in the limit, an infinite open branch. As in the Gödel completeness theorem we get a model described by this open branch. We know in advance what the domain of this model is: the ground terms. So we have a countable model.

□

Suppose now that Γ is the axioms for set theory. We suppose these are not inconsistent. So they have a countable model. The domain of this model is the ground terms. Within set theory, however, you can prove that the real numbers are uncountable. This result is called the Lowenheim-Skolem paradox.

Imagine a person named Fred who lives in this countable model of set theory. Fred is a mathematician and he often thinks about uncountable sets. He believes that such things exist. But we know that in his world there is nothing but the ground terms. Everything we can prove, Fred can prove. (Fred can even prove that there exists a countable model of set theory; and he can imagine a shadowy being, called $Fred^2$ who inhabits this world.) There is absolutely no way for Fred to realise that his world is nothing but a countable set of symbols.

Fred has the real numbers in his world, $\mathbf{R}_{Fred}$. He believes this is a set. Only we know that it is nothing but a ground term.

Of course $\mathbf{R}_{Fred}$ does, in a sense, have elements: those ground terms which are said to be real numbers in Fred's world. Fred proves that $\mathbf{R}_{Fred}$ is uncountable. This means that in his world there is no injection from $\mathbf{R}_{Fred}$ into the natural numbers. But we, looking down at his unattractive world, can construct such an injection, and thus we can enumerate all the elements of $\mathbf{R}_{Fred}$.

All of this begs a number of questions.

How do you know that you are not Fred?

What happens if Fred begins to suspect that his symbols mean nothing but themselves?

Quiz for chapters 3 and 4

1) Give a grammar for the language of statement forms.
2) L_N, the language of first order arithmetic, has the following grammar:

$F := (F \wedge F) \mid (F \vee F) \mid (\neg F) \mid (F \rightarrow F) \mid (F \leftrightarrow F)$

$F := (\forall Variable)F \mid (\exists Variable)F \mid$ Atomic-formula

Atomic-formula $:= (Term = Term)$

$Term := (Term + Term) \mid (Term * Term) \mid Term' \mid 0 \mid Variable$

and a *Variable* is a string of digits and lower case letters beginning with a lower case letter. A *Formula* of L_N is something terminal you can get from the above by starting with F. Classify each of the expressions in the list below as *Variable*, *Term*, *Atomic-formula*, *Formula*, or *syntactic mistake* with reference to L_N. Be very particular about syntactic details.

$(0 = 0')$,

32,

$X + Y$,

$(X + Y'')$,

$(0''''''''''' = 0'')$,

$(\neg(X + (Y + Z)))$,

$((X = 0'') + (Y = 0))$,

$(\forall X)(\forall Y)(\exists Z)(\forall W)((X = (Y + Z)) \rightarrow (W = 0))$,

$(p \rightarrow (q \rightarrow r))$,

$((X = 0'') \vee (\neg \exists W)(W = Y))$,

$((p * q)^{''''''''''} * W),$

$X * Y = Y * X$

3) Suppose a term T of L_N has three variables, X, Y, Z. In the standard interpretation of L_N, what does T represent?

4) Give a truth table for $(a \rightarrow (b \leftrightarrow c))$. Also give a parse tree for this expression.

5) If S is a statement form with n variables, how many rows are there in the truth table for S?

6) Define logical equivalence of statement forms. Prove that $(\neg(p \vee q))$ is logically equivalent to $((\neg p) \wedge (\neg q))$.

7) Define the idea of an interpretation for statement forms.

8) If v is an interpretation and $Sat((A \rightarrow B), v) = False$, what, if anything, can you say about $Sat(A, v)$ and $Sat(B, v)$?

9) Find conjunctive normal form, and clausal form for $((p \rightarrow (q \rightarrow r)) \wedge r)$

10) Unify $(cows \wedge (midge \vee shadow))$ and $((daisy \vee clarabel) \wedge horses)$. Give the substitution.

13.1.10 Quiz for chapters 5, 6, 7

Do either Part A or Part B

Part A

1) Define "logical equivalence" for statement forms A and B.

2) Either prove, or give a counterexample:

$((((p \wedge q) \rightarrow r) \wedge ((\neg q) \rightarrow r)) \rightarrow (p \rightarrow r))$

3) Find a conjunctive normal form, and also a disjunctive normal form for

$(((\neg cat) \wedge rat) \rightarrow trouble)$

4) Decide whether or not the following argument is valid.

"Zorn's lemma implies the axiom of choice. If the well ordering principle is true, then both Zorn's lemma and the axiom of choice are true. The axiom of choice implies the well ordering principle. Therefore Zorn's lemma and the well ordering principle are equivalent."

5) Define "interpretation σ" of the *proposition names*.

6) State the completeness theorem and the soundness theorem for the semantic tableaux system applied to statement forms.

7) What is a predicate? Give examples.

8) Write in Prolog:

"Every burglar from Bristol is a barber. Every barber who is a burglar is also a baker. Fred is a burglar. Fred is also from Bristol. Louise is a barber and a burglar. Bill is a burglar from Bristol."

9) Give a grammar for the statement forms, using only statement variable

p.

So you should have $(p \wedge p)$, $(p \leftrightarrow (p \vee p))$, etc.

Write a language recogniser in Prolog to recognise legal expressions in this language.

10) Prolog has a built-in predicate

$$X < Y$$

defined for integers, with the expected meaning. Using this, write a definition, in Prolog, for a predicate

   $sorted(X)$

which says that X is a list in ascending order. Hint: you can use

   $[X \mid [Y \mid Z]]$

for the list whose first two components are X and Y, and which goes on like Z. In other words,

   $append([X, Y], Z, [X \mid [Y \mid Z]])$

is true.

Please attempt either part A or part B, but not both.

Part B

Assume the following loop invariance theorem.

If T_{x_0} is any semantic tableau, and T_{x_n} is a tableau obtained from T_{x_0} by any number of steps of the semantic tableau process, and if σ is any interpretation then

   σ satisfies T_{x_0} if and only if σ satisfies T_{x_n}.

Use this to prove the soundness theorem for the semantic tableau process.

13.1.11 A final examination

1)

   (a) A *statement form* is an expression obtained by combining statement variables using any number of logical operators $\land, \lor, \lnot, \rightarrow, \leftrightarrow$. Write a grammar for the statement forms, assuming that we have previously defined the set of statement variables.

   (b) Explain what it means to say that statement form B is a *logical consequence* of statement form A.

   (c) Give a proof of the following, using semantic tableaux.

   $$(((p \rightarrow q) \land (q \rightarrow r)) \rightarrow ((s \lor p) \rightarrow (s \lor r)))$$

   (d) Decide whether or not the following argument is valid. You should say what you mean by validity and justify any assertions you make.

   "If Zorn's lemma implies the axiom of choice, then Zorn's lemma also implies the well ordering principle. The well ordering principle implies both Zorn's lemma and the axiom of choice. If the well ordering principle is false and the axiom of choice is false then Zorn's lemma is also false. Thus Zorn's lemma and the well ordering principle are equivalent."

2)

   (a) State the soundness and completeness theorems for the semantic tableau algorithm as applied to statement forms.

(b) What is an *interpretation* σ of the statement variables? What does it mean to say that an interpretation σ *satisfies* a semantic tableau T_x?

(c) Sketch a proof of the soundness Theorem for the semantic tableau algorithm as applied to statement forms.

(d) Explain very briefly how *loop invariants* can be used in proofs of algorithm correctness.

3)

(a) Find a conjunctive normal form for

$$(((p \to q) \to r) \land (r \leftrightarrow p))$$

(b) Find a prenex normal form for

$$(\exists W)((\forall X)(X \circ W = X) \land (\forall W1)((\forall X)(X \circ W1 = X) \to (W = W1)))$$

(c) Find a Skolem form, and a clausal form for

$$(\forall X)(\forall Y)(\exists W)(\forall Z)(Z \in W \leftrightarrow (Z \in X \land Z \in Y))$$

(d) What does it mean to say that two formulae in a first order single sorted language L are *logically equivalent*?

4)

(a) Explain what a *predicate* is.

(b) Give a Prolog definition for the standard predicate

$$member(X, Y)$$

which means that Y is a list and X is a component of Y.

(c) If A and B are lists, we will say that

$$sub(A, B)$$

if every component of A is also a component of B. Write a Prolog definition for $sub(A, B)$.

(d) Compare and contrast the behaviour of the following two programs.

(Program 1) **Ancestors**

```
p(a,b).
p(a,c).
p(c,d).
an(X,Y) :-p(X,Y).
an(X,Y):- p(X,Z), an(Z,Y).
```

(Program 2) **Ancestors**

```
p(a,b).
p(a,c).
p(c,d).
an(X,Y) :- p(X,Y).
an(X,Y) :- an(Z,Y), p(X,Z).
```

5)

(a) Describe, by a grammar or otherwise, a first order single sorted language L_r with one binary predicate symbol

$refine(X, Y)$

and one binary function symbol

$combine(X, Y)$

and no constants

(b) Either show that the following is logically valid, or give a counterexample

$(\forall X)((refine(X,A) \rightarrow refine(X,B)) \rightarrow ((\forall X)refine(X,A)$
$\rightarrow (\forall X)refine(X,B)))$

(c) Translate the following into the language L_r

"For any X and Y there is a Z so that Z refines both X and Y. In fact, X and Y can be combined together to make a Z so that not only does Z refine both X and Y, but it is also true that any W which refines both X and Y also refines Z."

6)

(a) Let L_N be the language of first order, single sorted arithmetic. Explain what the *standard interpretation* of L_N is.

(b) Give an interpretation of L_N in which

$(\forall X)(\forall Y)((X' = Y') \rightarrow (X = Y))$

is false.

(c) Translate the following into some first order single sorted language:

"Every animal is hunted by some other animal, except for the skunk."

(d) Translate the following into Prolog:

"X is stuck if X is next to Y and Y is stuck. X can also be stuck if X is below Y and Y is blocked by Z which is slack."

References

T. Amble, *Logic Programming and Knowledge Engineering*, Addison Wesley, Reading Ma, 1987

G. Birkhoff and S. MacLane, *A Survey of Modern Algebra*, Macmillan, 1965

G. Birkhoff and S. MacLane, *Algebra*, Macmillan, New York, 1967

Bratko, I. *Prolog Programming for Artificial Intelligence*, Addison Wesley, Wokingham, 1986

N. Chomsky, *Aspects of the Theory of Syntax*, MIT Press, 1965

W. F. Clocksin and C. S. Mellish, *Programming in Prolog*, Springer, Berlin, 1987

J. H. Davenport, Y. Siret and E. Tournier, *Computer Algebra, systems and algorithms for algebraic computations*, Academic Press, 1988

K. Devlin, *The Joy of Sets, the Fundamentals of Contemporary Set Theory*, Springer Verlag, 1993

W. Feller, *Introduction to Probability Theory and its Applications*, Vol 1, 2nd edn, Wiley, New York, 1975

K. Gödel, *On formally undecidable sentences in Principia Mathematica and related systems*, (1931), Oliver and Boyd, Edinburgh, 1962

R. Gupta, S. A. Smulka and S. Bhaskar, On Randomization in Sequential and Distributed Algorithms, ACM Computing Surveys, vol 26, No 1, March 1994

A. G. Hamilton, *Logic for Mathematicians*, Cambridge University Press, Cambridge, 1988

A. G. Hamilton, *Numbers, sets and axioms, the apparatus of mathematics*, Cambridge University Press, Cambridge 1982

P. Hill and J. Lloyd, *The Gödel programming language*, MIT press, 1994

C. A. R. Hoare, *Communicating Sequential Processes*, Prentice Hall, London, 1985

J. E. Hopcroft and J. Ullman, *Introduction to Automata Theory, Languages and Computation*, Addison Wesley, London, 1979

M. Kline, *Mathematical thought from ancient to modern times*, Oxford University Press

D. Knuth and P. Bendix, Simple Word Problems in Universal Algebras, in Computational Problems in Abstract Algebra, Ed by J. Leech, Pergamon Press 1970, pp.

263–97

R. Kowalski, *Logic for Problem Solving*, Artificial Intelligence Series: 7, North Holland, New York, 1979

I. Lakatos, *Proofs and Refutations, the logic of mathematical discovery*, Cambridge University Press, 1976

G. L. Lazarev, *Why Prolog? Justifying Logic Programming for practical applications*, Prentice Hall, N. J. 1989

J. W. Lloyd, *Foundations of Logic Programming*, Springer Verlag, Berlin, 1984

Z. Luo, *Computation and Reasoning*, Clarendon Press, Oxford, 1994, International Series of monographs on computer science

E. Mendelson, *Introduction to Mathematical Logic*, van Nostrand, 1964

R. Milner, *Communication and Concurrency*, Prentice Hall, London, 1989

J. Minker, An Overview of Nonmonotonic reasoning and Logic Programming, J. Logic Programming 1993; 17, 95--126

J. Minker (ed), Foundations of Deductive Databases and Logic Programming, Morgan Kaufmann Publ, Los Altos California, 1988

L.C. Paulson, *ML for the working Programmer*, Cambridge University Press, Cambridge, 1992

B. Russell, *A History of Western Philosophy*, Allen and Unwin, London; Simon and Schuster, New York, 1948

U. Schöning, *Logic for Computer Scientists*, Birkhauser, 1989

A. Tarski, A. Mostowski and R. M. Robinson, *Undecidable Theories*, North Holland, Amsterdam, 1971

Van der Waerden, Modern Algebra (1931), F. Ungar, 1950 in English

R. F. C. Walters, *Categories and Computer Science*, Cambridge Computer Science Texts 28, Cambridge University Press, 1991

A. N. Whitehead and B. Russell, *Principia Mathematica*, CUP, 1927

D. Williams, *Probability with Martingales*, Cambridge University Press, Cambridge, 1991

A few journals

Artificial Intelligence, Elsevier

The Journal of Logic and Computation, (D. M. Gabbay, Imperial College of Science, Technology and Medicine, 180 Queens Gate, London SW7 2BZ)

The Journal of Logic Programming (Dept of Computer Science, Syracuse University, Syracuse, N. Y.)

The Journal of Symbolic Logic (Association for Symbolic Logic, 1325 South Oak Street, Champaign, Illinois 61820, USA)

Logic Programming Newsletter of the Association for Logic Programming, (ALP, Dept of Computer Science, University of Melbourne, Parkville, Victoria 3052, Australia)

Index